POWER 101

The Harvard Report, Soul Music and
The American Dream

Dr. Logan H. Westbrooks
and
Schuyler Traughber

Ascent Publishing
Los Angeles, CA

Ascent Book Publishing
1902 5th Avenue
Los Angeles, CA 90018
www.Loganwestbrooks.com

Edited by Dee Robinson the Right Writer
Cover Design by J. Godbee's Design
Photo Digitizing by LaRita Shelby

Printed in the United States of America
First Edition: 2022

Library of Congress Control Number: 2022913574

ISBN 978-0-9987822-3-2

IMPORTANT MESSAGE:

This book was originally written in 2010, and for the most part is in its original form covering events primarily from the 1970s. However, we must note that in June 2020, ***Rolling Stone*** magazine ran a series of articles online, exposing today's music industry's charts deleting "Soul," "R&B," "Black Music," and "Urban Music," choosing instead to identify anything today that sounds like Black Music as either "Rap," "Hip Hop," or "Pop." The article goes on to say that the Harvard Business School "Study of the Soul Music Environment" for CBS/Columbia Records did not have this result for Soul/Black Music in mind when it was written/instituted at CBS Records in 1972.

Enjoy your reading and make up your own mind.

FOREWORD

Dr. Logan H. Westbrooks
Reflections of a Living Legend

by Playthell G. Benjamin

A few years ago, I attended a lavish affair hosted by the Living Legends Foundation in Los Angeles. It was the occasion of Logan Westbrooks' induction. As I looked around at the luminaries of the record industry gathered to honor those African Americans who had made outstanding contributions to the business of Black music, I felt as if I were among living historical monuments. I listened to the testimonies recounting his deeds, and my mind harkened back nearly half a century when I first met Logan Westbrooks. It was during the 1970s in New York, when he was the Director of Special Markets—a euphemism for "Black Music" by CBS Records.

It was during the golden era of the record business and its indispensable partner—the Black radio industry, as they had a symbiotic relationship, and one was unimaginable without the other. I had just left academia to try my hand as a bandleader and song writer, a dream I had harbored since my teenage years. I was introduced to Logan by Ulysses S. Kilgore, a New York based business executive and a mutual friend whom Logan had known since boyhood.

When I visited him at his office in the CBS building, it seemed like a wonderland where dreams came true by some unfathomable magic. As I watched various members of his staff flit about to and fro, with their latest "product" playing on the office sound system, I thought Heaven must be like this.

We became fast friends and he invited me to record parties, especially for Philadelphia International artists, since I was originally from Philly and knew some of the artists and was old friends with the legendary "Personality DJs"—Georgie Woods, "The Guy with the Goods," and "The Mighty Burner," Sonny Hopson. I recall one party for Gamble and Huff held at the famous Essex House, a posh hotel on 59th Street bordering Central Park. It was a storybook affair, with sharp cats and beautiful women everywhere.

The food and drinks seemed to have no limits, and the soulful "Sound of Philadelphia" provided the background music for the festivities. It was a bacchanal worthy of a Roman Emperor. I turned to Logan and asked, "Is it always like this?" He smiled and said, "Everywhere they go!"

I felt as if I had entered a magic kingdom where the good times always rolled. But I would learn that this was the glamour side of the business, and the thing that fueled it all was the dollars generated by hit records. And that was the result of some astute business maneuvering behind the scenes, away from the limelight. I discovered that it took an enormous team to make hits happen. They just didn't happen on their own no matter how talented the artist.

Behind every hit record there were songwriters, producers and arrangers, the right combination of studio musicians, Artist and Repertoire managers. It took all of these to get the record made. But nothing happened, no dollars rolled in from this enormous investment, until the record got played on the radio. That was the job of the marketing and promotion teams. It was here that Logan was the star, a Master of Music Marketing. In fact, that's how he got the gig over a host of impressive candidates.

Armed with a street level knowledge of the promotion hustle, Logan knew who had the personal relationships with the important radio jocks, and he understood from his years as a promotion man how important these relationships were.

It proved to be an ingenious strategy as Logan gained a reputation for possessing the Midas Touch when records turned to Gold, and the Gold records generated millions of dollars for CBS Records Group.

The fact that Logan was brought into CBS by the legendary Clive Davis—a Harvard trained lawyer with a love for music who was president of the Records Group—gave him the latitude to do his thing, as Clive recognized that he had found a rare talent in Logan.

All great record executives have an ear for a hit. And Logan had his own method of identifying a potential hit. Once, a record producer hyped a record he had just produced, assuring Logan he had a hit. Logan quietly listened then asked him to leave a demo for him to scrutinize.

After the producer left, Logan looked at me and said, "They are all hits in the studio." Logan's method consisted of intuition and marketing savvy. He told me, "First I see if it grabs me in the gut. Then I take the record to a disco, or a recreation center with teenagers, put in on the sound system then sit and watch their response. If it's a dance record, I want to see if the people get up and dance." Then he knew he had a potential hit; it was up to him to make it one. And the measure of his success was the way the record charted and the bottom line expanded, the magic of the music was in the money it made. And Logan made beaucoup money!

The inside story, the secrets of how he worked his alchemy, turning sounds into gold—much as medieval Moors were said to turn sand into gold—is revealed in his new book Power 101, his fifth book on the music industry. We are told that this book "takes you on that "other" journey, traveling deep behind the scenes of this profoundly important era of Soul Music set against a backdrop of an evolving America. Both America and Soul Music began as mom-pop, soulful entities in the 1950s, moving to corporate cultures in the 70s with challenging futures today."

We are reminded that Dr. Logan H. Westbrooks began his magnificent odyssey in Memphis, the city where W.C. Handy composed the first Blues song, introducing "blue notes" into western musical literature. Although the city was segregated, and the races were kept apart by law, Blues music evolved into various styles and seeped out of the Black community on radio waves.

Bewitching the Whites who heard it, this music turned Elvis Presley into a cultural mulatto that took this Black sound to Whites all over the country. Then Logan took this music, now evolved into the modern genre called Rhythm & Blues and made it available on records to listeners around the world through the global distribution network of CBS. This was an amazing contribution to world popular culture emanating from one southern town. It is the stuff of legend, and this book is the reflections of a living legend.

STATEMENTS OF SUPPORT

"This book illustrates the uncanny ability of veteran music industry insider, Logan H. Westbrooks, to unearth a nuanced evolution, complex character, and multifaceted significance of Soul music in dialogue with a racialized America. Through this seminal publication, the dynamic reality of Soul as musical expression and cultural manifestation intersecting with sociopolitical, racial, and commercial barriers among other definitive variables is unmistakable. This is a must read for any enthusiast of the musical tradition desiring to learn from a trailblazer who was there when it all unfolded. Here is Westbrooks' masterclass for students of Soul."

TYRON COOPER, Ph.D.
Director of Archives of African American Music and Culture,
Indiana University

"Dr. Westbrooks and his scholarly contributions to the music industry are legend! By taking a close look at Soul music and the soul of our nation, Power 101 looks backwards to remind us what we've come through and gives us context for the road that we are now traveling."

H. BEECHER HICKS, III
President & CEO
National Museum of African American Music
Nashville, TN

"Logan Westbrooks gave CBS Records the inspiration to help develop a staff of very strong executives. With that staff of music people, he guided the progress to bring Soul music to the life of CBS Records for radio and all of the artists he helped to develop for Columbia/Epic and the Associated labels."

RON ALEXENBURG
Former Vice President, Epic Records

"As a young African American growing up in the music industry, I know that Logan Westbrooks had visions echoing in his ear for many years culminating in this writing titled POWER 101: The Harvard Report, Soul Music, and the American Dream. I recall when I first had the opportunity to review the Harvard Report, after only a few pages I realized that I needed to investigate both the individuals who wrote it as well as their source of information. I was thoroughly impressed by the information contained within the report and immediately began to ponder how I could use it to my benefit.

With all that has changed within the last 40 or so years, I'm constantly told that the glory days are long past. However, this current writing by Logan Westbrooks and Schuyler Traughber reveals that those glory days may not be over, just in a different place. And I believe once you had a chance to experience the pages between the covers of the Soul of Black Music, you will find that the magic is still there and now you have the road map to take that journey once again."

EDDIE GILREATH
Former Sr. Music Executive, WEA Records

"Only Logan H. Westbrooks is qualified to write about Soul Music. He is Soul Music. Logan would never have to do any research on this subject because he has experienced the culture and lives—the Life of this Soul Music. Logan is a legend and warrior of Soul, and we respect and honor all that he has contributed to this World of Soul Music. "POWER 101: The Harvard Report, Soul Music and The American Dream" reflects all that."

BRENDA ANDREWS
Former Sr. V.P. Rondor Music

"In Dr. Logan H. Westbrooks' and Schuyler 'Sky' Traughber's compelling new book POWER 101: The Harvard Report, Soul Music, and The American Dream, the authors explore the cultural and economic impact, as well as the potent influence of America's majestic indigenous art form—Black music.

Dr. Westbrooks' life and career is consequential. He is an historic, pioneering music industry executive, author, educator and historian, who during his tenure at CBS Records as Director of Black Music, helped to usher other executives of color into the lucrative music business. He augmented opportunities for many songwriters, producers, and entrepreneurs like Gamble and Huff's Philadelphia International Records and the artists on their roster, Teddy Pendergrass, Billy Paul, Patti Labelle, Lou Rawls, and Harold Melvin & The Blue Notes.

Westbrooks co-orchestrated the landmark Harvard Report—a Harvard University Business School study commissioned by CBS in 1972 in order to understand how to garner a larger market share of the enormous economic engine generated by Black music and the flavor of its innovative culture.

Anyone interested in learning more about the development of the multi-billion Black music industry from the perspective of an insider and authoritative source, will find this gem both insightful and illuminating...Power 101: The Harvard Report, Soul Music and The American Dream is an inspirational, and informative must read."

DYANA WILLIAMS,
Co-Founder of June, Black Music Month &
CEO, influenceentertainment.com

On his decision to delve into Black music marketing in the early 1970s...

"I noticed the Black motion pictures were coming out such as "Shaft" and one or two others that were getting a large audience. It appeared to me that the time was ripe to sign artists with potential who could develop into album sellers, as well as singles sellers."

CLIVE DAVIS
Former President of Columbia Records Group
(CBS/Sony Records)

"Logan Westbrooks is a veteran music industry and record company executive. In fact, he is one of a very few pioneering executives in the "Black music" divisions of several major record labels. He has served in executive positions at Capitol, RCA, Mercury and CBS (now Sony Music). Logan has provided guidance, insight, mentoring and encouragement to countless young people seeking a career in the record industry. His books have helped explain the realities of the music business and how it really functions.

Notwithstanding Logan's success on the business side, he has been, and still is, following his heart with his life-long commitment to helping young people. He and his wife, Geri, established the "Helping Hands Home For Boys" where they provided for and cared for at-risk young boys. Later, Logan established his own record label, Source Records, which had the huge hit "Bustin Loose" by Chuck Brown and The Soul Searchers. Logan has an encyclopedic knowledge about the music industry and Black music within its overall framework. I can't wait to read this book so I can absorb his latest gift of knowledge and experience. Thank you, Logan"

MICHAEL FRISBY
Sr. Vice President Legal & Business Affairs
Lionsgate Films & Starz TV

"Back in 1972, I was the only woman of the six MBA students at Harvard Business School who chose to work as the researchers and co-authors of The Harvard Report. The report was commissioned because CBS/Columbia Records' then president (now legendary) Clive Davis and group vice president Larry Isaacson requisitioned an HBS consulting report/thesis on whether and how Columbia should enter the Soul/Black/R&B Music Business."

"Logan Westbrooks, Columbia's recently hired Director of Special Markets was our liaison and guide. As we did our extensive research, it made absolute sense to us that CBS should enter this arena of the record business...because Columbia had The Midas Touch as the dominant record distribution channel and marketer of the 60s and 70s. After our Report was published and adopted as a strategy by CBS, and graduating with my door-opening '72 Harvard MBA; Logan had the foresight to hire me as his Assistant to the Director of Special Markets.

It was a magic carpet ride as CBS zoomed to the top of the charts with Gold Records galore by Black Artists...led in the beginning by Gamble & Huff's Philadelphia Sound. Numerous "Soul" music hits (The Isley Brothers, Earth Wind & Fire, Johnny Nash and others) "crossed over" to the lucrative and coveted "Pop" charts under Logan's astute promotion and marketing direction.

Several years later in 1977 when I was Business and Investment Manager of MCA New Ventures (a sub-division of MCA/Universal Pictures, engaged in venture capital), I approached Logan about starting his own record label with some financial backing and resources from MCA. That collaboration resulted in Logan's own label—Source Records—which achieved a Gold Record with its very first release—Chuck Brown & the Soul Searchers "Bustin' Loose."

Logan Westbrooks has been my dear friend and mentor since my time with him at CBS Records 50 years ago. We have both pushed through glass ceilings throughout our careers. As a pioneering and successful Music Industry Executive and Entrepreneur, Logan is a fabulous soul, with depth of knowledge, empathy and philanthropy.

He is a guiding light in African American Music. He has guided so many young people in their careers.

CHEERS to you Logan for another marvelous book which shares your deep wisdom. May you live long and prosper. With love and deep respect always."

MARNIE TATTERSALL
Formerly with
ABC Radio, MCA New Ventures, Source Records,
and CBS Records

"I have read Dr. Westbrooks' other books, and I know this one will be as enlightening."

MILLER LONDON
Former Sales & Marketing Music Executive, Motown

"When I was hired at BRE in 1987, who knew that Dr. Logan Westbrooks—the pioneer and architect of Soul and Black Music Promotion—would take me under his wing as my music industry mentor and philosopher. He helped me realize the indelible contributions I had augmented in the 70s as the first WEA Black Music Marketing Coordinator in San Francisco in 1977.

Dr. Westbrooks was the first to take a live tour of Black American Soul and R&B groups to Africa in the mid-70s. As one of the architects of the Harvard Report and his profound history of his vision behind the scenes, Dr. Westbrooks is the quintessential Soul Man. POWER 101 is an enlightening spiritual experience of how his vision and focus shaped and evolved the position of Soul and/or Black music as a cultural force in the universe."

Michael Nixon
Former Executive
Warner Brothers/Elektra/Atlantic Records

Logan H. Westbrooks Special Dedication
to
Kenny Gamble (Luqman Abdul Haqq)
Leon Huff and Thom Bell

Prolific and visionary songwriters/producers who produced many songs
with a universal message along with countless love songs.
Because of the Mighty Three, we be!

Love Train – The O'Jays
Put your Hands Together – The O'Jays
Give the People What They Want – The O'Jays
Family Reunion – The O'Jays
Message in Our Music – The O'Jays
For the love of Money – The O'Jays
Wake Up Everybody – Harold Melvin & the Blue Notes
Show You the Way to Go – The Jacksons

***

Back Stabbers – The O'Jays
If You Don't Know Me by Now – Harold Melvin & the Blue Notes/Simply Red
The Love I Lost – Harold Melvin & the Blue Notes
Me & Mrs. Jones – Billy Paul
When Will I See You Again – Three Degrees
Ain't No Stopping Us Now – McFadden & Whitehead
The Sound of Philadelphia   MFSB
You'll Never Find – Lou Rawls
Enjoy Yourself – The Jacksons
Do It Anyway You Wanna Do It – People's Choice
Turn Off the Lights – Teddy Pendergrass

***

Created TSOP (The Sound of Philadelphia)
Philadelphia International Records
Mighty Three Publishing
Published over 3,500 songs
175 Gold and Platinum Records
Rock & Roll Hall of Fame
Lifetime Achievement Grammy Award

And Pat Shields from the Living Legends Foundation

A Special Tribute
to
Armand McKissick
The #1 Promotion Manager

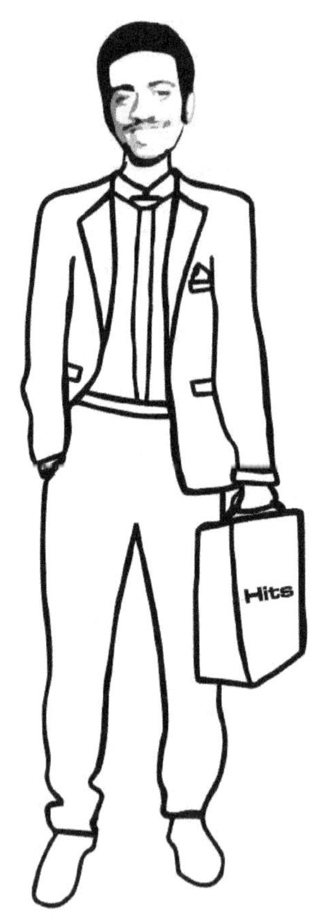

He never failed to deliver!!!

Sky Traughber
Special Thanks

To immediate family for bonding, acceptances, support: deceased parents Charles and Vivian Traughber; brothers Rayburn (wife Bonita) and Charles Melvin (deceased wife, Lois and friend Sandra); nephews Merritt and Charles Ayers, Charles A's wife Juanita and their children Ge-Ge and John Charles. Extended family in Nashville, Chicago, etc., for same attributes.

To Logan for the idea, unbiased interviews and follow-up on this book.

Actor Samuel L. Jackson, African-American Studies Professor /Blues artist Clark "Deacon Bluz" White, deceased Texas Southern U. Band Director George Edwards for allowing me to tag along in high school. Yeah…I paid attention. To everything: like learning how to dress/act for professional musical performances/interact with girls, stay away from syrup/pills popular by others, at the time and maintain a GPA to afford an option for college admission while I was playing bass at the Elks four nights a week on "everything-goes Ninth Street," Chattanooga, TN.

Billy Peak (Zulu Nation/Howard University) for electric bass lessons and my first professional band gig at the Elks.

"Too many to name" positive influences at Stax, CBS and Motown Records.

Doug Wilkins and Marsha Smith for big help with photos. Neda Shahram for the "sunshine" and Gold Record cover-idea in "POWER." Prof. Carolyn Wilkins for clear-memory.

Attorney and Carole King rabbi (at the time) Stan Levy, Herbie Hancock manager David Rubinson in San Francisco, CA. Bay Breeze Productions, in Oakland, CA, owners Craig Neely, and

Jay Ivey. J.C. Flores, Esq. All who are listed for valuable experience and wisdom.

MTSU's Geoff Hull and Recording Industry Management students. Berklee College of Music's Warrick Carter, Larry McClellan, Don Gorder, John Kellogg, Larry Simpson, Lee Berk and Music Business/Management students. Brian Price at Harvard Law School, for confirming that education and intellect in Music Business is okay.

To Mike Scott and Berklee's Faculty Union, Berklee's Association of Faculty and Staff of African Descent (AFASAD) for showing that organization and unity in higher education can work.

Medical Doctors Holbrooks, Levinthal, Hijikata, Reed, McIntyre (Cheryl), Maguire (Liz), Kingston (Donna and Debbie), Marcello, Blaha, Zanger and Fowler (Mercy), Jackie Meadows at North Shore Pain Management, Julie Fidler at Spaulding Physical Therapy, Danielle and Elizabeth for housing management in highly-scenic sea-coast township of Gloucester, Massachusetts, Helena and Y.M.C.A. of North Shore, Gloucester, Turner's "Fresh Seafood," Sawyer Free Library, Gloucester, and Buddhism Mind/Body Meditation. Billy with CATA. Without health, well-being and safe transport, my complete co-authorship of this book would not be possible.

LaRita "2 Jazzy" Shelby of SB Music, Media & Marketing for fantastic photo-pages guidance and edits. Dee Robinson for "close to miraculous" manuscript revision and edits.

CONTENTS

POWER 101

POWER 101

The Harvard Report, Soul Music and The American Dream

"Quincy Jones was the first African-American executive with a major label when Mercury Records named him Vice-President in charge of A&R (Artists and Repertoire) in 1961. But it was during the second wave in the 70s, when Black pioneers with street smarts and a strong yen for business success, such as Logan Westbrooks, really opened the door wider for Blacks as senior executives at major labels."

~~David Earl Jackson, *The Tri-State Defender*

INTRODUCTION

The richness of Black Music is a long and storied journey encompassing pain, joy, love, human spirit, the social, the business and the political. All fueled by a thing called Soul.

Soul itself is as indescribable as the results it produces. Crossing barriers in age, race, gender, income, religion and philosophy, it knows no discrimination. Actor Sean Penn describes a person's soul, in physical terms, weighing only *21 Grams* (the weight of a hummingbird), as his film title implies. The average human body weight is somewhere around 150 pounds. The soul carries the most intrigue of all body components. We always wonder if we have "sold our soul." How can something so small carry so much spiritual weight?

The turning point, musically and businesswise for Soul Music transpired during the 1970s. Grounded philosophers will say it is a natural evolution in its movement from small independent owner-ship to its controversial alliances with corporate America. Others tend to take a deeper look, eager to stretch that extra mile.

This book takes you on that "other" journey, traveling deep behind the scenes of this profoundly important era of Soul Music set against a backdrop of an evolving America. Both America and Soul Music began as mom-pop, soulful entities in the 1950s, moving to corporate cultures in the 70s with challenging futures today.

POWER 101 also explores a strong co-dependency between record labels and radio stations in the 1970s. Without record labels, radio stations would not have a steady stream of product to program. Without radio stations, record labels would not have a powerful exposure vehicle for its product. Particularly with the introduction of FM stations and its brand of programming LP cuts (selling LPs as opposed to singles), and long versions of songs, this co-dependency would become "by any means necessary" to keep it going, sometimes as an asset for Black Music. Sometimes as a detriment.

Picture a highway. Call it Power Highway 101. The main road is a document known as *The Harvard Report*. Commissioned by CBS Records (now Sony Music) for development at the Harvard Business School in 1972. This document leads us on a journey of intrigue, calculation, achievement, deceit, culture-clash and controversy arguably resulting in a head-on collision that contributes to the Soul culture finding itself in a constant search for a home. Power Highway 101 tells the story with exits and pit stops along the way, allowing time for reflection, thought and foresight. To some, Power Highway 101 may be the equivalent of riding through a college course minus the exams. Others may groove to this book as their favorite radio dial, POWER 101.

True Black Music is not about "oneness" in the singular. Rhythm sections supply driving back bones under Southern Baptist Church and Pentecostal keyboard riffs, holding the mid sections in a mournful, joyful idle, waiting for the voice, horn and orchestra to explode. Humans coming together while staying strong enough in their separatism to still ride as one in the plural. This is not only true of Black Music but, arguably, a part of the true American spirit. Like Black Music, defining a true American spirit defies simplicity.

Honest Black Music started in the South. The big business of America[1] we see today is rooted in the dark legacy of a slave trade unlawfully granting land, capital and network access to only a few. This slave trade had roots in the South but is never exclusive to any particular territory or culture. Everyone in America cries out to distinguish his or her soul within the realms of intellect, love, commerce and social awareness. Any attempt to separate the soul of

---

[1] Deyle, Steven, *Carry Me Back: The Domestic Slave Trade in American Life*, Cambridge University Press, 2008. The combined capital investment of America in 1860 for banks, manufacturing and railroads is $2.6 billion whereas slaves were valued at between $3-$4 billion.

America from its honest soul music and its roots is not only in denial but it also inhibits honest progress.

The co-architect of *The Harvard Report* and pioneering Director of Black Music at CBS Records in the 70s, Logan Westbrooks, begins his journey in Memphis Tennessee. The same South where the Berry Gordy family, Jesse Jackson, Bobby "Blue" Bland, the multi-racial Freedom Riders, early music business entrepreneur Sam Cooke, author Alex Haley, Stax Records, MCA Records legendary Jheryl Busby, martyr Dr. Martin Luther King, Jr., Jimi Hendrix, NAACP Chairman and former SNCC activist Julian Bond, actor Samuel L. Jackson, actresses Reese Witherspoon and Julia Roberts, television mogul Oprah Winfrey, Ray Charles, peace activist and former President Jimmy Carter, Elvis Presley, and film revolutionaries Melvin Van Peebles and Spike Lee can trace all or part of their roots of development. The same South where Blues, Gospel and arguably, Jazz, were born.

LOGAN H. WESTBROOKS

I learned Black culture entrepreneurship in Memphis at an early age. Then after high school graduation I spent two years at the Historically Black LeMoyne-Owen College in Memphis and developed my entrepreneurial skills at Lincoln University in Missouri—also an Historically Black College. After sharpening my expertise at Chicago-based Johnson Publishing Company, I entered a management training program at RCA and helped lead Black Music stalwarts Capitol and Mercury Records to prominence before answering a call from CBS Records honchos Clive Davis and Bruce Lundvall in New York.

The call was to organize and develop the *crème' de la crème'* of Black Music Divisions. The drama of the resulting division at CBS Records in the 70s defies oversimplification, and its consequences are felt today not only in America but worldwide. My wife Geri and I began to utilize the definition of "direct" community power in

America through our various business and spiritual ventures that were based in Los Angeles.

Everyone at some point, if not always, searches for freedom and love in some form or fashion. Black Music executives of the 70s found themselves in a search to further define the freedom and love emanating from the 60s Black Power movement. The conflict in the search for this definition comes from a changing corporate and social America, as people of all races and class underwent transformations from the turbulent 60s. This search for definition is, in many ways, still alive today.

We can create touching music, fine wines and intimate encounters with our souls. However, when commerce arrives, conditioning says the landscape must now add a traditional definition of control and capitalism to the mix or the inmates will run the prison. On the other hand, if everyone is in the same prison, then everyone is an inmate looking for a way out of the abyss into the light—searching for power, freedom and love. The only difference is perception. Soul knows no perception, only the truth.

POWER101 explores this conditioning, its perceptions, its truths and its lies. A wide and eclectic cast of characters and themes complement us on this highway, including the *Original Thirteen* soldiers of the CBS Black Music Division, succeeding CBS Black Music heads LeBaron Taylor, Vernon Slaughter and Paris Eley, James Brown, Sam Cooke's SAR Records and Publishing, the POWER of distribution, finance and content in entertainment, John Lennon, J. Edgar Hoover, Ronald Reagan, Philadelphia radio personality and activist Georgie Woods, Mighty Three super producers and entrepreneurs Kenny Gamble, Leon Huff and Thom Bell, the Congressional Black Caucus, Earth, Wind & Fire, Sly and the Family Stone, the Isley Brothers, the O'Jays, the Black Panther Party for Self Defense, Jesse Jackson's Operation PUSH, Don Cornelius, Dick Griffey and Soul Train, Stax Records and Al Bell, Otis Redding, Motown, Suzanne DePasse, Faye Hale, Larkin

Arnold, Wall Street, Quincy Jones, Michael Jackson, MTV, BET, Oprah Winfrey, Richard Pryor, Ruth Bowen and Queen Booking, Jo Bridges, the Mafia and gangster cultures, Madison Avenue, Russell Simmons, Rev. Al Sharpton, Sean Combs and the group of athletes that "get it" in the 70s, led by NFL player and Hollywood actor/ activist Jim Brown.

Jim Brown, while managing Earth, Wind & Fire, and Friends of Distinction at Warner Brothers Records, around 1970, suggested that the label create a strong national Black Music staff. Warner Brothers responded by hiring one person—Perry Jones. All are heroes and heroines but not all are perfect. Perfection creates ideals. Flaws create human beings.

As of this book's updated writing, first-time documentary-director *QUESTLOVE* has won an Oscar for his *"Summer of Soul"* six-week 1969 Harlem concert production featuring Epic/CBS multi-racial act Sly & The Family Stone, Gladys Knight & The Pips, The Staple Singers, Mahalia Jackson, Nina Simone, The Fifth Dimension and more. *POWER 101* transitions from this final-era of Pure Soul, Psychedelic Funk, popular message-tinged Gospel music styles to the controversial 1970s Black/Urban music styles. The Harvard Reports, also controversially, serves up a blueprint for major corporations, with deep pockets, to embrace and eventually control this transition.

Questlove's Oscar night included an act of on-stage violence between two highly lauded Black men in the entertainment world. *POWER 101* delves into some history of what Black people in entertainment, particularly Black men, have dealt with for decades in how we have had to deal *with each other* as a *second job* in addition to our primary job of dealing with other non-Black people in entertainment. As Malaco Records blues-soul artist Latimore would aptly proclaim in 1974: "Let's Straighten It Out."

Warriors don't always win, but Warriors do their best every day. Warriors identify the odds and the advantages, accept both and set forth in their mission regardless of consequence.

Warriors are also born of influence by others.

SKY TRAUGHBER
Before I became involved with Logan H. Westbrooks as a principal character and collaborator for this book, his persona served me as an inspiration to achieve a high level of character, study and professionalism in my works and relationships with others. My previous 15 years as a college professor covering Music and Traditional Business Management, Media and Society courses are a result of being influenced by Logan and having worked with, studied or met most of the characters in this book.

Part I of this book covers the era of the 1950s to the early 1970s— an important era in the Black cultural search for freedom. The search and the music actually begin much earlier, but its commercialization in the hands of two powerful labels, Motown and Stax, along with a short-lived and tragic Sam Cooke-SAR Records begins in the 50s.

Part II of this book, covering the era of *The Harvard Report* in the 1970s, is actually an extension of a book, *The Anatomy of a Record Company* written in 1981 by Logan and Dr. Lance Williams. The search for freedom becomes more complex during the 70s, in part because of the gains from the 1960s. In the 70s, defining a love for music excellence, a culture of greatness and Black manhood must be dealt with in the face of Black men having access and power to the same system previously identified as the oppressor. *Chain of Causation* is identified as controllable and uncontrollable events that further complicate what should be a rather simple search. The complexities are sometimes blurred across racial and class lines. *Everyone* searches for definition.

Part III offers some commentary and story of "the day after" *The Harvard Report* era.

Whether the reader of *POWER 101* is an aspiring warrior, currently in the game or in fascination of others, the power of *POWER 101* ends inside the reader's soul. There is no formula for stretching the intellect, the understanding, the emotion, the imagination, the cleansing, the inspiration that *POWER 101* offers.

PART I

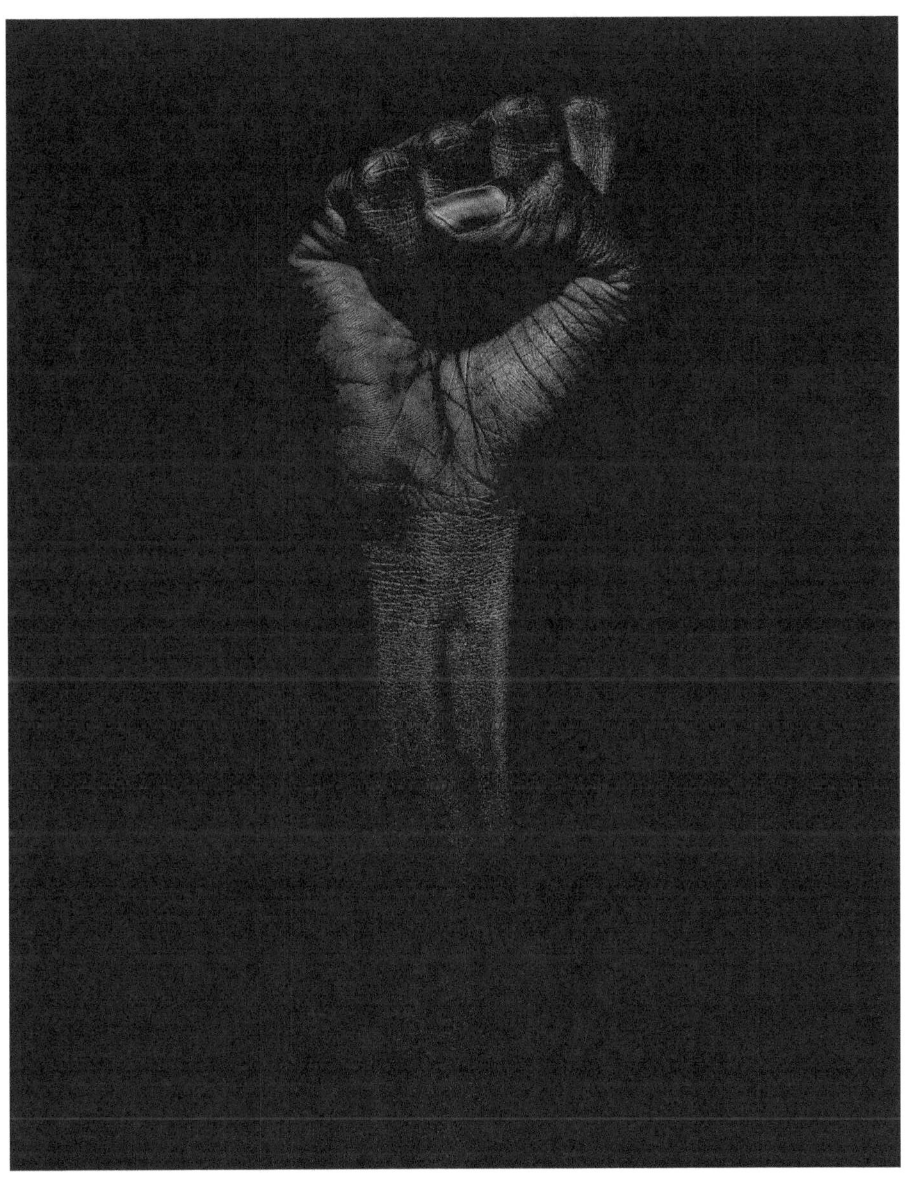

CHAPTER 1

What is Black?

1950s - 1970s

LOGAN H. WESTBROOKS
It's 1955. The Booker T. Washington High School Auditorium in Memphis, Tennessee.

Professor Blair T. Hunt, the high school principal, delivers a stirring speech from the podium:

> *You're Black, and as a Black person you've got to run faster and you've got to go further...jump higher...*

It is still 1955. Or maybe it is the year 2020. Professor Hunt continues:

> *It's from your neck up that counts, your abilities. You've got to read! More importantly, you've got to understand WHAT you're reading...*

Contrasts in the first and second quote from Professor Hunt lie in the specific versus the universal. Traditional thought and common-sense history tell us that the first quote refers to a person's skin color and ethnic heritage. This is specific and during this period these specifics are referred to, constantly, as Negroes or Niggers, from within and outside the specific culture. The second quote, though intended in Professor Hunt's speech to address the specific race we now know as Black or African-American, extends to everyone and is universal.

A non-desire or inability to understand the obvious, by any person, leads to a lethargic view of their surroundings. Reading, as an activity, can be viewed as a metaphor for a more universal meaning of just paying attention, listening, sharing, studying, even beyond the obvious. Being Black can go beyond the specific heritage resulting from an inherited identity at birth.

Roget's Thesaurus defines all references to White being 100% pure while only 50% of its references to Black are defined in the same meaning of purity. So, the second quote can refer to: how do we *read* this event? Is it just our conditioning that tells us what is Black and what is White, and more importantly are we conditioned to accept its meaning without rebuttal or reinvention?

A deep understanding of power, in our world, is to separate the specific from the universal. Though there is a connection to the physical definition of Black in our conditioning, anyone can be Black in a more universal context. Most of the problems regarding the Blackness of our world start with the physical but carry over to the universal. Definitions of freedom and power are usually not far behind.

"Reading" is for and affects everyone. Everyone can take reading and make a change.

SKY TRAUGHBER

As of writing this paragraph my vision is challenged in the left eye. Earlier today I stumbled from the subway platform in the Boston rail station because I failed to "read" that the peripheral vision on the left side of my face has changed. Luckily it was not a deep fall and not onto a third rail supplying live electricity. Reading can prevent and create profound events, but adjustments must be made from the reading for forward-moving results. Next time at the subway station…well, you know.

LOGAN H. WESTBROOKS

I see a reading of segregation in 50s Memphis. My eyesight cannot overlook the segregated swimming pools, zoos, theatres and libraries dotting the landscape in my daily walk from the "old" neighborhood to the "new" neighborhood for schooling and the like. Same scenery day after day as this is during the time when racism was firmly entrenched—absolutely everything was segregated. For African Americans it was a time of inferior schools, a lack of public accommodations, red-lined neighborhoods, being relegated to the back of the bus, limited job opportunities and many other barriers to upward mobility.

Still, my church leaders had faith, reinforced with scripture that assured a better day was coming. By attending religious Convocations through the years, I also began to see barriers and forms of discrimination disappear. Today, one of the segregated libraries in Memphis is named after former NAACP and FCC Director and Memphis-bred Benjamin Hooks, an African-American. Faith and dreams sometimes go hand in hand.

EVERYONE DREAMS! Research[2] shows that majorities of our waking hours are actually spent dreaming, in one way or another. Dreams can be Black or dark. They can also be described as bright. Conditioning in our world tells us which dreams are bright, which dreams are dark. A bright dream may be the traditional American definition of a healthy relationship, home and automobile ownership, a robust bank account or job and career fulfillment. A dark dream may involve being homeless, no loving relationship or no money in the bank.

Growing up Black in the cultural richness of the South in the 50s and 60s is an experience beyond words, both in the physical and the universal. Dodging, yet defying the Ku Klux Klan in the physical affects the universal. This type of experience can affect the color of dreams.

SKY TRAUGHBER

The leader of the lunch counter sit-ins in my hometown of Chattanooga, Tennessee, was an older high-schooler that lived across the street. Still in elementary school, my universal understanding of police protection comforted me to believe that the protesters, including my neighbor, would be okay. However, the police turned out to be the people who used their whistles to signal to the hidden attackers that the protesters were in a position to be attacked. The physical confrontation over a "Black" protest affected

---

[2] Radjindrababou Ramassamy, Are Dreams Unconscious or Subconscious? www.Quora.com, March16, 2020.

my universal belief in police protection for everyone. Today, there are incidents that do not require a protest event for the abuse of police power to rear its ugly head, in the name of "street justice."

During this same period, I had developed an extraordinary French-speaking skill from some television instruction and was selected to appear on the show. My universal glee of showing the result of my intelligence was quickly dampened when the television show moderator asked me to "dumb down" these skills. Having watched the show religiously, I knew that previous participants were allowed to showcase their learned fluency in this foreign language, but I was asked to play the dummy who could not get it. So much for the universal belief in equal treatment in education and media for one who was physically Black. Later, people like *Bill Cosby, Oprah Winfrey* and *Bob Johnson* will blend education and media to offer faith and dreams to others, though at times controversial in nature.

On the bright side, growing up physically Black in the South includes attending all Black elementary, junior and senior high schools, serving an *Al Green* "Love and Happiness"-style wooden-floored, musically rockin' Southern Baptist Church, watching mom and pop businesses of doctors, attorneys, car dealers, insurance companies and radio stations take care of serious but still soulful business.

Drummer *Louis Hayes* (Yusef Lateef, Horace Silver, Cannonball Adderley) took care of soulful business as my elementary school music teacher, followed by incredible music educators like *Dolphus Spence* and *Doc Kendricks* who demanded the learning of technique by not the sacrifice of, but the embellishment of soul.

LOGAN H. WESTBROOKS

This is the same environment that afforded me the priceless opportunity of selling national daily and weekly newspapers such as *The Memphis World, The Tri-State Defender, The Chicago Defender, The Pittsburgh Courier, Kansas City Call and Houston Informer* to a mixed clientele of barbers, GI soldiers, Pullman Car porters and waiters, lawyers and rubbing shoulders with the likes of

Benjamin Hooks and Universal Life Insurance President Maceo Walker, the son of Universal founder Dr. Joseph Walker.

SKY TRAUGHBER

One of the most defining experiences for me at this time was being allowed at age 15 to perform as a bassist four nights a week in the "chitlin' circuit" nightclubs on Ninth Street in Chattanooga. James Brown's drummer, *Clyde Stubblefield*, the *Impressions*, *Bessie Smith* in the 30s, the *Blind Boys of Alabama* and reportedly Roland Kirk cut their teeth up and down this street in the 50s and 60s. Learning syncopated rhythms like the "New Orleans back beat" heard in tunes like James Brown's *Cold Sweat* from cats like drummer *Joe Burke* and bassist *Lucky Scott*[3] on "nights off" makes this a full time job even when not performing.

Though actor *Samuel L. Jackson* would not join us[4] in the clubs, he exerted his high-range trumpet playing in the *Riverside High School* jazz swing band during the week after school, while crafting his drama and culture skills in the Riverside drama productions.

The horn men during this time would amaze me with their MIT-like skills in chord and theory progression knowledge. On a rare Sunday night off, the primary horn player, *Alvin Ellerby*, would pick me up in his folk's Chevy. After a friend hooked us up with some ice-cold beer and chips, we would drive around listening to the Holland-Dozier-Holland sounds like the *Supremes*. Alvin would *make* me listen and understand the coloring and progressions in their music.

---

[3] Joe Burke and Lucky Scott headed a group called *The Inclines* who landed a single deal on Atlantic Records during this time. Lucky would go on to play and produce with *The Impressions* and the solo career of *Curtis Mayfield.*

[4] "Us" at this time would include highly talented, but still high-schooled aged cats like *Alvin Ellerby, Ralph Ward, George Edwards* (later an Historically Black College band director), *Ricky Howell, Henry Gordon, Patrick Arnold* (later an Historically Black College music professor, *Michael Stubbs* (later a band mate with the *Temprees*) *Larry Flanagan* and *William "Billy" Peak*, who my brother, *Rayburn*, would pay to teach me the crucial transition from upright bass to Fender electric bass. Billy would go on to form the original *Zulu Nation* music group at Howard University. Future *Temple U., Northeastern U.* and *Morehouse/Atlanta U.* Black Studies professor and now-Atlanta-based Blues artist, *Deacon Bluz* aka *Dr. Clark White*, would jam in the Riverside jazz band on sax.

After school, another horn man, *George Edwards*, who was the Riverside Marching Band drum major, would brutally, but lovingly, drill me on the importance of precision and "snap" as I toted a tom-tom drum in our tight and precision-oriented replica of the *Florida A&M Marching 200*.

Amongst the chicken, ribs, and beans and wiener joints, the "smell" of this experience never leaves a person's soul. The Elks, the VFW, the American Legion Hall, the Malibu and a few "after-hours" jam and sex joints (someone of my age was not allowed) fill the air with music, drinks, food, squabble and weekend intellect.

Chattanooga high school sports and marching bands ruled the town on weekends, until 11 p.m. Then, the clubs took over until dawn. With this mixture, it is no wonder that our club band and high school Jazz band won every high school Pop and Jazz competition we entered, hands down.

LOGAN H. WESTBROOKS
I, in Memphis, experienced the regal influences of the legendary *Beale Street* clubs and lesser known, but equally jam-filled places like the *Flamingo*. Kansas City, Missouri, a pulse of the *Charlie Parker* Bebop[5] era is miles away, but you can hear and feel the music and the culture glide between both cities. In this environment, we learn class and culture from older, but "down" people who look like us.

SKY TRAUGHBER
The exposure to older Black women in these clubs helped create a sense of understanding and respect for people who look like your mother. One can also learn how a woman's spiked heel can be a "weapon of dangerous intent" if the situation necessitates such action. Overall, this early exposure helps develop a diplomatic, philosophical, soulful view of communicating with women that has no room for violence. Let's be clear, gender violence is not race-

---

[5] One of the most influential saxophonists and composers who modernized jazz was a principal innovator of Bebop.

based. Also, I am in no superior position to hold in judgment those who receive joy or attraction from gender violence if it is their prerogative. Just not this co-author's prerogative. We are all products of early experiences in our lives.

Being new to pumping an electric bass four hours a night, four nights a week creates blisters on the playing fingers. Sometimes this will occur early on a Thursday night with three more nights to go. Any thoughts of quitting or complaining because of the pain are not an option when liquored up, soul, pain and joy-seeking audiences need that bottom funk to light the kindling in their souls. You play on raw skin and enjoy it. It carries on in life.

Integration during this period has its merits also. Among the bass-playing nightclub jaunts and high school marching, concert and jazz band rehearsals, I joined a mostly-white symphony orchestra on Saturday mornings for some Stravinsky, Mozart, Bach and the like.

Let me be clear that the musical training with and from Blacks in and out of the schools covered the Classical as much as the Soul. Being "dragged" to listen and watch my namesake and Harlem Renaissance classical pianist *Philippa "Duke" Schuyler*—who is mixed race—jam like a combination of Jimi Hendrix and Mozart on that piano helped instill a confidence that I could play with anyone, anywhere, on any piece of music. On the flip side, ego aside, mixing my soul with the soul of these White kids, in musical unison, later helped in the appreciation and understanding of the works of people like *Henry Mancini, Gamble-Huff, Thom Bell-Linda Creed, Isaac Hayes, Quincy Jones, Karen Carpenter*, and *Burt Bacharach*.

People wondered how *Mike Tyson* could destroy taller opponents. Mike delivered from the bottom up, using his leg strength. As a bass player, I delivered the funk to the White kids in the same fashion. Bottom line, when the soul and the power surge from the bottom, everyone feels it and the physical sense of fellow musicians become insignificant. We were all playing "Black" in the universal sense.

Not that a Black sound has to come from the bottom by a Black person in the physical sense. In the 70s for instance, *The Average White Band*—a Scottish Band—supplied Black soul from the bottom. By the same token, just because a non-Black person, in the physical sense, grows up in a Southern-type funk culture does not *automatically* grant them a Black visa, in the universal sense. It has to be earned.

LOGAN H. WESTBROOKS

A Black person, in the physical sense, does not automatically receive a visa for Blackness in the universal sense, either. During economic hardships in the early 1900s Harlem, Black landlords charged their Black tenants higher rents for squalid living conditions than White landlords were charging their tenants for more desirable quarters.[6] This is not Blackness from the bottom up.

Black Quality from the bottom up enters my life early, waiting tables and gaining wisdom at the prestigious *Tony's Inn*, a night and dinner club in Memphis. Here, I was surrounded by the tradition and philosophy of social prestige, collective work and community involvement supplied by gentlemen from the *A. Philip Randolph*-inspired Brotherhood of Sleeping Car Porters.[7] Serving your own people, as well as others, at a high level of service and integrity removes the "negative" thesaurus definition of Blackness from the dictionary in one's mind. Tony's Inn in Memphis represented a "chain" of this Black nightlife culture. The chain stretches to other hot spots like *Club Delisa* in Chicago and *The Twenty Grand* in Detroit, before chains become less soulful, in their separate identities, in the 80s. I also witnessed the owners of the other nightclubs frequenting Tony's with girlfriends at some hours, while their wives would hold bridge meetings at Tony's at other hours. Well, you know. Nothing's perfect.

Black radio of the 50s and 60s on the AM frequency monaural stage emphasizes this bottom-up sound as most radio receivers in the home or car carry one speaker, keeping the music condensed and

---

[6] Abdul-Jabbar, Kareem, co-written with Raymond Obstfeld, *On the Shoulders of Giants,* Simon & Schuster, 2007.

[7] The Brotherhood of Sleeping Car Porters becomes the first Black union in 1925. Black railway workers in the 1920s comprise the largest category of Black labor in the U.S. and Canada, for this period. A. Philip Randolph and his men will prove a valuable asset to the Civil Rights movements of the 50s and 60s.

centered on the bottom. James Brown's "Papa's Got a Brand New Bag" literally tears this one speaker apart.

Most R&B stations signed off when the sun went down during this time and the Pop stations at night carried mostly Top 40, guitar and keyboard songs the likes of "Beautiful Morning" by the Rascals, "Love Makes the World Go Round" by Deon Jackson, some Paul Revere & The Raiders. This balance of listening has its positive attributes in rounding out a Black sound in the universal sense for the masses during this period, but will prove controversial in years to come.

In Memphis, amidst the wailing sounds of sax man *Hank Crawford* [8] and others, sanitation workers prepare for a daytime fight that will claim the life of a young preacher now cutting his chops in Georgia and Alabama. *Berry Gordy* captures the southern migration to the northern motor city of Detroit and polishes it for the masses. *Sam Cooke* contemplates leaving the highly successful Gospel group, the Soul Stirrers, to venture into the Pop world that many of his counterparts equate with the world of the devil. And to top it off, Sam is doing it in Sin City aka Hollywood. *Al Bell* is spinning and preaching his future at a Mississippi radio station.

Columbia Records (CBS Records) in New York, is moving from the early *Bessie Smith* and *Mahalia Jackson* recordings and its recent Okeh-subsidiary label era with crooner *Walter Jackson* to scratching their heads over how to record a soulful, church-inspired *Aretha Franklin* for their Pop audience. *Quincy Jones* owes Mercury Records for financing the return of his stranded band from Europe back to the United States.

As a payback, Quincy breaks new ground as a Black person in A&R at a major record label. The mob smells something brewing in owning the songs, recordings and concert business of people like "Mr. Dynamite" *Jackie Wilson* and teen crooner *Frankie Lymon*. President Dwight Eisenhower, upon leaving office, warns the country of corporations becoming too involved in the nation's war

---

[8] Tenor Sax man Hank Crawford will become a major fixture in the sound of the Ray Charles band as well as becoming an identity for dark, but soulful Jazz as a solo artist.

efforts. He also warns they are inching their way into business areas meant to be small mom and pop-controlled businesses as a result of FDR's New Deal in the 1930s. The New Deal gives government a greater role in the social and economic affairs of the country following the Great Depression.[9]

Athletes *Jim Brown* and *Kareem Abdul-Jabbar* set physical achievement records at Syracuse and UCLA Universities, respectively, while developing universal strategies of Black social and economic empowerment for later. *J. Edgar Hoover* and the FBI created COINTELPRO to thwart efforts of individuals and organizations, like the *Black Panther Party for Self Defense*, who are deemed a threat to "national security."[10] All of these beginnings will soon bump in a head-on collision of defining Black, Green and White American Dreams while the power of Soul Music becomes involved as a bystander.

---

[9] New Deal Programs: Selected Library of Congress Resources/Library of Congress, Symposium, <u>Art, Culture and Government at 75</u>, March 13-14, 2008.
[10] Jackman, Tom, The FBI Break-in That Exposed J. Edgar Hoover's Misdeed to be Honored with Historical Marker, September 1, 2021, http://www.washingtonpost.com>history.

CHAPTER 2:

What is Soul?

"Soul is just the way Black folks sing when left alone to themselves."
~~ Ray Charles

SKY TRAUGHBER
Contrary to the Introduction reference to Soul as "indescribable,"
let's give it a stab. We are on that "other journey."

Here are some Web definitions for Soul:[11]

- Deep feeling or emotion

- A secular form of Gospel that was a major Black musical genre in the 1960s and 1970s; "soul was politically significant during the Civil Rights movement."

- The True Self. The inner, most sacred part of each person. Soul exists before birth and lives on after the death of the physical body. It is the creative center of its own world.

- The name for a type of Rhythm and Blues built on elements of Gospel and spiritual music. Often, practitioners such as Sam Cooke maintained two careers simultaneously in Soul and Popular music.

- Acting within a shared experience of the world, where 'spiritual' is best understood as 'a sense of self and that which is greater than self.'

- The power of spiritual awareness and intangible things that cannot be explained in science.

Let's add one more:

---

[11] Also as explained to me by elder musicians and vocalists.

- Soul is love. No more. No less. Sometimes it is soft love. Sometimes it has to be tough love. No more. No less. Love is the ultimate power. No one, in actuality, wants to be tough. All human origins are from a female egg.[12]

Encompassing both love and emotion, it is easy to see where the hardness of commerce, especially in an emotion-based entertainment industry, can clash with soul. Blacks in America, in the physical sense, are the only group of people in the world without a "home." Sold by Africa and bought by America. Let a Black person commit a deportable crime and see where that person is sent. Prison, in America.

Even 1940s gangster and murderer Lucky Luciano was released from prison and granted the luxury of deportation to his "home" of Italy, in part for the mob's role in helping the American overseas effort in World War II. If a member of the Buffalo Soldiers all-Black WWII unit returns to America and crosses the street looking suspicious, they are jailed with no "home" for deportation.

So, soul has a special meaning for some people in the social and the love meaning as well as the entertaining value it offers. It gives something special to hold onto.

LOGAN H. WESTBROOKS

While still in Memphis, I find this something special in my wife *Geri*. Sam Cooke finds an assortment of special ones in Chicago, including the one that sticks the most, *Barbara*.[13] They say the sex (as a metaphor) with that special one lasts about ten minutes. Then the real work begins. I will find this real work a long-term proposition and a positive source for the events that are about to unfold in my life.

Male bonding during this period is a significant source of that special soul strength. Young people today are probably amazed at how groups like the *Dells* and the *Four Tops* or even *Aerosmith* can

---

[12] Moir, Anne; Jessel, David, Brain Sex/Random House, 1989.

[13] Wolff, Daniel; White, Clifton; Tenenbaum, David G.; Crain, S.R., *You Send Me: The Life and Times of Sam Cooke,* William Morrow and Company, 1995.

keep the same line-up for 30, 40, 50 years.[14] Shared experiences of the world, discipline and professionalism over long periods of time help to solidify this bond.

Soul, in itself, can set the Hammond-organ foot pedal bottom, embellish it with the mid-range moans, and handle the high screams in the music, but that music has to be organized, developed and maintained. The *people* involved have to operate on a higher level of commitment, understanding and tolerance than most humans are willing to endure. Not just during the good times or the bad ones, but during *all* the times. Robert Townsend's classic film, *The Five Heartbeats,* captures this essence, not only in the music, the male bonding and the women who enter and exit, but how commerce can affect this bonding.

Jesse Whitaker of the 50s and 60s Gospel group, the *Pilgrim Travelers,* explains:

> *....you had to try and treat each other like brothers.*
> *And that's the only way a group can get along—you*
> *got to be like brothers, and you got to be businesslike.*
> *Because the money isn't there, so you got to have that*
> *oneness between each other to make it.*[15]

SKY TRAUGHBER

Given time before commerce and its side effects arrive can make a difference in extending the start-up foundation necessary for bonding souls. Actor Samuel L. Jackson and his wife, *LaTanya,* and *Lionel* and *Brenda Ritchie* established this bond during their college days at Morehouse, Spelman and Tuskegee, respectively, before either Sam or Lionel hit the major leagues. *Al Green* and *Willie Mitchell* bonded running from rednecks with guns after a gig in Texas where Al opened for Willie Mitchell and his band. Willie loaned Al a few thousand dollars, on faith, to go home and clean up his business with

---

[14] A Doo-wop historian and co-founder of the Chicago Doo-wop group of the 50s, *The Magnificents,* Johnny Keyes, has an insightful book on this specific music life, titled: *Du Wop.* As of this writing, Johnny also has an accompanying web site: duwoplives.com.

[15] Wolff, Daniel, *You Send me: The Life and Times of Sam Cooke,* 1995

an agreement for Al to return to Memphis for an undetermined period of boot camp development with Willie's Hi-Records studio band. The results of this bonding with a commitment and purpose are now legendary, worldwide.

Put in charge of hiring and rehearsing a back-up band for the Stax, Memphis-based soul ballad group—the Temprees—with no income for three months of eight-hour-a-day rehearsals proved a turning point for me. Once the tour was announced to support the hit "Dedicated to the One I Love," the most rewarding thing I remember is not the thoughts of bright lights, travel, being paid to perform or the girls, but the comment, "We are proud to have you guys back us because you hung...," coming from the Temprees. Mission accomplished. Well at least Part I. Some relationships don't get that far.

Success of early Civil Rights and Revolution pioneers like Julian Bond, Congressman John Lewis, Stokely Carmichael and Huey P. Newton depended heavily on soul bonding, every day, as no one knew when the next bomb or gun shot from the oppressors would find them as the target for the day. Dr. Martin Luther King, Jr., was finally "forced" to buy a house shortly before his death, probably thinking of his family's shelter more so than any material or image gain for himself. His mindset was not material but he understood the power of television and press for the movement, with himself, as requested by the Southern Christian Leadership Conference, the image symbol for the movement. This is different than just an image gained solely for self.

LOGAN H. WESTBROOKS

I am now an ordained minister. I know my soul is rooted in the Church of God in Christ. This firm foundation serves as the basis for my accomplishments as a businessman, entrepreneur, record company executive, author, real estate investor, world traveler, college professor, child advocate, dedicated husband and family man and a proud and faithful pastor. From our early days of being ridiculed and scorned to where we are now six million saints strong, I have experienced COGIC through durability and faith.

The power in surrendering one's soul reportedly saves the life of COGIC Founding Bishop, Charles H. Mason in 1880. A 14-year-old Charles is given up for dead by others until he surrenders himself in prayer, regains life and eventually founds the now-powerful COGIC congregation.[16] Marvin Gaye has attested to the power of this Pentecostal soul base and these joys are consistently felt in his music.

SKY TRAUGHBER

I can remember the joy on my parent's face returning from Wednesday Night Prayer Meeting at our Baptist church, every week. I am sure that this surrender helped their union last until their deaths.

I used to reject prayer in the sense of thinking it was being sent to some "unknown person in Heaven." To be frank, I did not know where it was going and rejected it as nonsense. Then, I grew into a period of realizing that prayer can be what you make it. It can go anywhere but you must first "kiss this world goodbye" and enter a zone disconnected from any belief, judgment or expectation. Just do it earnestly in any way that fits your soul.

Soul may not be as indescribable as the Introduction states. It seems to cover some physical as well as hard to define out-of-body attributes. Packaging and protecting a soul environment can be the focus of dreams. Sometimes these dreams require a tangible degree of implementation before the dream can translate into reality.

---

[16] *From Prior's Farm to Heaven*, Bishop C. H. Mason, A Biography of His Life as Told By his Daughter, Lelia Mason Byas with Jack T. Hunt.

CHAPTER 3

The Dream

"It's not about where your dreams take you,
but where you take your dreams."

~~Maya Angelou

SKY TRAUGHBER

Reality begins with a dream. In a capitalist society, dreams can involve and benefit a single person, small groups of people, or an entire nation or planet. The dream world of the 50s and 60s in America defies oversimplification. On the one hand, America emerges from WWII of the 1940s and the Cold War of the early 1950s with a sense of invincibility, power, joy and optimism. On the other hand, the real power of the nation is divided between a government still immersed in the New Deal economic and social model, an emerging corporate culture and an organized crime syndicate becoming more legitimate and more sophisticated every day. Before long, the strength of Black people and its music are caught in the vice of the big picture.

Ray Charles invents something called Rock 'n' Roll, owns his masters at ABC Paramount and has a better overall deal than Frank Sinatra but gives way to the "look" of Jerry Lee Lewis. Chuck Berry takes a back seat to Elvis in the sense of universal acceptance. A majority of Black entrepreneurship is rooted in financing from the "numbers rackets" of the 1920s, 30s and 40s, universally controlled by organized crime.[17] Returning Black soldiers find it hard not only to find legitimate financial backing and corporate careers but a good place to eat and sleep in living and travel. On top of this, America is preparing to ask these same men to return to the battlefield in an upcoming Vietnam conflict that will not only deplete its reservoir of

---

[17] Marable, Manning, How Capitalism Underdeveloped Black America, Haymarket Books, 2015.

Black male potential in numbers, but in its belief in American principles.[18]

For example, in 1967, Black P. Stones gang in Chicago makes an historic and soulful effort to purge itself of the crime environment. The gang decides to rise above the esteem-deflating environment of the corporate and government cultures by incorporating itself, and under the guidance of credible advisors, operate legitimate businesses. Any hopes of this event creating a domino effect among other street gangs in Chicago, numbering 10,000 members from 40 factions, vanishes when Mayor Daley nonetheless orders the extermination of the Black P. Stones.[19] On the flip side of this extermination is a rise in violence from other gangs towards the Black P. Stones and other gangs attempting to go legit, reportedly of a jealous nature.

LOGAN H. WESTBROOKS

The Black P. Stones episode occurred two years into my marriage with Geri, as I was entering an RCA management-training program in Chicago. This is the environment that I, Berry Gordy, Sam Cooke and Al Bell will endure in our quests of implementing our wide-ranging and culture-defining dreams. Imagine the thoughts of not only having to identify motives of government, the mob and corporations, but also your own people, in the physical sense.

Immersing one's self among one's own people, in the physical sense, in a positive, soulful, intellectually challenging environment can eliminate the introduction of cancerous viruses such as jealousy, distrust and insecurity whether the cancer is introduced externally or internally. The resulting positive energy is too constant, too powerful for the negative virus to find an entry point and sustain itself. Much

---

[18] The number of Black soldiers serving and dying in Vietnam was actually in proportion to the Black U.S. population. Twelve percent of Vietnam soldier deaths were Black (Wikipedia). However, the climate of injustice to Blacks during this period raised debates of whether Black soldiers should fight for America on foreign soil. 16.3% of drafted soldiers were Black; 23% of combat troops were Black (time.com). This war cost boxer Muhammad Ali many years in his fighting prime as he refused to serve in Vietnam not only on religious beliefs but also because of the aforementioned debate.

[19] *Street Gangs-A Secret History*, History Channel Documentary.

like the anti-virus programs that pop up in our computer programs today that are sometimes annoying, we know the long-term benefits are worth the short-term expense.

I immerse myself in this positive environment, first, at LeMoyne-Owen College in Memphis courtesy of a two-year Elks scholarship. Then, at the Historically Black Lincoln University in Jefferson City, Missouri, studying and practicing business, though I am drawn to Lincoln from my older brother's studies in the top-notch journalism environment of the college. In this environment, entrepreneurship can find a steady and appreciative consumer, not only on campus, but also in the surrounding city limits, for the most part[20]. One must understand the power of direct contact and be wise and aggressive enough to move on it.

I observed a shortage of dormitory space for male freshmen students at Lincoln and rented some two-and-three-story homes. I then observed that Lincoln owned some veteran's barracks not being used, but they had beds and mattresses. So, Lincoln loaned me the beds so I could furnish the homes and rent them to the students without housing. This became a profound event in my future in real estate and property investment and is called "management where everyone wins."

SKY TRAUGHBER

One must also be "down" enough to be flexible in their communication and energy skills, while still remembering the bottom line. Without respect for the profit equation, there is no re-investment capital to create repeat business and spread whatever product or service one is selling over the long term.

Tending bar at our Kappa Alpha Psi party one night, at Knoxville College[21] in Tennessee, our chapter president respectfully assigned me to another post, as I was giving away all the profits at the bar. On a tight budget, this means that once the original capital is depleted,

---

[20] Spike Lee's film *School Daze* has a dynamic scene that illustrates a sometimes very real conflict between the Black College and Black inner-city environments.

[21] I was actually the first Kappa member at The University of Tennessee in Knoxville, but had to pledge, willingly, at Knoxville College.

any desperate run to the liquor store for replenishing the stock is taken from the same capital the frat began the night with. No gain in income and maybe a loss. Sooner or later, that's one less organization able to offer some much-needed jam time for a needy clientele. Sean Combs learned this while at Howard University in Washington, D.C. The difference in Logan, the Kappa business and Sean Combs in contrast to the Black P. Stones is the ability to isolate and control the operating environment from overwhelming viruses.

LOGAN H. WESTBROOKS

This knowledge and ability will serve me well in graduating from Lincoln and moving to the fast-growing Johnson Publishing Company, entering the world of corporate labels RCA Victor, Capitol, Mercury, CBS Records and CBS International collaborating with the world's most profound base of business intellectualism, the Harvard Business School, entering the 70s.

Berry Gordy, after discovering the difficulty in getting paid in full for his songwriting hits on artists like Jackie Wilson, immerses himself with his "dream brother" Smokey Robinson. Smokey reasons that if Berry can deliver the content, then why not isolate and control it under his own label. Berry is smart enough but also "down" enough in his communication and energy skills to enlist the best of the burgeoning Detroit Jazz musician scene to create the "oneness" we know now as Motown. Berry was also fortunate in his family's already positive outlook on entrepreneurship and equally important, their courage to take a chance with Berry after his first venture, a Jazz record shop, went belly-up.[22] Positive energy works better against viruses when it is sustained over time.

Sam Cooke, during this time, epitomizes the phrase: *"women love you and guys want to be just like you."* Fresh from "knockin' 'em dead" every night with the gospel-tinged and southern-performance circuit *Soul Stirrers* and his national, Art Rupe-owned Specialty

---

[22] Berry's family was already established in legitimate printing and nightclub photography businesses, among other ventures. The family was also organized as a lending-institution for family members with solid business plans. The family loan of $800 to Berry proved to be the initial capital financing for what became the Motown Record Corporation.

Records Pop hit "You Send Me," Sam's dream encompasses a desire for independence and the creation of a new image for recording artists:

> *It wasn't meant to be a record company at first. It was just a production company to go along with the music publishing, KAGS. But Sam was beginning to want a financial base stronger than the success of his next single. He understood that the industry saw artists as disposable: "pains in the asses" as Roulette's Mo Levy[23] put it. There were examples of Negroes owning labels-John Dolphin and Dootsie Williams in L.A., Berry Gordy and his still hitless Tamla/Motown in Detroit, but NO rock & roller of any color owned his or her own label.[24]*
> ~~Sam's lifelong partner, J.W. Alexander

Doo-wop expert Johnny Keyes recalls that Sam and his brother L.C. were also firm believers in owning the publishing rights to songs, and Sam and L.C. would educate and inspire others to study and enter this arena of ownership.

Al Bell's dreams of taking the *Holy Ghost* to the masses through the channels of radio, ministry, political, social and economic empowerment. Al graduates from the Historically Black College Philander Smith, in Little Rock, Arkansas, with a degree in Political Science, where he begins spinning records and preaching the Soul sound in radio. Later, Al adds a Bible College degree from Oakwood College in Alabama to establish a background to realize this dream.

---

[23] Morris "Mo" Levy is the notorious and reputed mob-connected controversial owner of Roulette Records and the famous Birdland Jazz nightclub in 50s and 60s New York. Besides holding the keys to artists like Frankie Lymon and Jackie Wilson, Morris develops a penchant for questionable ownerships of songwriting and publishing material of the artists he signs and at one point owns the term "Rock 'n' Roll." Morris later becomes the first music executive to be sent "up the river" to prison under the Federal RICO ACT, prohibiting interstate racketeering. Morris dies in prison in the late 80s, supposedly signaling the end of the gangster and rip-off cultures of the record business.

[24] Wolff, Daniel; White, Clifton; Tenenbaum, David G.; Crain, S.R., *You Send Me: The Life and Times of Sam Cooke,* William Morrow and Company, 1995.

Al then joins Dr. Martin Luther King, Jr.'s Southern Christian Leadership Conference for a spell to embellish these credentials. However, it is the economic empowerment of the dream that will help change the course of history in Black Music.

Al explains:

> *I left Dr. King's SCLC because I was not about passive*
> *resistance. I was about economic development,*
> *economic empowerment.*[25]

While my dreams of empowerment mirror those of Sam Cooke, Berry Gordy and Al Bell, there are developments in radio ownership from people like James Brown, of Augusta, Georgia, and A. G. Gaston, of Birmingham, Alabama, that, when set against the channels of distribution, will translate and take us into the world of POWER.

---

[25] Bowman, Rob, *Soulsville, USA: The Story of Stax Records*, Schirmer, 1997.

CHAPTER 4

The Power

"Power is building things that last." ~~ Schuyler Traughber

Sam Cooke's tune "A Change Is Gonna Come" illustrates power in life. Profoundly placed toward the death scene in Spike Lee's film *Malcolm X,* it can also signal the passing of power from one entity to another. The mid-to-late 60s offers a series of change unequaled in the soul of American culture.

The death of Malcolm X, reportedly due in part to his discoveries of hypocrisy and transformation from some of the teachings of the Nation of Islam,[26] the assassinations of John F. Kennedy, Robert Kennedy and Dr. Martin Luther King, Jr., the Tet Offensive in Vietnam, the Manson-Tate murders, the Monterey Pop Festival, Woodstock, the mystery of Otis Redding's plane crash are just a few events signaling a change of power during this period.

The intrigue carries equal significance in the widely accepted James Brown tune "Soul Power" and the equally powerful but confusing-to-some and career devastating to James, "Say It Loud, I'm Black and I'm Proud" tune. When the masses of America hear "soul power" it carries a universal meaning, though emanating from a Black experience. However, when the physical nature of being "Black" becomes associated with power, it causes alarm for some, not necessarily Black or White.

---

[26] Numerous books, documentaries and films chronicle Malcolm's discovery of the many illegitimate children fathered by The Honorable Elijah Muhammad, the treatment of the mothers and the Nation of Islam's controversial acceptance of donations from The Ku Klux Klan, in exchange for the Nation's vow not to disrupt any Klan rallies. The Nation justified this pact in the belief that both organizations promoted segregation. *Only In America,* the Don King bio-film also explores some behind-the-scenes business practices of the Nation in managing boxing Muhammad Ali. On the other hand, the Nation is credited with instilling pride and strength in Black men, particularly incarcerated and recently-released-from-prison, and the Nation was instrumental in organizing the successful *Million Man March* on Washington.

To be "proud" of this power can add insult to injury. Some Whites wonder if they will be left out or destroyed. Some Blacks wonder if the movement is strong enough to succeed in providing financial, social and emotional security for all willing to join.

The Black American race is the only group of people that, when placed in a position of universal power, can be unsure of its footing. Japanese and Chinese have Japan and China. Germans have Germany. Africans have Africa. Canadians have Canada. Mexicans have Mexico.

Black Americans are often torn between a sense of territorial homelessness, a sense of squatting in a nation they helped build and a sense of tremendous power and soul in being able to deal with this while progressing and influencing others.

Both concerns, Black and White, are by-products of the human conditioning process. And both concerns will affect the development of the rising power of Black Music during this period and into today.

<u>The Holy Ghost and The Music</u>
What the hell is a Holy Ghost?

This is where the democracy of a country like America allows individual exploration and interpretation. More censor-based nations may equate the term with some type of religion or mind-altering regime.

SKY TRAUGHBER
To be frank, the term and its feel scared me as a child in attending a Southern Baptist Church. The wooden-floored balconies and choir stands would sway and rock, the congregation would feel the spirit and a youngster would wonder if the world is coming to an end. The older folks just called it "gettin' happy."

LOGAN H. WESTBROOKS
The spirit of the Pentecostal music just lets it flow.

SKY TRAUGHBER
Though the bottom-up spirit of this experience carries forth in acts like James Brown, the Bar-Kays and Al Green, the mid and top minor-chord, "blue" note layered top can inspire.
The Bar-Kays explain:

> *Your love is like the Holy Ghost*
> *...Shakin in my Bones*
> *...I never felt such a feelin'*
> *...In all the days that I've been born*
> *Your love is like the Holy Ghost*
> *...The antidote that freed my soul*
> *...And no [psycho] can ever describe*
> *...This feelin' that sets my soul on fire*
> *...This feelin' I have within*
> *...Makes me feel like I've been born again.[27]*

Sly Stone, his brother and sister took their Oakland church-inspired musical souls, joined with bassist Larry Graham and created the first universally commercial multi-ethnic group in the Family Stone. Inspiring millions with "Take You Higher," "Sing A Simple Song," and "Everybody is a Star," Sly and the Family Stone deliver an endless supply of Holy Ghost-meets-commerce funk.

Earth, Wind & Fire leader Maurice White experienced this in Memphis before migrating to Chicago, joining his brother, Verdine, New Orleans-soulster Al McKay, "twang master" Johnny Graham from the group *New Birth*, Denver falsetto-voiced Phillip Bailey and others, creating some Holy Ghost-meets-commerce music no one thought could exist.

Even Jazz-saxophonist Cannonball Adderley "gets some" with the tune "Mercy, Mercy, Mercy."

LOGAN H. WESTBROOKS
"Mercy, Mercy, Mercy" was actually recorded live at a Saturday morning community meeting of Operation PUSH's *Breadbasket*

---

[27] Excerpts from the Bar-Kays tune: "Holy Ghost."

program. I was the Capitol Records Promotion Manager and accompanied the group to the center that morning. Tom Nixon, then ahead-of his-time engineer of Motown and later Stax fame was at the controls, and I was able to witness the workings of his sound magic.

While other Jazz greats like Horace Silver and Bobby Timmons also hover in the neighborhood, Quincy Jones takes a European, Boston and New York classical and Jazz experience into outer space. Jimi Hendrix, fresh from the Isley Brothers chitlin' circuit road experience and Tennessee State University Jefferson Street-vibe in Nashville is more than willing to join this party. Their versions of the Holy Ghost take the spiritual into another place.

The Holy Ghost can be what you make it. Its strength, power and everlasting nature can also scare and confuse. Anything that is this powerful sheds pretense, comes from within, inspires and emanates from true talent. It carries commercial appeal as well, if marketed correctly.

The Business of Mass Communication

SKY TRAUGHBER

Reaching a mass of people can be one of the most powerful means of influence known to man whether the signal is to entertain, enlighten, or a combination of the two. This is why it is also one of the most protected means of influence.

Today, the internet offers an opportunity to carve a niche audience or to create a mass network through small pockets. Or as in the case of *Google* and *Twitter* reaching millions instantly, as of this writing.

The mass media of the 50s and 60s and into the next 30-40 years, however, mainly revolves around radio, television, print and film. Just as you cannot overlook the "brick-laying" of slavery and its effects on the power structure of today's America in finance and business, the early developments of these media outlets figure in the mix of today's mass audience influence.

Radio has always been a kindred soul to not only Black Music, but also Black culture. In 1938, *Jack Cooper*, reportedly the first Black disc jockey, started a "search for missing persons" program on his radio show.

This program was meant to help find separated Blacks during the Great Migration of Blacks from the south to northern cities (this must have included some serious "quick" exits). Anyway, Jack's program united 20,000 people over a period of twelve years.

In 1927 CBS Radio broadcasted live shows from the fabulous *Cotton Club* five or six nights a week, giving its hungry audience a steady dose of early music kings like *Duke Ellington*.[28] This media power also broadcasted the controversially funny *Amos 'n' Andy* radio show featuring white voice-overs, followed by the television version featuring Black actors and actresses.

Both versions will eventually catch the wrath of censorship from a growing image-conscious Black audience. Actor *Stepin Fetchit* aka Lincoln Perry had already demonstrated the amount of money one could earn portraying Blacks as ignorant and lazy in various film roles. *Hattie McDaniel* became the first Black to win an Academy Award for Best Supporting Actress for her role in *Gone with the Wind* in 1938.

Not all Black actors played stereotypical roles, such as actress Juanita Moore in the movie *Imitation of Life*. I can remember not being able to pick up my date from her dorm in the early 70s because she and her sorority sisters were still crying from the dynamic funeral scene in *Imitation of Life*, set against the music of Mahalia Jackson.

LOGAN H. WESTBROOKS

So, the early media exploits of Blacks portray some negative, some positive material and almost none of the media outlets delivering the material is owned or controlled by Blacks. Moving into the 60s and

---

[28] Abdul-Jabbar, Kareem; co-written with Raymond Obstfeld, *On the Shoulders of Giants: My Journey Through the Harlem Renaissance*, Simon & Schuster, 2007.

70s, some of this begins to change in radio ownership through Black businessmen like *A.G. Gaston*, who owned multiple stations in Birmingham, Alabama.

Gaston is an extraordinary case as he amasses his fortune, estimated at $30-$40 million, in the early-to-mid 1900s in just one city, Birmingham. This Alabama city is a beehive of racism in America during this time. Adding to this feat, he understands the real power of money at a time when it is unthinkable for a Black person to understand such things:

> *"Money is no good unless it contributes to the community, unless it builds a bridge to a better life. Any man can make money, but it takes a special kind of man to use it responsibly"*[29] ~~A.G. Gaston

People wonder how multitudes of jailed civil rights demonstrators in the South were instantly sprung through bail money. It was through people like A.G. Gaston. Like any story there are two sides to A.G.'s economic power at this time.

Some believe A.G. is afforded this power by not representing a threat to the racist core of America during this period. On the other hand, bail money puts warriors back on the street to do their best another day.

Other Black radio entrepreneurs to follow include *Percy Sutton* of Inner City Broadcasting in New York, *Regan Henry* owning WGIV in Charlotte, the Johnson Publishing Company's Chicago stations, KPRS owners in Kansas City, the James Brown Enterprises chain of stations, former Green Bay Packer defensive standout *Willie Davis* and Motown legend *Stevie Wonder* owning KACE and KJLH, respectively, in Los Angeles.

The purchasing price of top radio stations during this time is relatively minimal (maybe in the $1-5 million range, give or take

---

[29] McKinney, Jeffrey, 45 Great Moments in Black Business, No. 24, "A.G. Gaston Amasses $130 Million in today's dollars," Fortune/www.blackenterprise.com, November 17, 2017.

some figures) in contrast to the price of top stations today, starting probably in the tens of millions.

This is an important contrast in understanding the economic power and mindset of Black businessmen during this time set against the major media purchasing prices of today. This economic condition in major media affects the power mindset of not only Black business-men, but today's media moguls in general. A.G., Willie, Percy, Stevie, and Regan were able to mix business and community.

The mix of the two was affordable, fit the times and showed up okay in the bottom line. A difficult mix for today not only in Black culture but American culture, taking for granted there is still a difference in the two.

The Power of Distribution

Any media of mass communication is held hostage by the power of distribution.

LOGAN H. WESTBROOKS

I learned this early after graduating from Lincoln University. In Chicago Johnson Publishing Company had a corner on the Black print market nationally in the 1960s and continues to be a player today through digital publishing.

The early days of selling daily and weekly Black newspapers in Memphis showed me the power of information dissemination along with the networking opportunities it presents if one is savvy enough to listen and talk to one's client base.

Johnson Publishing founder John H. Johnson,[30] a Black entrepreneur, fits in the mold of Sam Cooke, Berry Gordy and A.G. Gaston in recognizing and moving on the power of direct contact with a consumer base. In publishing profound economic, educational

---

[30] John H. Johnson founded Johnson Publishing Company in 1941 with a $500 loan from his mother to publish *Negro Digest*.

and entertainment pieces and using the captivating medium of photography to its fullest extent, Johnson Publishing was the Black culture version of *Look* and *Life* magazines but with its own content freedom.

This was an important distinction. Especially in a period when Black culture is moving from the *Amos 'n' Andy*[31] and *Buckwheat/Little Rascals* era that presented Black persona from a non-Black base of content control.

SKY TRAUGHBER

My problem with the French-speaking television show in the late 50s was probably due to them not having a clue of how a nine-year-old Black kid could be anything *but* Buckwheat. Johnson Publishing helped change some of this through its publishing and distribution of magazines like <u>*Jet*</u> and <u>*Ebony*</u>.

Though the magazines profiled celebrities, their homes, cars and luxury lifestyles, it also touched the everyday person. You could turn from a page featuring the NAACP helping a poor person win a court case to the next page showing Nat King Cole's estate and feel a connection to both.

Slowly a more diverse image of the Black experience begins to emerge, though the Black culture was already rich through eras such as the Harlem Renaissance period. With Civil Rights coming to the forefront and more Blacks taking a serious look at the behind-the-scenes buttons to push, the power of Blackness now takes on a deeper meaning in the 60s.

LOGAN H. WESTBROOKS

This is the environment that sets me forth into the powerful worlds of content control and distribution. Coming from a co-operative entrepreneur environment at Historically Black Lincoln University

---

[31] *Amos 'n' Andy* is still considered by some to be a masterpiece of a production. The timing of the social, media and business environment when it was presented contributed to its early demise, though today there is still debate over media content presentations involving Black culture.

to Johnson Publishing leaves little or no room for that negative, esteem-deflating virus to find a nesting place. Of course, one has to be willing to immerse oneself in this power no matter the background.

Many Black leaders have never attended an Historically Black College or worked at a Black-owned powerhouse and still immerse themselves in recognizing this power. One may have to work harder to "feel it" without a strong Black environment to build on. Some may have to work equally hard to place a strong Black environment into perspective by not "missing the forest by looking at the trees."

This is the true beauty of Black in a universal sense. It can travel on many roads, blast into space, hit and miss a few galaxies and still find the funk.

Having an open mind serves me well in my acceptance into an RCA Victor Management Training Program in Chicago following the Johnson Publishing stint. Also accepted in this program at this time is future Warner Brothers Black Music head Tom Draper, though I believe that Tom more clearly fit the profile for corporate management than myself.

This type of distinction will prove a major clash in later years as major labels integrate their Black Music Divisions with a more "street" label culture.

The RCA training gig put me in a position of Inventory Clerk in an era where the physical distribution of albums and singles dominated sales. It was a crucial entry-level position ensuring that the communication and data between retail, wholesale and the record company is timely and accurate.

Miscommunication can affect the availability of a hot record to the public. It can also disrupt pressing priorities, say, if a hot record is selling out of the warehouses and stores, nationally, and the record company is pressing other records as priorities, due to a lack of this information.

Today, computer technology assists in this vital chain of information flow, but the basic concept remains the same. Know what is hot, make sure it is available for purchase and make sure the consumer knows where to find it. Online, offline, crossing the line, whatever.

Also generated in the distribution side of not only records, but also film and to a degree, print are revenue collections. Print and television collect their major income through ad sales. "Cooking the books" is easier when you control the flow of product into the marketplace along with the return flow of money from the consumer back through the channel of retail to wholesale to manufacturer/supplier. Product and inventory accounting is part of this process.

Picking up networking skills served me well at RCA. My assimilation into the "lily-white" world of sales distribution informed me of a sales rep opening at Capitol Records in Chicago.

SKY TRAUGHBER

Two things are of importance here. First, all the radio airplay and exposure in the world will not help an act if the record is not distributed and sold, especially during this period. Secondly, even though I spent a couple of years at powerhouse CBS Records in the late 70s in promotion and marketing, I did not even "see" a Black record company sales person until I arrived in Los Angeles and this person worked for Motown.

To go even further, there was a time in the 50s and 60s when only White promotion men promoted Black records to R&B and Pop radio. Pioneer Black promotion men like Dave Clark, Fred Ware and Granville White[32] benefited, in part, by Black radio disc jockeys, probably in the likes of Birmingham radio legend Shelley Stewart, refusing to play an R&B record not delivered by a person of color. Not only does the culture thing come into play, but also an

---

[32] Dave Clark is reportedly the first Black radio promotion person. Fred Ware is a pioneering Black promotion person who started in promotion and sales at Liberty Records. Fred, in Atlanta, and Granville, in Chicago, later help form the nucleus of power at the CBS Records Black Music Division with respect from radio, distribution, prominent artists and the Black underworld.

examination of employment opportunities generated by Black Music.

Radio airplay analysis and applications as well as wholesale and retail sales operations can require a high-level of math and counting numbers. As with reading words, having opportunities of employment utilizing these analytical skills are part of the American Dream.

LOGAN H. WESTBROOKS

I was aided in my Capitol sales rep exploits by hot-selling artists Cannonball Adderley, Lou Rawls and Nancy Wilson demanding that Capitol employ Black sales people. A key element here is "hot-selling artists." All the social and morale considerations aside, entertainment is still a business and a voice that helps keep the lights on at a company is usually a voice that has to be at least heard.

Though film does not have the Black base legacy as Black Music, it is an equally powerful medium for the culture and its stories. Denzel Washington and Spike Lee are two film figures that come to mind in using their box office clout to speak out on some issues regarding employment in areas of control in the film industry, though Denzel, in particular, distinctly draws the correlation between box office power and opportunity when he speaks on this subject.

Recently a report surfaced showing the fact that not one Black person in Hollywood is in a position to "green light"[33] a movie. However, over recent years Nicole Brown at Tri-Star Films, Shonda Rhimes at Netflix, Ava Duvernay, and film producer Debra Chase Martin have come close to achieving or have achieved positions of power in deciding film production deals.

Samuel L. Jackson has spoken out on behind-the-scenes controls in writing and story content. This can be dangerous territory for a new artist or actor or even an established one looking to expand their career or business interests.

---

[33] "Green light" in film is whether or not the project receives funding.

Again, perfection creates ideals while flaws create humans. Record company execs, television producers and film studio heads have the same human traits of fear, confusion, retaliation, etc., as everyone else and the power of distribution eventually makes its way into the world of content. At the same time, warriors usually carry forth even in the face of danger.

While people like Cannonball, Nancy and Lou helped open the door for me in the sales position at Capitol, the changing business climate also played its hand as Chicago, at this time, had the highest number of Black retail outlets in the country.

The mob still owned the distribution of music through the jukeboxes in the speakeasys during this time and their influence easily spread into the pinball machines and video games of later years. I would find myself opening a Pac-Man arcade years later. Some of this organized crime influence will make its way into the core distribution networks of not only Black Music but also all popular music to retail.

Meanwhile, Motown and Stax Records are entering their own worlds of realizing the power of distribution. Acting on Smokey's suggestion of direct empowerment and his family's financial investment, Berry transfers the "get it right" production model he learned at an auto plant assembly line[34] in Detroit to the studio.

With the Funk Brothers supplying a steady base of tracks, writers penning an endless stream of relatable stories, singers releasing their souls in a pop surrounding and producers mixing the parts, the *Sound of Young America* aka the *Motown Sound* is born.

SKY TRAUGHBER

Just for the record, there are rumors of "luck" with Berry and Motown. I had the privilege of heading the Quality Control Committee in the A&R/Creative department at Motown in the late 70s, reporting to Berry. Though this particular version of this important decision-making facet of the Motown Sound was not the

---

[34] Reportedly the Lincoln Mercury assembly plant.

original version, this privilege involved a first-hand experience of learning that the music production model of Motown was not founded on luck. The string of hits coming from Hitsville was a mix of intelligence and talent, though it occurred in good timing.

Motown's music was getting massive and consistent play on R&B stations but receiving resistance on the Pop side. Enter a radio-advertising broker named Jerry Greenberg who reportedly withholds advertising dollars from the Pop stations not playing the well-deserved Motown wax.[35] Without advertising income, a radio station is dead air. Play the records the advertisers pay for. While creating a healthy demand for distribution, this reality between advertising and airplay will have an even more defining influence on the music content in Urban and Pop radio during the Hip Hop era.

Okay, so the Motown wax is spinning across the board now, but how does Motown *meet* the mounting wholesale and retail demand? Enter Faye Hale. Faye becomes a key person for Motown to meet its growing wholesale and retail demand by organizing the multitude of regional distributors necessary to feed the hungry consumers hearing the music.

In discussing crucial release dates with Faye, while at Motown, I would check the wholesale order board in her sales and distribution office for a quick and accurate glance of the hot music and *where the music is hot*. Again, the organization involved in shipping records to multiple distributors, tracking those shipments and *collecting from those distributors* was not the result of accident or luck at Motown. At least from what I saw and dealt with businesswise.

This need for massive shipping and collections will create disturbing rumors of mob connections and ownership for Motown as the label expands and experiences a need for capital infusion to meet its overall operation expense.

Stax takes a different route at this time and it becomes a highway exit eventually contributing to its early demise. Like Motown, Stax uses multiple independent wholesale distributors to piece together

---

[35] Conversation with Jerry Greenberg in 1989

regional hits, but unlike Motown, is unable to garner consistent national distribution. Enter New York-based Atlantic Records. Stax (then also known as Satellite Records) heads Jim Stewart and Estelle Axton and Atlantic honcho Jerry Wexler recall from Rob Bowman's book:

Soulsville, U.S.A.: The Story of Stax Records:

Atlantic proved to be especially assiduous at discovering small labels to distribute. When "Cause I Love You" (Rufus and Carla Thomas), had sold about 5,000 copies in the Memphis area (and according to Estelle, another 5,000 in Nashville and Atlanta), either Buster Williams (a Stax distributor) or his employee Norman Reuben, picked up the phone and hipped Jerry Wexler to the record. Wexler was impressed ("I liked everything about it that bespoke Memphis") and, in turn, sent one of Atlantic's promotion men into Memphis to talk to Jim about the possibility of leasing the master.

As Satellite was in no position to even begin to afford to market the record nationally, Jim was more than interested...

...The original signed contract with Atlantic covered only Rufus and Carla Thomas records. A couple of months later, via a handshake deal, Atlantic acquired first refusal rights on the distribution of any subsequent Satellite and later Stax release.

This "handshake" deal eventually turns into a signed contract between Stax and Atlantic. In actuality, it is a "master purchase" deal as opposed to just a "license" deal where Stax would still own its masters. The license fees Atlantic pays to Stax are minimal and Atlantic acquires Stax valuable masters like Booker T. & The M.G.'s and Sam and Dave[36] at a very low cost.

---

[36] The Sam and Dave deal with Atlantic is complex as the duo are actually signed to Atlantic and "loaned" to Stax for production, similar to early film studio deals on an actor.

One may say that Stax should have remained with independent distributors, but when you have music deserving of a national audience, you move. Jim Stewart, coming from a banking background, and Jerry Wexler, reportedly believing in the morals of Atlantic[37] were unaware of this deceiving contract language. Again "reading" comes into play. *Someone* at Atlantic knew what they were doing. Anyway, this loss of future income from its catalog sets Stax on a series of distribution deals involving Gulf and Western, bank loans and the final deathblow at CBS Records in the 70s.

LOGAN H. WESTBROOKS

Building on my experience at Capitol, I accept a Regional Radio Promotion Manager position for the Midwest Region at Capitol in Chicago. Then a series of opportunities present themselves that will build my experience and vision in both radio and sales, aided by the upward movements of promotion men like Ron Granger at Capitol.

With Black Music sales growing at a breakneck pace, opportunities in radio promotion seem to open every week. Ron Granger becomes the Vice President of Pop Promotion for Capitol in Los Angeles, directing *all* of the Capitol releases for radio airplay. This is a feat equal to my entry into the taboo area of sales in Chicago and will later influence my vision at CBS Records.

I join Ron in Los Angeles, becoming an Assistant to the Vice President of Marketing at Capitol, then back to Chicago as the National Director of Black Music Promotion at Mercury Records. This swift but crucial series of activity in radio *and* sales, and doing business with rack jobber accounts like *Sears,* as well as the smaller but equally powerful one-stops[38] afforded me an understanding that

---

[37] Wexler, Jerry with Ritz, David, *Rhythm and the Blues: A Life in American Music*, Knopf Publishing, 1993.

[38] Retail stores like Sears and Woolworth comprise the drop-off outlets for the wholesale distributors known as rack jobbers (their "job" is to supply the music racks at these stores with albums and singles). One stop distributors drop-off their albums and singles at smaller mom and pop outlets but these outlets usually serve the heart of inner-city communities. The combined power of rack jobber and one stop accounts in the 50s and 60s are necessary comrades for any record label to stay in business, leading to the addition of "major account" outlets like Tower and Strawberries as the record business approaches the 70s and 80s.

radio play is just the beginning, as Motown and Stax know. While the Ron Granger episode during this stretch shows a willingness for corporate labels to include Blacks in an overall plan, my new bride encounters an awakening attachment to this willing-ness. Through the normal social encounters of top executives and their wives, Geri discovers that my salary was substantially lower than my White counterpart's salary in the Los Angeles Capitol Marketing gig. This became a staple for Geri "watching my back" in subsequent major label's *equal but separate* displays of discrepancy.

Business, Human Flaws and the Movement

Black Music's move from the 60s to the 70s, like America, either invites the corporate culture to the party or it just crashes in. The rawness of James Brown, Isaac Hayes, Woodstock, Women's Rights and the Black Revolution begin a head-on collision with maybe an inevitable marriage.

Everyone is looking to reap some benefits from the revolution, struggle and disobedience mindset of the 60s. Expansion is the tone of the day. Stax moves into film with the ground-breaking and street-oriented music-film *Wattstax* featuring Stax acts like the Staple Singers, *Operation PUSH* founder Jesse Jackson and fast-rising political and social comic Richard Pryor, among others.

Motown joins in with the classic drama productions of *Bingo Long and the Traveling All-Stars* featuring Billy Dee Williams and James Earl Jones and *Lady Sings the Blues* with Diana Ross, Billy Dee, and Richard Pryor. James Brown increases his radio chain, issues his own food stamps, builds restaurants and buys jet planes.

Stax flexes its economic and content power by self-financing Wattstax and using Columbia Pictures only for distribution. This is not total empowerment, but a major distributor is more prone to stay out of content control if they are not paying for the production of the content. At least at this time, in this case.

Though Sam Cooke challenges Pepsi with his own cola and "Try a Little Tenderness" Stax-great Otis Redding plans on building his publishing and concert ventures to new heights, neither lives to join this turn-of-the-decade era. Sam Cooke's move from Gospel to Pop involves some marital infidelity, not an uncommon lure for anyone now immersed in fame and fortune, though perhaps more so for entertainers. Not creating any stereotype. There are countless entertainment figures that deal with their spouse and their spouse only.

Sam's case ends with a gunshot from a seedy motel owner after a hooker reportedly robs Sam.[39] Sam's case begins, rumor-wise, by his brave move into the record company[40] and publishing ownerships expressed earlier as part of his empowerment dream not only for Blacks but artists.

Even as Sam was becoming more careless with his social life, friends and associates for many years strongly question the "randomness" of his killing.[41] Some point to a possible set-up for "getting too big for his britches" and not sharing the pie with others who believe the pie is theirs to share, regardless of who created the recipe.

At the time of this death Sam was the number-two seller on the RCA label behind Elvis Presley. Presley's manager—Colonel Parker— reportedly used the Cooke killing as a negotiating tool in amassing his eventual 50% share of Presley's income. Parker would insinuate that Elvis was better off with him alive at 50% as opposed to being dead dealing with more "underground" power figures in the music business at that time.[42]

A similar rumor of underground figures "sending a message"[43] revolves around Otis Redding's plane crash, resulting in Redding's death as well as decimating the original Bar-Kays lineup. Some of the Bar-Kays were still of high school age.

---

[39] Wolff, Daniel, *You Send Me: The Life and Times of Sam Cooke*. 1995
[40] Sam Cooke's SAR Records had signed future R&B, Pop, Rock and Blues greats Bobby Womack, Johnnie Taylor and Billy Preston by 1961.
[41] Wolff, Daniel, You Send Me: The Life and Times of Sam Cooke.
[42] Nash, Alanna, *The Colonel,* Simon & Schuster, 2010.
[43] Conversations with veteran Stax musicians during the early 70s.

Moving into the 1970s, Black business in America is becoming more powerful but so is American corporate business. The number of executives truly dominating the Black Corporate core within the African-American[44] political economy grows from the 1960s to the 1970s, but still amounts to less than 200 individuals.[45] The capital worth of legitimate Black corporations at this time looks something like this:[46]

Motown Record Corporation	$64 million
Johnson Publishing Company	$61 million
Fedco	$45 million
H.J. Russell Construction	$41 million
Johnson Cosmetics	$35 million

Black banks at this time have an average capital of $60 million, while North Carolina Mutual Life Insurance and Golden State Mutual Life of Los Angeles average $3 billion.

Still, Mobil Oil Corporation could purchase *all of these corporations* with its liquid assets.[47]

Numerically speaking, Blacks in America usually comprise about 10% of the total population. So, the numbers themselves work against any massive percentage of Black economic power when set against the total economic power of America. A slow start, due to slavery, discrimination and lack of access to legal and illegal power, say, like the Kennedy family partnership in bootleg liquor with the mob,[48] has to also be considered in this disparity of wealth and economic power.

An illegal activity like numbers running[49] offers an economic base starting in the 1920s, but it is illegal and usually part of a larger headquarters not controlled by Black capital. Illegal business

---

[44] The new identity phrase for Blacks beginning to emerge during this time.

[45] How Capitalism Underdeveloped Black America, Marable, Manning.

[46] *Black Enterprise* 100 Black Companies, 1970s.

[47] How Capitalism Underdeveloped Black America, Marable, Manning.

[48] *The Kennedys: The Curse of Power*, History Channel Documentary, 2000.

[49] A forerunner to the now-legalized state-betting lotteries, this street version is reportedly still alive in America.

operations can present a powerful base but this base is always subject to a lawful or a government intervention, no matter the ethnic origin. The Taliban (terrorist?) organization, as of this writing, reportedly makes $600-700 million a year from illegal drug trafficking.[50] They don't care about legal or government intervention. In their eyes, they are their own government and ruling power. They pray to a higher power not connected to the planet earth. Unless a movement or enterprise can operate under this premise and "kiss this world goodbye" in this manner, illegal money assets are always under a threat of lien.

As Black Music, film, entrepreneur and athletic empowerment begins to reap some benefits from civil rights, better education and collective partnerships with each other, it also crosses over the radar line and into the "signal pickup" of not only the illegitimate but legitimate radar screen of an American culture creeping further into a capitalist rather than social mindset. Bottom line: there are not enough legitimate Black business enterprises with enough capital to capture, manufacture, bottle and distribute its own culture.

However, this rise in Black economic power is *astounding!* There is a saying:
If you don't use it, you can lose it.

Enter the *Black Panther Party For Self Defense*, Jesse Jackson's *Operation PUSH*, Stokely Carmichael, Julian Bond and *SNCC* (Student Non-Violent Coordinating Committee) and athletes Jim Brown, Kareem Abdul-Jabbar coming on the heels of the fiery and uplifting speeches of Malcolm X and Dr. Martin Luther King, Jr., and Curtis Mayfield's Impressions shouting "Keep On Pushing." Acting as forerunners to the 2008 Barack Obama *"Yes We Can"* slogan of optimism against the odds there emerges a consciousness of, "…let's pull together and do what we can with what we have, 'cause it ain't too shabby…"

At the same time, enter J. Edgar Hoover's FBI and COINTELPRO, the corporate culture that President Eisenhower warned of in the 1950s and a more sophisticated organized crime syndicate. The

---

[50] *The Taliban,* History Channel Documentary, 2008.

Vietnam War battles claim human lives in the physical sense, but the culture war within America at this time will have far-reaching physical, emotional and economic repercussions in the years to come.

Drugs, Sex and Payoffs are as much a part of the American legacy as Babe Ruth. However, the reportedly deliberate distribution of cheap and sometimes powerfully deadly heroin into Black communities during this time is noteworthy as its origins reportedly originate in the American government, organized crime and Blacks themselves.[51]

Why?

President Richard Nixon explains:

> *[President Nixon] emphasizes that you have to*
> *understand that the <u>whole</u> problem is really the*
> *Blacks. The key is to devise a system that recognizes*
> *this while not appearing to.*[52]

Contrary to major media outlets deleting *"For Self Defense"* and referring to the Panthers only as the *Black Panthers*,[53] the Panthers original mission, like the Black P. Stones incorporation, is a positive, intellectual and business mission. Initially, violence is used only in defense of their community against racist police. However, some renegade members later adopt a "shoot first and ask questions later" philosophy that mirrors their oppressor's tactics.

The Panthers *Free Breakfast for Kids* program is positively revolutionary at the time. Panther philosophers like Bobby Seale and Eldridge Cleaver share intellect with communities and the Panther legal-advice seminars inform an otherwise neglected clientele.

---

[51] Films Panther! and American Gangster.

[52] *The Haldeman Diaries, Inside the White House.* Nixon's controversial and conflicting relation with Blacks continues during this time as entertainers Sammy Davis, Jr., and James Brown endorse him. Nixon also commends Jim Brown's Economic Union as a "brilliant example of how a charitable organization should work," though the organization is actually established as an economic empowerment venture.

[53] Bobby Seale, *Seize the Time*, Vintage Books, 1970.

Black music becomes involved as Stax's alliance with Jesse Jackson and Motown's release of Dr. Martin Luther King, Jr.[54] albums take Black Music into the FBI radar screen along with the Panthers, Dr. Martin Luther King, Jr., and John Lennon.

Lennon, at the time of his death, is also under surveillance as an undocumented alien and a threat to U.S. security for his affiliations with revolutionary figures.[55]

Motown's mission of "Pop crossover and acceptance" somewhat dilutes the extent of its public involvement in some of these movements, helping to extend its shelf life, somewhat.

SKY TRAUGHBER

Just for the record, my contact with Berry, other family members, and key Motown personnel showed more concern and empathy for Black empowerment than the company image projected.

I never witnessed Berry Gordy suppressing anyone's dreams. In fact, he seemed to encourage entreprencurship, quality and achievement as an integral part of Black Power.

When one attempts to figure out the ownerships, distribution of income[56] and power affiliated with *Motown as a company,* it may require a good shrink.

As Berry would tell us: "Don't try to figure out Motown...just do your job." The most profound wisdom Mr. Gordy ever laid on me, *personally,* is: "I don't want you to make the same mistakes that I did."

---

[54] A Motown Vice President, Junius Griffin, wrote or co-wrote some of MLK's speeches and served as the Motown emissary to civil rights and Black power movement organizations.

[55] John Lennon Documentary.

[56] The bi-weekly salaries to Motown artists and the bi-weekly "work for hire" payments to Motown/Jobete writers are the subject of many discussions both pro and con. On the one hand, any consistent paycheck or advance to a creative person can help keep that person focused on their work as opposed to illegal activity, starvation or homelessness. On the other hand, it may present a conflict in independence and accounting.

Berry knew he had allowed Motown, as a company, to enter some areas of imperfection. Some of this revolves around "employee" vs "entrepreneur," the meaning of true power and the decisions surrounding making pacts with the devil for the ride to heaven.

- Berry would emphasize to us that not only was Motown "*not a Black Music company* but a company that recorded primarily Black acts," but that "*everyone* played and listened to Motown." This was true in in the 1950s, 1960s and early-1970s with only *two* major radio formats: Top 40 and R&B. However, by the late 1970s we had Top 40, Urban Top 40 (mostly singles), Urban Progressive (mostly FM including LP cuts), AOR (Album-Oriented Pop and Rock), Alternative, Progressive Jazz, AM R&B, and MOR (Middle of the Road), equaling EIGHT formats as opposed to the TWO earlier formats. MOR was a key format for "hard to classify" acts in the 1970s that may have been great exposure for, say, Teena Marie at Motown with a mostly White audience.

  My personal professional take, as an example, was "if everyone plays Motown, in 1980, then why am I sitting in all these meetings, as Teena Marie's A&R person catching hell trying to get her pushed on Pop radio (at times getting her pushed, internally, at Motown, at all). Just as an example of how times had changed on Motown's music-and-radio philosophy. This was, in part, a heartbreaking reality for Berry, I'm sure, as more *formats* meant more *payoffs*. How could Motown keep up with deep pockets of, say, CBS and Warner Brothers in this respect?

- Berry, in 1980, still preferred that Motown acts not use their own attorney, implying that "Motown will always take care of you." In reality, yes, a number of early Motown acts and staffers, no longer active at the company, were still on the payroll. However, Motown's competition, as in major-corporate labels, were fine in dealing with artists having their own attorney, sometimes *requiring* this as a way of ensuring acts could not come back at them later claiming they were discouraged from this right.

Nashville music-industry professionals, such as Billboard's Bill Williams and ASCAP's Charlie Monk, who helped initiate Middle Tennessee State's soon-to-be-powerful Recording Industry Management program would constantly tell us they were doing so not only because "...Nashville has too many hand-shake deals..." but because the "entire music industry was growing too fast to not have more iron-clad contractual and marketing strategies. And that these new-strategies would require a new-breed of executives to manage the industry going forward to the 1980s, 1990s."

Berry's early songwriting partner with Jackie Wilson and at Motown, Billy Davis, strongly agreed with Bill and Charlie's assessment of the MTSU program and future of the music industry at that time, as he would speak to us while cutting commercials in Nashville studios after penning the very-popular commercial for Coca Cola "I'd like to teach the world to sing..."

- Though Motown was "indie-distributed," who were some of the people controlling some of these key distribution networks?

To this day I still commend the man for the honesty in this bit of education.

Another bit of education I received after leaving Motown was from Reggie Andrews—my replacement in A&R who was involved in hits by *The Dazz Band, DeBarge, Teena Marie,* and *Lionel Ritchie* in one calendar year at the label. But he was still told by Berry, "It was not enough." Though considered a "small" label by major corporate standards, Motown needed enough hits, like everyone else, to off-set its costs. Some costs were *full* LP costs to "test" an artist.

Nevertheless, all of this social power connected to a rising music power like Motown is bound to draw conflicting attention, confusion and suspicion from Blacks and Whites alike.

Let's go even deeper. Why do people do drugs, drink and have sex? *Because it feels good.* Dopamine is the "feel good" human brain chemical that we all fight to control or resign ourselves to at different levels and methods of enjoyment. Entertainment and revolution cultures already have a high level of estrogen, intrigue and danger. To a degree, it is only natural for this "thrill" to manifest itself in other mannerisms as an extension or escape from the work.

People like Berry Gordy, Sam Cooke, Jesse Jackson, Al Bell, Marvin Gaye, Al Green, don't necessarily have to look very far for these temptations. So, when we enter a discussion of how these temptations fit into a power environment, it is not from any judgmental view. This is not to insinuate or implicate any of the mentioned people, just giving an example of another thing they usually have to deal with.

It is well-known that Huey P. Newton, the Black Panther founder, died in a drug deal on an Oakland street after the Panthers were placed in a position of easy access, reportedly through infiltrators and the aforementioned alleged government and mob involvements. Drugs, alcohol and sex have always been a successful lure to distract the "dangerous" minds of revolutionaries.

Having access to willing women (or men for the female power group) narcotics, parties, gambling, exotic trips, etc., also became a natural part of doing business between record labels, radio and artists, and it finds its way into the social and political scenes.

During this time these exploits are generally civil, enjoyable and affordable. R&B radio jocks during this period are for the most part underpaid in relation to the income their broadcasts and personalities generate for others. A lot of the payola activity is actually to supplement their basic lifestyle or help provide for their family. But, as the stakes rise, the costs of either a normal or erotic lifestyle can also rise.

This will prove to be a "honeynet" for companies that have deep pockets to enter the world of Black Music, along with the power of distribution and the ease of collecting the funds necessary to fuel the cycle of business, life and fun.

<u>*Artist Development and Image*</u>

LOGAN H. WESTBROOKS

The travels of my world at this point are diverse, but they all revolve around a "richness of culture." Looking at films representing Black Music culture like *Bird* (Charlie "Bird" Parker), *The Cotton Club, Ray, The Five Heartbeats, Dreamgirls, Cadillac Records*, etc., a certain culture emerges, rolls into one's skin and never leaves.

A lot of this is the music itself. Honest soul and Black Music are just an inner experience manifesting itself through a self-taught or formally trained vehicle. Before his prison execution, Crips gang founder Tookie Williams said: *"You can't practice redemption by study, you have to live it."*[57]

When a lived experience is groomed through planned mechanics, it becomes what we call a "developed image" or in the music business, "artist development." This represents the middle ground between the *conception* and the *presentation* of an idea or expression.

Some of the most profound and deeply felt images are really people and expressions just being themselves. However, the process of how this rawness is captured, packaged and delivered is sometimes what an audience perceives the person or product to be.

My journey from Beale Street, the newspaper network, and Tony's Inn in Memphis to Johnson Publishing and music-rich Mercury and Capitol Records in culture-rich 60s Chicago and Los Angeles have given me a sense of what a powerful, yet soulful Black Music company can be.

Undoubtedly, this background figures in the call I received from CBS Records President and CBS Vice President of Marketing Clive Davis and Bruce Lundvall, respectively, to give the powerhouse label the one thing it is missing in the early 70s – *Black-oriented product.*

---

[57] Williams, Stanley Tookie, *Blue Rage, Black Redemption: A Memoir*, Simon & Schuster (Touchstone), 2007.

Bruce Lundvall announced:

> *It is with great pleasure that I announce*
> *the appointment of Logan H. Westbrooks*
> *to the newly created position of Director,*
> *Special Markets. Mr. Westbrooks will be*
> *responsible to me for directing the overall*
> *marketing efforts of Columbia, Epic and*
> *custom label R&B singles and album product.*
> *To help achieve this new concept in Black*
> *product marketing, he will directly supervise*
> *the field activities of our R&B promotion*
> *managers and will also provide special*
> *marketing direction in all aspects of R&B*
> *product, including advertising, cover art*
> *and design, sales and merchandising.*[58]

The CBS Records commitment to me and the development of a strong Black Music presence in the marketplace was admirable, fit the times and created jobs, record deals and concert revenue for Black artists and executives. However, the memo illustrated <u>three areas of concern</u> that will create problems for the venture in light of a Harvard Business School document, the venture became, arguably, based on:

1. The Special Markets division reports to the Vice President of Marketing, not the Label President or CEO of CBS, Inc.
2. There is no clear autonomy for the new division in the areas of A&R, which signs and develops the music content or Business Affairs, the department that cuts the deals.[59]
3. There is no clear autonomy for the new division in the area of Distribution, which establishes sales quotas, develops

---

[58] Westbrooks, Logan H., Williams, Lance A., *The Anatomy of a Record Company*.

[59] Some of this will change, later, with the CBS A&R appointments of CBS Black Music *Original Thirteen* member Gerry Griffith, former RCA veteran A&R executive Jerome Gasper and former Blue Note Jazz legend Dr. George Butler. The arrival of A&R and attorney heavyweight Larkin Arnold, of Capitol Records fame, at the label, in the early 1980s signals some A&R autonomy for a Black Music executive at the leading Black Music major label.

wholesale and retail account relationships and deals, tracks invoices and collects the dough.[60]

This is no insinuation that Clive or Bruce deleted these three concerns, intentionally.

SKY TRAUGHBER

I arrived at CBS after Clive was dismissed, but I had the opportunity to communicate with Bruce in his position of CBS Records President, and later when he held the same position at Elektra and Blue Note Records, and he always seemed honorable.

Like Berry and the imperfections at Motown, Jim Stewart, Estelle Axton and later Al Bell with the imperfections at Stax, Jerry Wexler at Atlantic, these are some flaws in early Black Music that will figure into both a magical and disturbed future of Black Music, affecting all popular music.

Nevertheless, the *Original Thirteen* staff [61] assembled at CBS have the opportunity to build on the profoundly rich artist development and image beginnings at Motown, Stax, and despite the Stax episode, Atlantic Records.

Also setting the stage for this surge in Black Music are labels like the Chicago-based Chess Records, Curtis Mayfield and his Curtom label, the raw Gene Chandler,[62] the socially aware Jerry Butler, Ewart Abner's[63] Vee-Jay Records and the Thom Bell-*Delfonics*, a

---

[60] Some of this will change, much later, with the appointment of Jimmy Starks, a former Temptations-bassist and CBS promotion person, to the CBS (Sony) Sales and Distribution Division.

[61] The first members of the newly organized Black Music Division, though there were Black promotion representatives like Fred Ware and Granville White already employed at the label.

[62] Gene Chandler's *"Duke of Earl"* single in the 60s is considered to be one of the first widely successful "sing along" records of R&B.

[63] Ewart owned one-third of Vee-Jay Records, the label that although immersed in R&B, initially brought the music of the Beatles to America. Ewart graduated from Historically Black Howard University with a degree in accounting and became a pioneer Black person on that end of the business. Later, he managed the Temptations and the Supremes and served as President of Motown.

smooth-Philadelphia sound that will also provide the strongest indie production team for the CBS venture.

The difference in the Stax and Motown image and the other labels at this time lies in the Stax and Motown Black-ownership "full-service" perspective and the mass public recognition of Stax and Motown.[64]

Motown's approach to this image is a formal approach. A "charm school" is established to train and groom Motown artists specifically for appearances at places like the *Copacabana Club*, the *Ed Sullivan Show* and the White House (sound familiar?). The thinking is to further embellish the Pop and crossover music sound with a more polished artist image than most Black artists are known for at this time.

Maxine Powell, who graduated from the highly regarded John Robert Powers School of Modeling in Chicago, and had Berry's sister, Gwen, as a student is brought in along with legendary choreographer Cholly Atkins.

Though some artists, like Marvin Gaye, rejected the school, most artists will later credit this grooming with expanding their appeal base and prolonging their careers. Even Marvin was able to pick up some tips on stage performance that helped in his quest to mix his church, soul and R&B background with a more Frank Sinatra-type presentation.

People like Suzanne DePasse, Bob Jones and Billie Jean Brown help implement this philosophy of presentation at the label on a daily basis. Suzanne figures prominently in the image development of acts like the *Jackson 5* and the *Commodores* and later heads the creative (A&R), television and film divisions of the label.

Bob Jones heads the Press and Publicity department for many years and later continues behind-the-scenes in the press development of

---

[64] It is during this time that the 100% ownership of Stax begins to change hands from Jim Stewart to Al Bell. Berry owns at least 51% of Motown, on the books. "Full Service" implies that a label can carry a record from inception to distribution and collection without the aid or dependence of a major distributor or label.

superstar Michael Jackson, though Michael and his brothers leave the label. Billie heads the original and crucial Quality Control Committee entrusted with deciding the product suitable to represent the Motown brand in weekly releases. Everything still begins with the music.

The key word for Berry in developing what would become the industry's first formally structured Artist Development Department is *presentation*. What people hear is an important thing, but what they see and read are also important.

Stax takes an equally profound but less formal approach. The artist development image for most Stax artists to the public becomes *"whatcha ya see is whatcha ya get,"* ironically becoming the title of one of the label's biggest hits with The Dramatics. Being based in Memphis as opposed to Detroit or Los Angeles with that southern realness probably contributes to this approach also. Not that the Motown approach is any less real or the Stax approach lacks crossover potential. Again, this is the true beauty of Black. Hard to define but it can still be felt.

People like Deanie Parker, Josephine Bridges and Larry Shaw head the Stax media and public relations image. Deanie's down-to-earth but still classy style emanates through the Stax artist and executive roster during this time.

Jo Bridges leaves a teaching position in the Memphis school system and lends her socially active but always classy and business acumen to acts like Isaac Hayes and the Temprees. Larry Shaw crafted many of the advertising campaigns for the label and is a major force in having *Wattstax* filmed.

Jo and Larry saw the benefits of higher education and arranged for me to attend Memphis State University on the first Stax scholarship even as I was receiving an equally eye-opening education on the road playing behind the Temprees. This was during the "Dedicated to the One I Love" tour and the Temprees were headlining and opening for acts like Curtis Mayfield and Kool & The Gang. Part of this education included observing Stax recording sessions.

The Stax studio education was courtesy of the Temprees and Rufus Thomas producer, Tom Nixon, who also invented some of the industry-defining engineering techniques at Motown before joining Stax and forming the We-Produce label with Tom, Josephine and Larry, never hesitated in spelling out the realities of not only the beauties but the battles Black Music was experiencing during this time. I only came in contact with Deanie recently, but the same education value seems true there.

Having been a musician for a Stax group, a promotion and product management person at CBS Records and an A&R/Staff Producer person at Motown, I will say that each of these important stalwarts in Black Music have their positive culture influences. However, I am glad that I started in the Stax environment. Being taught it is okay to see things as they are, early, can help put everything in perspective later. I acknowledge this blessing daily and never take it for granted.

LOGAN H. WESTBROOKS

I walked into a heavy dilemma in carrying forward these image and development pioneers while forming and directing the new CBS division. Stax and Motown are in a friendly competition for market share, but now the stakes in capturing this market will take on new meanings industry wide.

Like the mob model of business, money will flow upstream while image and control will flow downstream, only under a powerful corporate hierarchy. My background is drenched in Black ownership, culture and networking. My religious background has the Holy Ghost all over it. I have seen segregation from many angles.

Booker T. Washington High School, LeMoyne-Owen College, Lincoln University, the Johnson Publishing Company, RCA, Capitol and Mercury Records helped educate me. Now I must not only set a precedent for a "full-service" Black Music division within a suspect but powerful major label system, but also oversee a formalized blueprint being written at the world's most recognized center for business organization, in intellectual terms, the Harvard Business School in Boston.

Marrying a strong partner in Geri, in 1965, proves to be a good move for me in this quest and in the years to come.

Education

LOGAN H. WESTBROOKS

As of this writing, some may associate Harvard University's legacy with Black Culture to the widely publicized conflicts between former Harvard President Lawrence Summers and the African American Studies professors Dr. Cornel West and Dr. Henry Louis "Skip" Gates. Some of the conflict revolved around Dr. West's teaching and grading methods along with his entry into the Rap and Hip Hop worlds.

More controversial is the timing of this conflict, as Dr. Gates has amassed a "dream team" of African-American expert scholars at Harvard prior to the conflict. Due in part to this conflict, Dr. West and Dr. Anthony Appiah, key members of the team, leave Harvard for Princeton University.

Years earlier, Harvard Law Professor Derrick Bell, the first Black tenured professor at Harvard Law, refused to return to the college after an unpaid leave in protest over the lack of women of color on the faculty.

SKY TRAUGHBER

To go even further with Harvard's history, as of Tuesday, April 26, 2022, (reported by CNN's Ray Sanchez), Harvard has committed $100 million to create a fund to research and redress its "extensive entanglements in slavery" as stated by university President Lawrence Bacow.

Numerous writers have also, at this time, including Craig Steven Wilder (democracynow.org) harvard_slave_report, April 28, 2022) exposed Harvard's attempt, over the years, to "erase the story of slavery" from the university's history. To say that CBS's commission of Harvard Business School to research and come up with a report that eventually creates a strong era of Black Music while creating numerous job opportunities but also, controversially, plays a part in ending Soul/Black music's strong indie distributed ownership is like "Dr. Jekyll & Mr. Hyde" may be an understatement. For younger readers, this "title" is from a story by Robert Louis Stevenson about a person with a two-sided personality. One good. One questionable. This is strictly from an "historical" and "aftermath" perspective and does not reflect the positive intentions of the report in 1972.

LOGAN H. WESTBROOKS

The Harvard University of the early 1970s that I will co-ordinate an important <u>Study of the Soul Music Environment</u>, known as *The Harvard Report,* faces an equally controversial environment in higher education.

This Harvard University is dealing with its own Psychology Professor, Timothy Leary, leading the LSD-Mind Expansion Movement while UCLA is dealing with its own former Professor Angela Davis becoming one of the FBI's Most Wanted for alleged Communist ties and murder charges connected to a prison escape attempt.

San Jose State track athletes Tommie Smith and John Carlos defy American patriotism with Black-gloved clinched fists at the Olympic Games. Oakland-based Merritt College and the California Berkeley Campus are in the heart of the northern California Panther and Black Power Movement and the Kent State and Jackson State student massacres by police still resonate through academic life.

A student body migration from Historically Black Colleges and Universities to White Institutions of Higher Learning created a dilution and expansion of Black social awareness and power in America, all at once.

Much of the intellect surrounding these events had a potential to overthrow a now-Richard Nixon led government and became standard classroom fare in the curriculum of many colleges at this time.

It is said that everything has a breaking point. Everything must change. As the American Dream and Black Music move from a more social and rebellion stage to embracing some of this change within a corporate culture, so does Harvard University.:

> *Bureaucratization changed Harvard in profound and unexpected ways. The growth of a corporate infrastructure that reported to the president diminished the structure of the faculty while boosting that of the central administration. The culture of the university changed as well. Harvard's dominant values had once been those of scholars, but increasingly the university was defined by the bottom line standards of corporate lawyers and MBAs.*

> *At points in Harvard's history, the faculty had essentially run the institution. Now they became more and more like mere employees, with less and less of a sense of investment in the university as a whole…Bureaucratization created a corps of behind-the-scenes powerbrokers whose decisions had great impact on both the students and faculty – yet the students and faculty frequently didn't even know who those decision makers were.[65]*

This change of decision-making power set against one of the most profound turn-of-the-decade eras in American history created a "heck of a time" for me and others to embellish yet attempt to protect the rawness, honesty, magic and equity of Black Music.
As early Pop impresario Phil Spector said,[66] *"All popular music is affected by what happens in Black Music."*

---

[65] Bradley, Richard, *Harvard Rules,* Harper Collins, 2005.
[66] Brown, Mick, *Tearing Down the Wall of Sound: The Rise and Fall of Phil Spector,* Vintage, 2008.

PART II
"Bridging the Gap in the 70s"

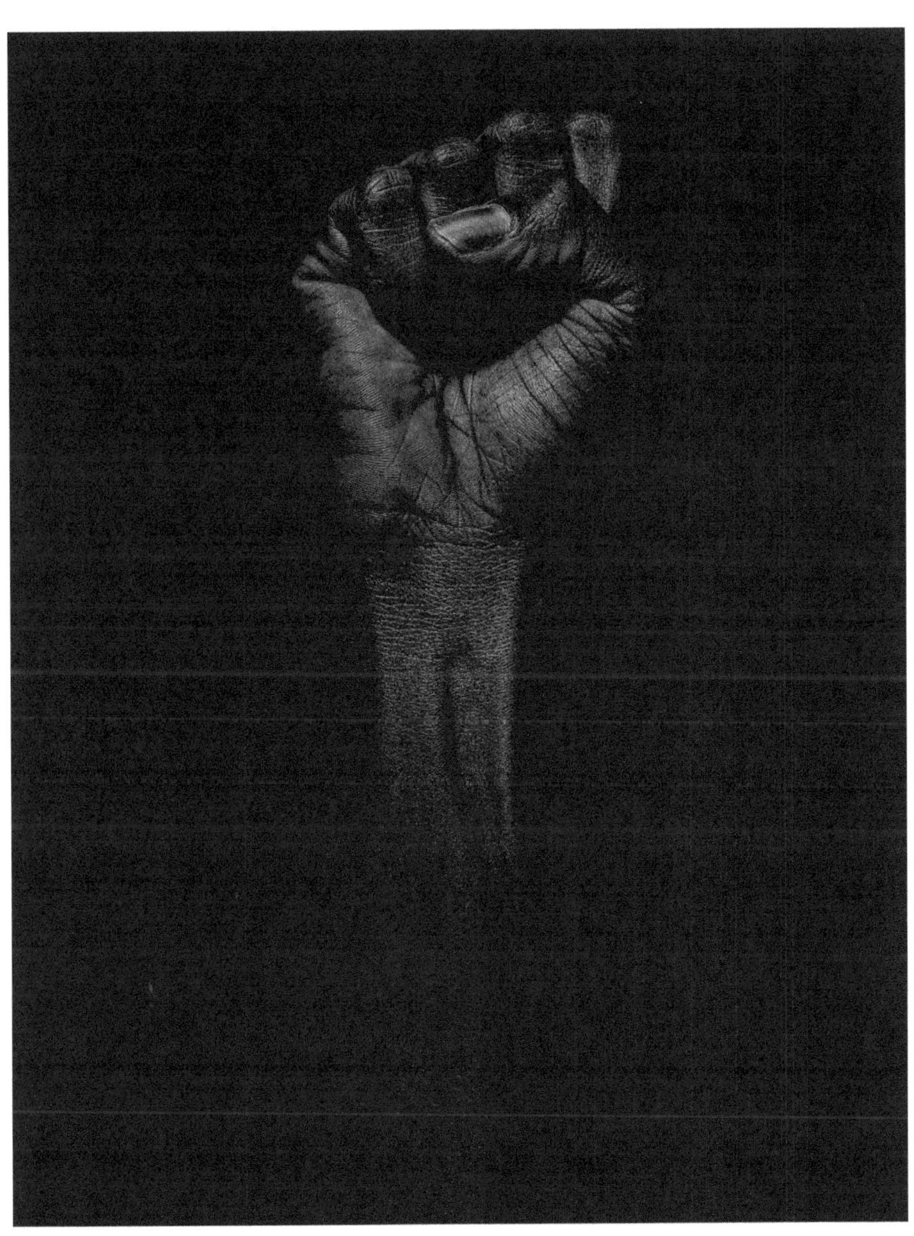

CHAPTER 5

The Mission

You know how it feels
You understand
What it is to be a stranger
In this unfriendly land [67]
      ~~ Bobby "Blue" Bland

LOGAN H. WESTBROOKS

As with any new business venture, a mission establishes a blueprint to follow—in the long term as well as the short term. Black Music, entering the 1970s, has endured in a consistent and steady pace, both musically and socially.

Economically, Black Music revenues at this time are estimated to be worth an estimated $60 million, annually[68] and the projected potentials are like the free-flowing water in the Tennessee River, waiting to be harnessed into the Hoover Dam, supplying its soulful force to a bigger clientele.

CBS Records in the early 1970s has essentially two top groups targeted to Blacks, *Sly and The Family Stone* and *Santana*. This roster will boom to over a hundred in less than ten years. The years following 1971 and up to the early 80s are considered a critical point where Black Music "turns the corner" in more ways than one.

Arriving at the top Pop label in the music business, now committed to an entry in Black Music, puts me in a position to elevate the *Original Thirteen* staff and myself to new heights never witnessed in the power of Black Music. But it also puts me in a position to help place CBS Records in the company of labels like Motown, Stax and

---

[67] Bobby "Blue" Bland tune, *Lead Me On.*
[68] Mills, Fred, *Behind the Rhythm, Urbaninsite.* A previous footnote lists Motown Record Corporation at $64 million, alone. That footnote is for the mid-to-late 70s and reflects Motown's total capital worth.

Atlantic, who are considered the leading labels in Black Music market share at this time.

My short-term vision has already been established with Clive Davis and Bruce Lundvall:

Build a strong Black Music presence from the ground up.

Articles, books and documentaries have chronicled this short-term mission for years.

What I now share was my long-term vision, previously unknown:

Build a strong enough presence within CBS so that the entire label reports to a Black Music-based presence, thereby placing everything on equal footing.

This long-term vision was ahead-of-its time and preceded America reporting to a "Black President," in Barack Obama. It also shows a changing definition of *freedom,* from a "rights gaining" definition of the 50s and 60s to a definition of commanding power within the same system that only recently denied Blacks and lower-class citizens some basic constitutional rights.

One must understand the complexity as well as the foresight of this mission set against the 70s, in contrast to today. Many people label Bobby Seale, Huey P. Newton and Richard Pryor as "crazy niggas" during this time. Bobby and Huey studied California gun laws and sold Chinese Red Books[69] on the Cal Berkeley campus to finance the open armament of the Panthers in protecting their community against racist cops.

Richard Pryor openly exposes the sometimes racist, offensive and oppressive nature of White people in his works, makes them laugh and ask (and pay) for more.

---

[69] The Chinese Red Books of the late 1960s were a limited representation of the doctrines of then-Chinese Chairman Mao Tse Tung. The Panthers bought the books wholesale for $.30 and sold them at $1.00. In developing the Panther mission, Huey frequently replaced the words of "oppressed Chinese people" with "American Black people."

As this long-term mission for CBS Records was not shared with Clive and Bruce, it is unknown what their reaction would have been. *"Another crazy nigga..."* OR *"maybe he's on to something."* Today, at least this vision may be making some headway in some areas with Obama.

In the 80s and 90s we have CEO appointments of *Ken Chenault* at American Express, *Sylvia Rhone* at Atlantic East-West Records, and so forth. As of this writing, Xerox has named a Black female, Ursula Burns as its CEO. During the 80s, former CBS and Motown A&R executive, Gerry Griffith, headed *all* of the EMI Records A&R efforts, appointed by Bruce Lundvall.

Major record labels during the early 70s, however, have *no* Black Presidents and practically every Black executive works in the Black Music Division, centered primarily in radio promotion. On the positive side, this ensures that people who live the culture are involved in its presentation. It also creates employment and development opportunities for Blacks in the industry. On the other hand, it tends to stereotype and limit Blacks to a specific area, though a *powerful* one.

SKY TRAUGHBER

All of my Music Business professors at Middle Tennessee State University at this time were Country Music professionals[70] and country music was a basic culture emphasized at this ground-breaking program. I was employed as a disc jockey at a Top-40, Country Rock radio station.

All of this is in addition to continuing to develop a Black base in my radio and live DJ works. However, I was sent straight to the Black Music department at CBS, in promotion. There are no complaints from this straight arrow direction, but the long-term mission at CBS Special Markets at this time is meant, in part, to tear down some of these stereotypical perceptions and barriers within major record labels.

---

[70] *Bill Williams*, the *Billboard* Country Music editor at this time, became a primary mentor to myself before his death, which occurred shortly before my graduation. Bill is the brother of Boston Red Sox baseball great *Ted Williams*.

LOGAN H. WESTBROOKS

I realized, as time moved on, that my vision may tear down barriers but may also take away overall employment opportunities for Blacks, as Whites would begin to assimilate more into Black Music just as Blacks would be assimilating into other culture and department areas.

SKY TRAUGHBER

Though America has now experienced a Black leader in the White House and its first Attorney General of color, there are still some discrepancies in how this country views the staffing in certain critical areas of operation. The entertainment industry is no different.

So, even with an honorable intent for cross-assimilation, Whites taking a stab at Black Music and a few Blacks destined to succeed in, say, Rock, there is usually some disparity in the hard "behind-the scenes" crossover numbers involving Blacks in certain areas.

To be fair, preparation and qualifications have to be considered and are sometimes a result of access to education, exposure to training and a desire from an individual, no matter the color. Still, both sides have to be willing to operate in a "colorless" environment for this mission to flourish.

But first, the new CBS Special Markets[71] staff must organize and develop what would become the most powerful Black Music Division of a major label, maybe even into today.

Ironically, in 1971-72, athletes Jim Brown, Wilt Chamberlain, Bobby Mitchell, Willie Davis, and others were also setting forth on an equally powerful, but more isolated Black-empowerment mission, known as the *Negro Industrial Economic Union* (or *Black Economic Union*):

> *The basic principle was simple: When a potentially*
> *Black-owned business could not receive funding from*
> *traditional means, such as White-owned banks, the*

---

[71] The CBS Black Music Division is initially named a Special Markets Division. Reportedly, the first corporation to install a Special Markets Division with its own promotion staff is Pepsi in the 1940s, headed by Walter Mack.

NIEU would either provide those monies, or arrange backing from an institution that could.

While there is great dispute about just how successful the organization was, few high-profile Black athletes had tried anything like this before. Jackie Robinson, the groundbreaking baseball player, had opened his own bank, providing millions of dollars in loans to businesses in Harlem and other locations. Brown's attempts were larger in scope, and much more politically risky.[72]

The Jim Brown mission is far reaching, expressed in a different tone than the CBS mission and will come under a more serious FBI scrutiny than the Black Music environment at CBS. Again, the beauty of Black is chronicling both missions.

---

[72] Freeman, Mike, *Jim Brown:, The Fierce Life of an American Hero*. William Morrow and Company, 2006.

CHAPTER 6

Power Begins with the Music

LOGAN H. WESTBROOKS

For the most part, I inherited seven Black-oriented acts, *Sly and the Family Stone, Carlos Santana, Earth, Wind & Fire, Ronnie Dyson, Ramsey Lewis, Johnny Mathis*, and *O.C. Smith* though neither act was a lightweight at that time.

Not only will the number of Black acts at CBS begin to rise in a concerted and swift manner but the label will remain in the heavyweight division, musically,[73] with a keen ability to identify, resurrect and extend the careers of many deserving Black artists.

The Isley Brothers became one of the first acts to enter this rehab. From their classic *"Twist and Shout"* and *"This Old Heart of Mine"* days at labels like Motown, the Isley Brothers stretch themselves both socially and musically with the *Givin' It Back* album.

The LP chronicles the Kent State and Jackson State killings with the eerie "Ohio/Machine Gun" tune among other soul and folk-rock offerings including the James Taylor cut, *"Fire and Rain."* This leads to the Carole King[74] tunes inspired *Brother, Brother, Brother* album, *Live It Up, 3+3*, and the list never stops for the next ten years or so.

Like the Eveready battery, once the Isleys hit CBS, they just go "on and on and on…" though their productions are registered to their own label T-Neck Records. Ernie Isley replaces the Isley Brothers' guitar spot previously held by Jimi Hendrix in the 60s. Whereas Jimi

---

[73] There will probably be many acts left out of these musical discussions for various uncontrollable and unintentional reasons.

[74] Carole King began as a writer with Phil Spector in the 60s and during this time was riding high success with her *Tapestry* album, one of the top-selling works in Pop music history, reportedly at 20 million units, worldwide.

tended to "blast into space" (which he eventually did on his own), Ernie has some of the same power and expansion but with a tighter fit into the Isley's sound.

This signals a "serious" transition for a label whose legacy is immersed in Bessie Smith, Mahalia Jackson, Johnny Mathis and Broadway show tunes.

As the Isley Brother's T-Neck Records sets the stage for a production deal with the giant CBS, musically controlled outside of the Black RockTower,[75] producers Kenny Gamble and Leon Huff join this still-developing model. Kenny and Leon have many years as artist, writer and producer, specializing in a smooth, yet soulful Philadelphia-based sound. From *"Cowboys to Girls"* by the Intruders to *"Drowning in The Sea of Love"* by Joe Simon, Gamble and Huff now find some gems to place under their new Philadelphia International production label.[76]

Sometimes magic can't be explained. The *O'Jays* have been tearing girls' hearts out for years with tunes like *"I'll Be Sweeter Tomorrow"* and meet the Gamble and Huff team when both entities are ready for a more provocative musical sound. Even more magical is the Philly International deal with powerhouse CBS and its new Special Markets Division ensuring the exposure of this magic to a mass audicncc.

Reportedly, the first few singles on other acts that Gamble and Huff deliver to CBS, before the Special Markets department is fully instituted, don't work the magic and Kenny and Leon call a meeting in New York to ask for a release from their deal.[77]

---

[75] Black Rock is the legendary headquarters for CBS, Inc., during this period. Located at 51 West 52nd Street, in the heart of Manhattan, it stands tall and dark among its surroundings.

[76] In contrast to a production company, like, say a T-Neck Records, Philadelphia International added some of its own radio promotion people as part of its staff, though it depends on CBS for the majority of its packaging, manufacturing, promotion and distribution.

[77] Jackson, John, *A House on Fire: The Rise and Fall of Philadelphia Soul*, Oxford University, 2004.

There were records from Philadelphia International like *Johnny Williams "Put it in Motion"* that were not that great and then there were records like the *Ebonys* song *"It's Forever"* that were great but did not get the proper promotion. I was urged by CBS to appease Kenny and Leon. Kenny had a very loud voice and would sometimes intimidate the brass.

We would drive down to Philadelphia on Sundays, sometimes in limos, and hear the Philly product. Many labels used this "product presentation" model but CBS would, in years to come, take it to a higher level and do it right. Anyway, this is how we got turned on to the *Back Stabbers* project. And as they say, the rest is history.

Had the Special Markets department been in full force during a record like "It's Forever," I am certain we could have taken it further. What the Special Markets department did for the CBS/Philly International relationship was *solidify* it. The lesson is that it takes great material *and* great promotion.

SKY TRAUGHBER

The O'Jays music wastes no time in arousing the smooth funk everyone wants. *Back Stabbers*, as an album as well as a single, burns this honest, social, yet romantic sound across *all* airwaves, pop as well as R&B and is followed by *Ship Ahoy, Survival, Family Reunion* and *Message in Our Music.*

The Pop airplay becomes dependent on the record achieving a Top 5 status on the R&B charts first, and stresses the importance of the CBS Special Markets department and its ability to get this done.

Billy Paul worked as a vocalist with the likes of *Dinah Washington, Miles Davis, Roberta Flack* and *Charlie Parker* and recorded solo for Jubilee records in the 1950s and Neptune Records in 1970. Though it's a ballad, *"Me & Mrs. Jones"* on Philly International/ CBS, hits America like a thunderbolt, not only in its honesty that everyone from lower to upper class could relate to, but in its smoothness in blending orchestra, strings and band.

A trait also found in the O'Jays' music. The second single, though, "*Am I Black Enough for You*" took a similar fate among the crossover crowd as James Brown's "*Say It Loud, I'm Black and I'm Proud*" again raising the issue of how "Black" can one go across-the-board without causing confusion or alarm.

Without taking a minute to catch its breath, the Gamble and Huff/ Philly International/CBS machine churns out an equally powerful and aware production in "Wake Up Everybody" by *Harold Melvin & the Blue Notes*, featuring future super star solo vocalist, *Teddy Pendergrass*. Soon equally successful but less social commentary hits by *Lou Rawls,* the *Three Degrees, Jean Carne* and *Patti Labelle*, among others, will follow, along with the still-rockin' *TSOP (The Sound of Philadelphia)*, Soul Train Theme.

A small underground and college crowd becomes attached to a group called *Earth, Wind & Fire* through its Warner Brothers album release, *Earth, Wind & Fire* in the early 70s. Eventually, the group draws the attention of CBS President Clive Davis who flies the group to perform at the CBS Convention in London. Again, the rest is history. Led by former Ramsey Lewis drummer, *Maurice White,* the group successfully blends R&B, Pop, Jazz, Afro-Cuban and voices in a way that a *lot* of people believed Maurice was crazy in attempting to create. Magic knows no insecurity.

Enlisting his brothers *Verdine* and *Freddie* along with *Ralph Johnson* to help hold down the bottom, Maurice rounds out the group with top Chicago inner-city musicians *Al McKay, Andrew Woolfolk, Larry Dunn*, and *Johnny Graham* and soon adds falsetto-chief *Phillip Bailey*[78] and a blasting horn section. The Columbia-debut *Last Days & Times* album captures the soul of the group's raw Warner Brothers days, but a CBS-style polish is evident, allowing greater radio access.

With production and writing veterans like *Charles Stepney, Skip Scarborough* and *Jerry Peters* now collaborating with Maurice, it is no wonder that album follow-ups *Head to the Sky, Open Our Eyes,*

---

[78] Though *Earth, Wind & Fire* is established in Chicago, its members hail from cities as wide as Los Angeles, Louisville, Memphis and Denver.

That's the Way of the World, Spirit and *All 'n All* would follow, with each one becoming more profound in its production and band sound. Though not as openly socially conscious as the Isley's *Givin' It Back* and the O'Jays' early albums, Earth, Wind & Fire works a power influence into their music:

> *We are people of the mighty*
> *Mighty people of the sun*
> *In our heart lies all the answers*
> *To the truth you can't run from*
>   *- Mighty, Mighty* from *Open Our Eyes*

In my touring days with the Stax Temprees during this time, we noticed that *everywhere* we traveled, the O'Jays, the Isley Brothers and Billy Paul where now blasting on Pop as well as R&B radio. We took *some* notice that all of this was coming from CBS. However, when I became a full-time "night owl" disc jockey while studying music business at Middle Tennessee State, I took *extreme* notice that now Earth, Wind & Fire, Harold Melvin & the Blue Notes and seemingly every other record I played was on the CBS label.

This included Jazz great *Herbie Hancock*, whose cut *Chameleon* would have a frat party jumpin' though he emanated from a fellow Columbia Records-Miles Davis and Howard University-professor Donald Byrd beginning. They've got *Minnie Riperton,* too?

What I did *not* know at that time was the story of the Special Markets department that was directing the action and that much of this action was, arguably, laid out in a "blueprint" document for CBS Records to follow.

CHAPTER 7

The Report

LOGAN H. WESTBOOKS
Shortly after my hiring at CBS, I joined Bruce Lundvall and CBS Records Consultant Larry Isaacson on a trip to Boston. The purpose of the trip was to coordinate a *Study of the Soul Music Environment* with an MBA class at the Harvard Business School. Clive Davis did not make the trip, and to this day says that the study has never influenced his interest, management style or operational philosophy when it came to Black Music. Clive, however, is a graduate of the Harvard Law School and Larry Isaacson is a graduate of the Harvard Business School.

The Harvard association of Larry and Clive may have influenced the decision to consult the Harvard "B" School on the CBS entry into Black Music, as opposed to, say, a self-study by CBS or perhaps commissioning the study at an Historically Black College in the likes of maybe Howard University in Washington D.C., Fisk University in Nashville or the Morehouse/Spelman Center in Atlanta. All of these Black Institutions have long and proud legacies in Black Culture. However, it is important for one to accept certain facts surrounding the trip to Harvard.

First, the tone of the study is for a corporate *business* venture not a *culture* study, though the purpose of the study is to *identity* the culture in addition to recommending a plan for CBS to capture some of its magic and earning power.

As mentioned earlier, not only America but also higher education is entering an era of corporate intrigue and control in the 70s arising from the mom & pop business, social conscious uprisings and raw music eras of the 50s and 60s. Taking this into account, it is understandable why CBS would venture into what is perceived as the top business research and education center in the world.

Secondly, my background is already heavily drenched in Black culture and business. I hold a business degree from an Historically Black College and will be the CBS point person in the liaison with the Harvard students. So, the study is not without a Black College-edged input.

Six students were enrolled in the class that devoted six months to the study. However, a foreign-bred student named *Marnie Tattersall* emerged as the leader in the study:

> *I got involved in the study because I was at the*
> *business school and had to do a research report.*
> *It's a half-year requirement.*
>
> *There wasn't a whole lot unusual about the*
> *Request for the study. Many companies are able*
> *to develop fresh, bright ideas through student*
> *research at a very low expense. I think it cost*
> *less than $5,000 for the whole thing—including*
> *personal expenses, airfare, meals, hotels, taxies.*
> *I did most of the interviews and footwork.*
>
> *Six of us were involved in the study, for six*
> *months. Most of the data was derived through*
> *personal interviews, with the math part coming*
> *from a small sample in the Boston area. Priorities*
> *were established by our professor as an academic*
> *exercise. All of us envisioned ourselves as already*
> *in the corporate world in our training.*[79]
> *~~Marnie Tattersall*

I recall maybe one or two of the students as being Black. As with my mission of a "colorless" CBS Records, the ethnic diversity of the students involved in this important study is ahead of its time, though it is estimated that a majority of Motown's sales base is White going into the 70s, the Stax house band of Booker T. & The M.G.'s is

---

[79] Westbrooks, Logan H, and Williams, Lance A., *The Anatomy of a Record Company*, 1981.

evenly divided between Black and White and the legendary Muscle Shoals[80] house band is primarily White.

An intense *academic* study of Black Music in a diverse nature does not occur again, to my knowledge, in a major fashion until Hip Hop, though the book by myself and Dr. Lance Williams re-hashes the report in the form of a self-published manuscript.

The report begins with a brief introduction of PURPOSE, SCOPE and MAJOR CONCLUSIONS. In brief, this section establishes the study's goal as researching both the *Soul market* and *CBS's current business environment of operation*. Its conclusion is that the two could co-exist at CBS, but CBS must "significantly modify and substantially broaden its current efforts to cultivate that market."

A disclaimer both identifies the report as being somewhat limited in its methodology and suggests that "any degree of uncertainty associated with the resultant conclusions is not inordinately high."

The disclaimer is important as, especially during that time, quantified data surrounding the record business is usually private and/or considered unnecessary. Some of this is the lack of technology and software to analyze data in a credible manner, the "mystique" of the industry itself and a belief that the music business thrives on "instinct" as Clive Davis attests to in his statements of not only not *using* the report but also not *needing* the report.

Only a few privileged souls were privy to the report for many years. However, during the CBS/Stax court trials of the mid 70s (covered later), Stax enters the report to the court as evidence that there was a *concerted* effort on CBS' part during that time to gain a certain level of control of the Black Music market.[81]

---

[80] Most of the Atlantic Records rhythm tracks on artists like Aretha Franklin and Wilson Pickett are cut at Muscle Shoals Studio, in Muscle Shoals, Alabama, during that time.

[81] Bowman, Rob, *Soulsville, USA: The Story of Stax Records*, Schirmer, 1997.

SKY TRAUGHBER

Even as a diligent student of the behind-the-scenes activity of the record business during that time and having spent three years at CBS before moving on to Motown in the 70s, I, myself, was not aware of the report until 1992.

In 1992 I was fresh out of graduate school, beginning a career as a college professor and FULL of research juice in starting a book titled *Green Music at Black Rock*, just chronicling the CBS Black Music Division. *Fred Ware*, one of the *Original Thirteen* members and one of the first Black executives at CBS Records, overall, hipped me to the report during an interview. After reading the report and conducting other subsequent interviews, I became, in all honesty, uncomfortable with the subject matter. I was unprepared to face the *intent* vs the *actual influence* the report may have had on Black Music.

When discussing this project (which also includes a screenplay) with my students over the years, many suggested I not write or produce this story until I was either ready to die or separate myself from the music business. Not that the report is any "nuclear bomb secret," but one must consider the controversial content and control development of Black Music into today to understand why these students see this project, somewhat, as *"spilling the beans,"* historically. And in a sense, it does that.

Not sure if I am ready to die, but I have *"kissed this world goodbye,"* as of this writing, on the music business due to reasons not necessary to divulge. Well…hell, much of it revolves around content and control. *What?* A Black man can't get angry about something today because we have experienced a "Black" President in America? Just for the record, none of this disillusionment is directed towards anyone connected with developing the report as there is honorable intent there.

LOGAN H. WESTBROOKS (from 1981)

The significance of CBS' moves should be well framed in the light of subsequent events. The action of the largest record company in the world to establish a forceful presence in progressive Black Music begins a *chain of events* among all the majors. The reaction becomes a greater focus and better-structured handling of Black Music as commercial product.

CBS' initial actions were copied throughout the industry. Suddenly every company doing even *traces* of R&B business had a Black Music Marketing Division with a token executive force. Whites still maintained the lion's share of control and power. The motives? Clearly *financial,* as the "B" school study notes. $60 million pretty little green bucks were going untapped as a market base, because Columbia and most of the other majors were ignorantly under-exploiting Black sounds at the time.

Other benefits the "B" school study outlined were ancillary to the market potential. These involved the power to institutionalize Black commercial music as a legitimate Pop art form; more jobs for Blacks, other fringe benefits. Shall we name one direct result? CBS during this time now has a consistent power base with acts like Earth, Wind & Fire and the numerous Philly International acts.

One must put the power granted the CBS Special Markets Division through the vision of Clive, Bruce, Larry Isaacson and *The Harvard Report* in perspective with how power works in the entertainment business. Though power begins with the content, as in planting a seed in fertile ground, the most powerful content or seed planted needs proper sunlight and water before it can sprout and become a part of the bigger world above its underground world of creation.

There is a legal term for civil and criminal actions known as *chain of causation.* Though there may be a primary interaction between, say, two entities or people to cause subsequent results, the action(s) of a third-party entity or person is insignificant, legally, in determining cause and effect between the primary principals involved. The CBS Special Markets Division has a certain level of power, influence and control in the operations of this division at CBS Records. It also contributes heavily to the positive embellishment and development of Black Music inside the world's largest record label.

At the same time, there is *no one* in the division empowered at the levels of deal-making, inventory, collections and monetary payments that will figure in some controversial chain of causation events at CBS with Black-owned labels such as Stax, DeVille, Invictus and Philadelphia International in the years to come.

SKY TRAUGHBER

In doing some consumer market research in determining consumer interest in a screenplay on *The Harvard Report*, I found the most consistent reaction from consumers and a few industry people to be *surprised* that such a report even exists. As in Clive's assertion that instinct guided his Black Music vision and operations, most people assume that Black Music became a part of the corporate environment through natural osmosis. Maybe so. Maybe not.

However, the mere presence of *The Harvard Report* and the fact that most, if not all, of Black Music will eventually come under the control of non-Black-owned corporations cannot be ignored. The pre-production trailer producer for *The Harvard Report* screenplay asked me during a filmed interview if *every* genre of music has a similar formal research study to determine its base and capital worth.

To my knowledge, no. But one must understand that Rock, Country, Folk, etc., were already a part of the corporate record label system. Black Music, to the extent of a designated intent to capture and fully capitalize on its worth, was an unknown area for a powerhouse like CBS Records and other major labels.

If you are interested in a girl for not only her looks but maybe some money, then you look behind the designer clothes and makeup and you go into the family tree and portfolio. *"I'm not a gold digger...just ain't messin' with no..."* (you know the song).[82]

The study continues with an analysis of the Soul Music Environment. An historical essay on Black Music's treatment by major labels is included along with the music's evolution from a singles and regional-based music form to its current potential in a national album form at the time of the study.

---

[82] "Gold Digger," Kanye West, 2005

The report is honest in its assessment of how Black musicians and singers were for the most part taken advantage of in many instances in dealing with major labels in the 1940s and 50s. Some of this is due to lack of access to information and financial desperation on the part of the musicians.

Not all of these stories are dark. Ray Charles, as mentioned earlier, after leaving Atlantic Records and signing with ABC Paramount negotiated a better deal for himself than Frank Sinatra was enjoying at the time.[83] Still, the report has to be applauded for bringing this legacy to light and for the most part CBS gained a reputation for paying high dollars to its Black artists in years to come. Miles Davis, reportedly, negotiated[84] a deal unheard of for a Jazz artist, while signed to Columbia/CBS.

LOGAN H. WESTBROOKS

As time progressed, many artists in the industry wanted to be signed to the *Big Red* label, which is Columbia. Sly and the Family Stone were on the *Yellow* label, which is Epic. But Big Red became a "drawing power" for CBS in attracting quality acts to the company.

SKY TRAUGHBER

Earth, Wind & Fire, Miles Davis and *Deniece Williams* are three acts that come to mind, instantly on Big Red. When I saw the *Red and Black* of the Atlantic label, I knew to expect some soul and quality from acts like *Aretha Franklin, Ray Charles* and later *Donny Hathaway, Roberta Flack* and the *Average White Band*. In the same respect, the Big Red label of Columbia Records meant something. After Sly, it did not surprise me that "Lady Marmalade," by *LaBelle,* would be on the *Yellow* (which turned to *Orange*) of the Epic label.

---

[83] The film *Ray*, 2004

[84] The term "negotiate" may be in terms of an artist working in conjunction with their attorney and/or agent. Most of the "intermediaries" during that time were not African Americans. Though someone like James Brown would employ a Black manager, there would be a need, many times, for a "white face" involved in high-level discussions to secure the deal. Deep behind the scenes, some of this is still true, as of this writing.

The report then moves into identifying the importance of radio in exposing the music and capturing its current and growth potential market. With payola a growing concern during this time, the report recommends that: *"Using good public relations and consistently high-quality product can probably go a long way toward overcoming the obstacles posed by payola for companies who are not willing to engage in that practice."*

Though the product quality and the Press and Public Relations Department of the CBS Special Markets Division would both prove to be extraordinary, it would become CBS' power in radio that propels it to the top of the Black Music hierarchy, both in its staff relations with radio and "outsourcing" its product to the crucial and secretive independent network of radio promoters.[85]

LOGAN H. WESTBROOKS

In hiring my radio promotion staff, a "recommendation" from a radio programmer or powerful disc jockey would figure prominently in the hiring of that person. If a radio person recommends the hiring of this person, it means they will most likely play the records that person brings into the station.

SKY TRAUGHBER

It took a while after being a staff promotion manager at CBS and joining a top management firm representing a major CBS artist for me to fully understand the importance of having the indie network

---

[85] A "staff" promoter is employed exclusively by that label and has to work more closely with legal and moral business parameters in representing the label. An independent promoter is "independent" of any particular label employment and works by contract for a number of labels. This contract usually includes an "indemnification" clause, removing the label from any connection or liability for "illegal or immoral" payoffs to radio. By law, payola is only illegal if it is not reported in tax filings and not "disclosed." This relationship between labels, indie promoters and radio stations will evolve into what is known as "non-traditional revenue" tax reporting by the radio stations, allowing the money to go directly to the stations in a more legal and moral manner though the disclosure requirement will remain unclear and the subject of various investigations. Former NY Governor Elliott Spitzer headed a formidable investigation into payola only to be removed from office after being caught using a high-priced call girl ring, himself.

and lots of cash on your side. It's just the American way of business. Anyone who believes that Obama's record-breaking monetary war chest had no effect on his election victory is not paying attention.

Categorizing Black Music artists by the degree of soul content in their works is realistic and necessary in *The Harvard Report* team's job of communicating effectively with the CBS brass. However, the team does add this disclaimer:[86]

> *The issue is very complex, and there is no generally accepted definition. Efforts to define it in terms of a 'certain sound' lacks precision. Defining it in terms of specific artists can be problematic, because a given artist may produce a Soul record one day, and a Rock record the next. At the same time, artists do manifest tendencies in one or another direction.*

Acts like *James Brown* and *Wilson Pickett* are seen as: <u>Almost All (Soul content)</u>

Isaac Hayes, Roberta Flack, The Fifth Dimension and *Sly Stone* are: <u>(Mixed)</u>

Miles Davis, Johnny Mathis and *Dionne Warwick* have: <u>Almost Nonc (Soul contcnt)</u>

Interestingly, Isaac Hayes, Roberta Flack and Sly all have a *lot* of soul in the root of their content, but the use of orchestral instruments for Isaac, Roberta and the Fifth Dimension and the mixed-race and "rock' edge of Sly take them to a "mixed" bag in the eyes of many. *Parliament-Funkadelic* will expand on the James Brown bottom-up funk shortly. *Luther Vandross* and *Al Jarreau* will satisfy a growing crossover demand in the 80s.

Rap will explode in the 90s, predominantly featuring a rapper over beats (usually by machine), diminishing the need for formal musical training and the genre will soon be controlled and distributed to the masses entirely by major record labels.

---

[86] Westbrooks, Logan, *The Harvard Report*, Ascent Book Publishing, 2017.

The report then ventures into areas that show the team has done its homework while also leaving room for a wide range of CBS interpretation and implementation:

- *"Experienced Soul personnel would have to be hired in the areas of A&R, production and promotion."*

- *"Coordination of Soul music sales activities with the existing sales force."*

- *"Integration of the Soul music group with other functional activities within Columbia, which will be necessary for support. (e.g., legal, advertising, physical production, and sales).*

- *"The Soul music group should be semi-autonomous with the Director reporting to the President of CRG."*

- *"IMPLEMENTATION of the recommended strategy is intended to be accomplished in three phases:*

  1. *During phase one, emphasis should be placed on establishment of market position by expanding the existing custom label operation.*
  2. *In phase two, market position should be further established, and industry reputation developed by utilizing more externally generated product.*
  3. *When the third phase is reached, emphasis should be placed on internal product, and the development of a distinctive Soul music sound for Columbia.*

"The purpose of this sequential arrangement is to indicate to the industry Columbia's interest in Soul music, and thereby attract more talent and product while providing some initial operating results."

A Special Markets presentation at the CBS Sales meeting in 1974 also emphasizes the importance of relationships with and assisting Black retails outlet in their financial and expansion needs.

The presentation also suggests that it would be up to each CBS Branch[87] to enlarge its involvement with the Black community.[88]

The Harvard Report team shows great insight into an inevitable future for Black music. If CBS had not entered the genre in such a formal and swift manner, another major label would have surely taken its place. The CBS program proves to be as much analytical as creative and will add a *class polish* to Black Music from a *different* perspective than labels like Motown or Stax.

In my disc jockey days, during that time, as I began to notice the quality and quantity of CBS Black product hitting the street, there also seemed to be a certain "mystique" of substance and meaning in these releases—at least from my view. Though my plan after graduation was to rejoin the Stax scene in Memphis for life, CBS Records, along with Motown and Warner Brothers were added to the "exclusive and narrow" list of record labels I believed to be worthy of my services as an executive.

I could afford some confidence (not cockiness), as I was about to become one of the first persons ever to earn a full Bachelor of Science degree in the record business to compliment my practical experience as a musician, disc jockey and television cameraman for an ABC affiliate.

LOGAN H. WESTBROOKS
Though I was born and bred in Memphis, the various encounters in the South from the Pullman Porters to Lincoln University in Missouri to the Johnson Co., RCA Victor; Capitol, Mercury record labels in Chicago; CBS Records in New York; CBS International in Paris; and Soul Train Records and Source Records in Los Angeles had made me "citified."

---

[87] A branch distribution system with regional outlets in cities like Washington D.C., Atlanta, Chicago, Dallas, New York, Los Angeles and San Francisco can help de-centralize the national effort, while allowing a centralized, regional focus on national priorities, though some localized autonomy is certain to surface in this system.

[88] Westbrooks, Logan H. and Williams, Lance A., *The Anatomy of a Record Company*, 1981.

While this class and polish was setting new standards, some of *The Harvard Report* recommendations will fall short of any implementation by CBS. Specifically:

- No A&R appointments for the Special Markets Division were made immediately.

- I (and subsequent division heads) DID NOT report to the President of CBS Records.

- Though there was some integration of the division into areas such as Legal and Business Affairs, Sales and Distribution, the division was not autonomous in these areas and, for the most part, no Black person held any position of authority in these areas. However, Jim Tyrell[89] would become a Vice President of Marketing for Epic during this time.

Some of these discrepancies between the *recommendations* of the report and any *perceived implementation* of the report will cause a controversy regarding the integrity and sincerity of the CBS move into Black Music by some.

For instance, Invictus Records will leave Capitol Records with acts such as *Freda Payne,* the *Honey Cone,* and *Chairmen of the Board* and sign with CBS Records. Invictus executive Clarence Tucker saw the three stage CBS implementation as:[90]

1. Understand Black Radio
2. Realize that CBS does not have the internal capabilities, at this time, to produce Black Music.
3. Recognize that the Black-oriented and/or owned labels that CBS does business with for production, could walk away from CBS with these artists and CBS should direct its efforts to signing these acts directly to CBS.

The correlation between Clarence Tucker's assertion and the actual job descriptions of the Special Markets Division is important here in terms of any potential association of blame to the division for

---

[89] Jim was a former bass player for Patti Labelle & the Blue Belles, or Labelle.
[90] *Band of Gold: The Invictus Story,* TV movie, 1999.

perceptions such as Clarence's. No one in the division has a job description or level of responsibility in deciding which acts are signed, how the acts are signed or the deal structures, just as no one is directly involved in distribution.

Equally important is that *The Harvard Report* projects a fifteen percent market share of the Soul Music environment for CBS in five years, which would be in 1977. The projections show five percent of this market share coming from Atlantic and the other ten percent coming from independent labels' market share in the likes of Invictus.

While Stax is projected to increase its own market share by five percent and is not part of the CBS projection, it, too, will be the subject of "artist takeover" assertions in the years to come, though the report does not identify any plan for CBS to assume its market share by intentionally raiding other labels. As mentioned before, though, CBS will soon increase its Black-oriented artist roster from two to over a hundred in about five years.

However, it now becomes time for the division to find and hire its original warriors.

CHAPTER 8

A Staff That Delivers

LOGAN H. WESTBROOKS

The national staff began in the Black Rock Building with me and Marnie Tattersall. There were two or three offices on the sixth floor. Outside of a few Blacks in positions like telephone operators, there were no Black executive personnel entering the CBS building before we started the Special Markets Division. As I remember, Clive Davis had a Black secretary, as did high-level CBS executive Goddard Lieberson, and there were maybe some Blacks doing temp work. But there were no Black men.

There *was* a Black Music executive person, *Carl Proctor*, in and out of CBS Records, earlier, though not as a full-time staffer.[91] Carl was connected to legendary *Chi Sound Records* founder *Carl Davis* of Chicago and indirectly connected to Roulette founder and rumored-mob connector Morris Levy. Carl was found murdered in Central Park, though I cannot necessarily connect any dots of this Levy association to his death.

Nevertheless, getting through CBS security, for a Black person, could be somewhat traumatic at that time.

SKY TRAUGHBER

This changes pretty swiftly. In the mid-70s, one of my former professors at MTSU, Charlie Monk,[92] advised me to "start at the top and work my way down" as I was walking up and down music row in Nashville looking for a label job. Upon leaving Charlie's office at ASCAP, I saw the "gigantic" CBS RECORDS sign appearing

---

[91] Carl Proctor is reportedly, during this time, the road manager for Jazz vocalist Sarah Vaughn. His wife, Barbara Gardner owned the second largest Black advertising agency in the country during this time.

[92] Charlie would later become a key executive for the CBS Music publishing division.

against the sky like a sign from some higher power and figured this is as big as it gets. I easily walked into the CBS Nashville office, was directed to the CBS Atlanta office and after an easy entry there, would notice the easy entry and joyous brain and culture center both the New York and Los Angeles CBS Records offices offered its Black clientele.

In his book,[93] CBS Records Group head *Walter Yetnikoff* recalled how the CEO of CBS, Inc., became upset and concerned when Kenny Gamble and his Philly International staff parked five or six limos outside of Black Rock, New York, in the mid-70s.[94] Then Walter reminded the CEO of how much money Black Music and Philly were bringing into the CBS building at this time. End of discussion. *Green Music at Black Rock.*

Little did I know, at this time, that CBS was desperately looking for someone like me: qualified, clean from payola due to a recent federal "Newark Investigation" (covered later in book) implicating CBS Records, Stax Records, and Philly International Records with payola. There were 20 other applicants for the Charlotte, North Carolina, position that I was awarded. I was later told that all were at least loosely connected to that era. My "never-heard-of-before" Bachelor of Science degree in Recording Industry Management from MTSU did not hurt either in helping CBS make a fresh start.

LOGAN H. WESTBROOKS

Though I would coordinate important marketing development areas like album covers and advertising with the CBS Records product managers, the main focus in hiring the Special Markets staff would be to gain airplay for the CBS Black Music roster. Clive would preside over the overall CBS Records marketing meetings that would include Black Music discussions. Richard, Marnie, and I would be included in those New York meetings for a national strategy.

---

[93] Yetnikoff, Walter, with Ritz, David, *Howlin' at the Moon,* Broadway Books, 2004.

[94] Some of this concern may have been due to the ongoing FBI, IRS and Newark payola investigations of CBS, Stax and Philly International at that time.

Weekly conference calls with the regional staff around the country would then be the primary means of communication for direction, discussion and feedback on the Black Music operations, though impromptu and daily interactions between Richard, Marnie, and I, and the regional people would occur frequently.

A difference in *speaking* and *communicating* is crucial in a situation where territorial disbursement is wide and there is a combination of emotional and business concentrations. Split-second decisions, clear understandings and follow-ups can be paramount in not only achieving weekly, quarterly and yearly goals but also in fending off any unnecessary negative or disruptive viruses from the operation. It is sort of like a group of people in a marriage without sharing the same bed.

SKY TRAUGHBER

When I was hired at CBS, one of the first things the then-head of National Singles for CBS Special Markets, *Vernon Slaughter*, told me was: *"Don't take anything for granted."*

I learned to keep a good sense of organization, clarity and follow-through in working with the CBS Black Music unit. It sometimes disturbs people when a person is focused in this manner, but what must be done must be done. The CBS experience also taught the art of exercising some class (in style) and human consideration in getting this done.

LOGAN H. WESTBROOKS

In addition to establishing our base at Black radio, we had to deal with the lie of *"Top 40 radio [95] will not play Black records."* The Pop field staff was actually somewhat prejudiced in this mentality but it also goes deeper.

One must understand how embarrassing and problematic it could be for the Pop staff if Black staff promotion persons were to use their expertise at Pop radio to show that *"Top 40 radio will play Black*

---

[95] A radio format that primarily plays "Pop" records, or records considered more acceptable or appealing to a "crossover" or white-based audience.

records." So, a Black record had to become a Top 5 or Top 10 *Billboard* R&B Chart[96] hit at R&B radio before it became eligible for the Pop staff to take it to Top 40 radio. This tends to not only establish a criterium for crossover, but it keeps the Black Music staff busy at its own stations, further establishing "territorial rights" of *who* can take the Black record into Pop radio. Some of this is business. Some of it is not. So, in hiring and managing my staff, this environment of "results oriented" while also encompassing some dissonance had to be considered.

SKY TRAUGHBER

I have experienced the pleasure of working with most of the original CBS Special Markets staff. The qualities of *identifying the business from the bullshit* while maintaining a professional and strong presence for the culture existed in the persons brought into the division. To an extent *everyone* has to deal with this, but it is also a reality of the "homeless but connected" aspect of being Black in America.

LOGAN H. WESTBROOKS

In some cases, I had to show empathy for a person's financial and/or family situation. This may have involved arranging an advance on salary and/or expenses immediately so that person could clear their head and be in a state of mind and condition to deal with the mission.

As we were initially a small staff with a big task, I also had to evaluate investment and reward. If a person was already connected to or recommended through strong radio connections, the probability of investing in that person's hiring would probably pay off. At the same time, if a person did not work out in a particular territory or position, I would try and transfer that person to another area of operation or responsibility.

If I saw some genuine effort and potential.

---

[96] *Billboard* is the leading record industry trade publication.

SKY TRAUGHBER

After a series of interviews at CBS by driving back and forth to Atlanta from my radio sales and television cameraman jobs at *WNOO* radio and the *ABC Television* local affiliate, in Chattanooga, Tennessee, I was flown to New York, unexpectedly, for a couple of days of interviews with the top CBS brass.

The CBS Atlanta branch manager, *Joe Mansfield,*[97] after questioning why I would want to quit *two* good jobs for *one,* came out of his pocket to make sure I would be okay for a couple of days "in the big city."

My hiring required an immediate relocation to Charlotte, North Carolina, but CBS footed all lodging, food and incidentals until my American Express card arrived and I found a place to live. Subsequent promotions to Atlanta and Los Angeles included this ease of transfer also.

On the one hand, it shows concern for a person's welfare but it is also good business to keep that person in a "working" state of mind while in transit. I know of people that owned homes and were being promoted to another city. CBS would buy that person's house at market value or above to ease the transition for that person. CBS used its deep pockets well in this respect.

LOGAN H. WESTBROOKS

Marnie Tattersall's presentation of herself in terms of interest, enthusiasm and qualifications during the Harvard Report study made it a no-brainer to bring her in as my assistant. *Richard Mack* was the top man for Henry Allen[98] over at Atlantic. If you were the best in the business we came after you.

---

[97] Joe Mansfield came from Texas radio and eventually rose to Vice President of Marketing positions at CBS/NY, Capitol/LA and Capitol/Nashville and was instrumental in breaking Garth Brooks. And yes, I had to pay him back for the "pocket change." Joe is also a believer in education and made a great presentation to my Record Company class during my graduate student/teaching days at MTSU.

[98] Known for "honor" in business deals, but also for doing what's necessary when this honor is broken, Henry Allen is a prominent figure in radio promotion and record label management.

I would have no problem in hiring a strong presence like Richard. Bring in the best just pushes me further up the ladder.

I inherited people like *Fred Ware* in Atlanta, *Granville White* in Chicago and *Lou Woodard* on the West Coast. Fred became a *great* inheritance and kept the southeast region "locked up" in airplay of CBS artists.

Armand McKissick, in Philadelphia, was an example of someone recommended by a strong radio person *and* could get those records played. Kenny Gamble and Leon Huff also advocated on Armand's behalf. Armand was an outstanding promotion manager with the uncanny ability to spot a hit record and secure almost instant airplay. He was so well thought of by program directors that they were quick to follow his recommendations and advice on programming a record.

Bill Craig,[99] in Detroit, would find a way to work with the Pop staff or take the Black records directly to the Pop stations. At the same time, he was no ass kisser. Neither were people like *George Chavou* or *Speedy Brown,* and, for the most part, the entire staff. We picked up Speedy from the James Brown organization.

Sometimes a member of the staff would make a recommendation as in the case of Richard Mack putting in a word for *Richard Outler* and Granville White recommending *Gerry Griffith for* Chicago.

I stuck with *Chuck Offuitt* after initially hiring him for the New York market and then sending him to Texas, which did not work out. I simply brought him back to the New York market.

Leroy Smith replaced Lou Woodard on the West Coast and I remember *Glen Wright,* in the Midwest as one of the youngest staff members with a college-edge, and he could get the job done.

---

[99] Bill would go on to become a key point person for the controversial Joe Isgro-led national independent network of radio promoters chronicled in the book, Hit Men: Power Brokers and Fast Money Inside the Music Business. Attention focused on this network's possible link to organized crime when Isgro was consistently photographed with Mob figures during a major journalistic and FBI investigation of mob activities.

SKY TRAUGHBER

One of the first things I noticed about the Black Music staff at CBS when I joined was a diversity in background and entry-route to the company. Still, there was a singular, team-oriented concept of pride, focus, intelligence and class. Vernon Slaughter was a former football player in Nebraska, and I remember getting airplay priority sheets every week that would include the team *running a blitz* on certain singles that week at radio.[100]

Fred Ware became my immediate boss in Atlanta, and though he was known as a tough promoter who could just sit in his office and lock up all the southeast stations with a few phone calls, his strategy and personnel management skills were impeccable. I worked with *Gerry Griffith* in the CBS West Coast office and later under him in the A&R department at Motown. He would calmly explain things in an honest but strong manner, giving a young start-up some education but expressing the reality and importance of showing results under pressure and/or anger.

I replaced *Ralph Bates* in Atlanta, though he would still drop by and chat with Fred. At first Ralph, and others, seemed surprised at my physical size in an occupation known for having to "kick some ass," if necessary, on a record or otherwise. I later ran into Ralph when he was involved in the management of Isaac Hayes and I could tell that, by then, there was a mutual respect for profound communication and business skills.

LOGAN H. WESTBROOKS

A lot of labels in Black Music at this time would create a demand in the marketplace *then* hire a Black Music staff to meet and expand that demand. At CBS we put a strong staff in place *first,* then built from there. This probably figured in CBS' ability to attract a huge and profound artist roster in the years to come.

---

[100] National priority sheets were a crucial part of determining which records are to be promoted by everyone as a top priority, a second priority and so forth. A national team not in synch with each other in this respect can find itself losing hits because there is no weekly concentrated and organized effort. Running a blitz, as in football, meant that *everyone* would hit radio *hard* on this record, all at once, before they knew what hit them.

With the nucleus of a staff that delivers radio airplay on quality-produced music and the power of CBS, the Special Markets Division of CBS Records will grow into a honeynet of a magnet for artists, producers, labels and executives at almost a break neck pace.

CHAPTER 9

CBS and the Lure

CBS was incorporated in 1927 as United Independent Broadcasters, Inc. Its name was changed a year later to Columbia Broadcasting System, and in 1974 it adopted the name CBS, Inc.

*Under the direction of longtime chairman **William Paley,** CBS made media history beginning in the late 1920s. Paley, whose father owned the company that made Palina cigars, invested in the Columbia Broadcasting System, which was then a small, struggling radio network, in 1928. Realizing that the key to radio's success was large audiences that would attract advertisers, Paley offered programming free to affiliated stations in return for having a certain part of their schedule devoted to sponsored network shows. From 22 stations in 1928, the network grew to 114 stations in a decade.*

*Ratings grew during the 1930s with stars such as **Phil Harris, Fred Allen, Bing Crosby** and **Kate Smith.** As television grew more popular during the 1940s, and the appearance of performers became as important as their voices, Paley raided rival <u>NBC</u>, signing up stars such as **Amos 'n' Andy, George Burns** and **Gracie Allen** and **Jack Benny**, who proved as popular on television as they had been on radio. In subsequent decades**, Ed Sullivan, Lucille Ball, Mary Tyler Moore** and newscaster **Walter Cronkite** were among the personalities who made CBS the most watched television network in the country. CBS remained the dominant network until the late 1970s.*

*In 1938 CBS acquired the American Recording Corporation, which later became **Columbia Records. Peter Goldmark** of CBS laboratories invented high fidelity long-playing records, and the Columbia record label introduced them to the public in 1948.*[101]

~~Excerpt from the Britannica Online Dictionary

---

[101] *Britannica Online Encyclopedia*

SKY TRAUGHBER

One of my favorite movies from the 70s is *Network*, with William Holden and Faye Dunaway. That movie has CBS all over it. An industry-leading entity built on firm ground spewing drama and controversy galore.

LOGAN H. WESTBROOKS

Costs were never a factor in putting this thing together. Let's take a scientific business view of this. If you analyze the costs of, say, a <u>*Billboard*</u> magazine ad versus the cost of an *Essence*[102] ad, at that time, the CBS money mentality was already higher than the cost mentality it would occur in reaching a Black base.

CBS Records was already the "Rolls Royce" of record labels going into the 1970s. Adding a solid, thought-out Black Music Division only changed the grade of gasoline that propels the fine machinery from premium to high premium without auctioning the auto dealership. In the context of the Soul record label environment at that time, the lure of CBS offered an apparent and much-needed relief for some.

Stax Records was sold into a deal at *Gulf and Western* while it was standing[103] on one leg from the Atlantic Records deal, and the company emerged from the Gulf and Western deal on crutches. The Gulf and Western deal could have gone either way for Stax. Both smartly and with a gambler's model, the label's deal at Gulf and Western was an all-stock agreement.

Though this type of deal will bring in hundreds of millions for David Geffen and his Geffen Records sale to MCA, later, the Stax deal is somewhat ground breaking at that time and is based on the projected fast-rising value of Gulf and Western. Deals involving companies like *Google* being acquired by a larger firm, today, have this all-stock model. Had another company bought Gulf and Western *at this projected value*, as in the purchase of MCA by Japanese giant

---

[102] A leading Black-female based magazine, currently still popular.

[103] Stax kept its own distribution network, as opposed to using the Gulf and Western branch distribution system.

Matsushita, Stax would have benefited, monetarily, in a swift and profitable nature.

Had the stock market *only retained the value* of Gulf and Western, Stax would have been okay. Instead, the stock value of Gulf *declined drastically and swiftly*, leaving Stax without any substantial financial windfall from this deal.

There was also a serious "culture" barrier between Stax and Gulf and Western:

> *According to Jim Stewart, no one at Gulf and Western knew anything about the record business. The head of their music division, Arnold Burke, had come out of the motion picture business. "He was a real nice guy," says Jim, shaking his head, "but he knew absolutely nothing about the record business. They never had any record people [and] they had no idea what a Black record was all about.*[104]

Stax musician Wayne Jackson continues:

> *Here they were from Los Angeles in their suits and we're eating baloney and cheese on the floor in shorts and they didn't understand it, just didn't understand it.*[105]
>
> *~~Wayne Jackson*

The Atlantic and Gulf and Western episodes also forced Stax to obtain loans from Union Planter's Bank in Memphis. Though some of the culture differences would later emerge at CBS, one can understand why Al Bell would make the call to Clive Davis during that time, considering the deep pockets, radio and distribution power affiliated with CBS.

Kenny Gamble and Leon Huff's new Philadelphia International Records label had an aura matching the aura that lured the label to

---

[104] Bowman, Rob, *Soulsville, USA: The Story of Stax Records*, Schirmer, 1997.
[105] Ibid.

CBS. Though CBS was entering Black Music, its brand was still not entrenched in "deep Soul music." Philly had a smooth-layered but raw bottomed sound with strong lyrical content. Adding a Jazz edge at times, it was not entrenched in "deep Soul music"[106] and seemed to fit CBS.

CBS's crossover power also proved to be a good fit for the Gamble and Huff music potential and their branding mission of moving beyond a traditional Black sound in their music. Still, there were industry skeptics about CBS's ability and sincerity about being able to understand strong Black Music.[107]

The *Invictus* label was emerging from a disappointing deal at Capitol Records. Though the label was founded and musically run by Motown-exiles *Holland-Dozier-Holland* and carried a strong artist base of *Freda Payne,* the *Honey Cone* and *Chairmen of the Board,* the label felt it was not understood nor promoted and marketed correctly at Capitol. The label also interprets Clive Davis's offer from CBS to suggest that Invictus will become a promotion and marketing priority at the giant conglomerate.[108]

Motown at that time was paying its artists a salary, reportedly in the range of $250 a week, as an advance against future royalties. Some artists that were also writers may be able to draw a separate salary as a Jobete writer. This business arrangement will serve to keep some artists at the label. It will also present a label like CBS a negotiating lure for attracting artists that may have otherwise signed with a label like Motown, in offering a high advance figure as opposed to a weekly salary.

SKY TRAUGHBER

My A&R days at Motown were primarily musical, not business. So, I can't give any credible dissertation on who was getting what. However, I could sense that my primary acts of development—

---

[106] Previously, Kenny and Leon were involved in deep Soul hits, "Cowboys to Girls" by the Intruders and "Drowning in The Sea of Love" by Joe Simon.

[107] Jackson, John A., *A House on Fire: The Rise and Fall of Philadelphia Soul,* Oxford University Press USA, 2004.

[108] *Band of Gold: The Invictus Story,* Documentary, 1999.

Teena Marie and *DeBarge*— were receiving at least an artist salary if not a writer's salary, or maybe some combination of the two. A salary would give a developing artist a means of maintaining a focus of developing their craft, on a daily basis, minus any distraction of a major financial strain or the distraction of having to pick up odd jobs that may dilute this development. On the other side, minus a sizable advance, you have to wait on your money every week dribbling in, slowly.

Sure, there are some creative advantages in starvation and struggle. One has to dig deep into their soul and surroundings. The key is to not cross the "point of diminishing returns" where the starvation presents a distraction to the creative process or one's health and welfare.

As in the case of Teena Marie eventually suing Motown, winning, and signing with CBS/Epic, there could be *accounting* issues somewhere in this mix that could cause problems, somewhere down the road. Not to single out Motown or any other Black label at this time. But in all honesty, a prevalent mentality either by choice or conditioning, during this time, is that a major, White record label's "sugar may be *s*weeter."

The Holland-Dozier-Holland split from Motown was a complex example of perception versus a possible reality of "whose sugar is sweeter." In the *Band of Gold* documentary, it is stated that the mighty production team left Motown, in part, because of a reneged offer of stock ownership in the company from Berry Gordy.

Berry would tell us that he owned 51% of Motown. However, some of my observations and conversations in the distribution division of the company revealed that the other 49% owners *might* have actually owned a great deal more when you add the *on the books totals* with the *off the books totals*.

So, how can a man give stock in a company where he is not a *total* majority owner? Some of this is informed speculation but it shows where someone like Berry Gordy or Al Bell would have a profound intent of spreading the capital but, in reality, not be able to do so in the manner they would prefer.

Al Bell did not gain a 100% ownership in Stax until the CBS deal, which fell apart swiftly and heavily, dealing the deathblow to Stax. Some of the CBS/Stax drama revolved around the high *percentage* deal (actually a high distribution fee) Clive gave Al and the label, which also financed Al's 100% purchase of the label. More on this later.

As this book points out earlier, there is not enough Black financial capital to service everyone in the growth of Black Music during this time, so the "spillover" of artists and executives from Black labels is bound to find a home at White, major labels. This makes the Jim Brown's Economic Union mission of building Black capital, owned *by* and primarily *for* Blacks, even more profound at that time.

LOGAN H. WESTBROOKS

I personally know of some artists that would not have made it without the weekly salary at Motown. Still, artists at this time were also becoming more educated in their understanding of the different types of deals available and the different income streams available for accumulating these incomes. A lot of this now becomes more available at White, major labels.

SKY TRAUGHBER

As a contrast, I know of a major Black CBS artist in the early 80s that was receiving a monthly stipend of five or six thousand dollars to live on. This is the FRONT END of the business, in advances, and is subtracted from the BACK END of the business, in royalties, after any additional charge backs such as marketing, packaging, videos, tour support, clothing, real estate purchases, etc., are deducted against the artist account.

So, really, whether an artist is accruing a monthly debit of one thousand dollars or five thousand dollars, it will be subtracted on the back end. However, as in managing one's life or in the recent awakening of America's huge financial debt, the higher a life style or spending pattern one adopts, *on credit,* can dig a deeper hole to climb from and, in a sense, further enslave that person or entity to its creditors.

Nevertheless, the CBS Black roster will grow by almost a hundred artists in the next five years and will include a healthy dose of veteran acts leaving their label for CBS. This number will also include the artist rosters of numerous Black Music labels acquired by CBS during this period.

With a power base in media heavily built on acquisition and quality, the CBS legacy will carry over to album cover designs, photography and the mass consumer marketing of artists, while this acquisition period was in effect.

As a radio, club and mobile disc jockey at that time, I began to take notice of visual presentations like the cover photography of Marvin Gaye's *What's Going On,* the *Ernie Barnes* mural for the Gaye *I Want You* album cover and the deep-meaning of Stevie Wonder's *Innervisions* album cover art. Stax and Curtom were also beginning to present their product, visually, in a very soulful but quality-based fashion.

As a college student, I, like most of my comrades, did not have the discretionary budget to buy a lot of magazines and we probably viewed television less frequently than in high school. However, my course of study at MTSU was under the College of Mass Communication, so it became part of my academic as well as professional radar to take notice of media, journalistic and advertising happenings.

Just for the record, this is when I daily viewed *Oprah Winfrey's* newscasts at a Nashville television station,[109] as part of a television and journalism course assignment. Her presentation grabbed me every day, even back then, as she has grown to grab people over the years.

Being a semi-playboy and frat guy, my apartment was decorated cheaply, but in a very hip fashion with a lot of album covers, posters and magazine photographs. During that time, I also learned an

---

[109] Middle Tennessee State University is located in Murfreesboro, only thirty miles from Nashville, and receives strong television and radio signals from that city. Oprah was a student at the Historically Black College, Tennessee State University during that time.

important lesson in the music business: *get the girls and you will get the guys* (for the most part*)*. The Afro hairstyle in a lot these visuals also presented an allure to the culture of Black music as well as a reminder of the depth of its meaning and profound talent.

LOGAN H. WESTBROOKS

To support the massive airplay our artists were now receiving, we saw the need to match this music quality with top-notch photographers. *Howard Bingham*, for example, was the official photographer for Muhammad Ali and possessed the largest photo collection of the champ. I accompanied CBS artist *Johnny Nash* to Los Angeles to do the Soul Train Show and present him with a gold single for "*I Can See Clearly Now.*"

Howard Bingham was on the set and took numerous pictures of Johnny Nash. All were excellent. I selected one for the album cover. His photos were superior. It was very important to have artistically-designed album covers to match the quality of the music.

After one of our marketing meetings in New York, Clive asked our staff member Ralph Bates to collect 15 or 20 album covers of Black albums from other labels. We were both able to learn and enhance this profound movement in Black visual culture by studying what others were doing. Larry Shaw at Stax, for instance, was doing some amazing things with the bald-headed Isaac Hayes *Hot Buttered Soul* cover and later the same is true with artists like the Dramatics on the *Whatcha See is Whatcha Get* cover.

Cinematographer *Gordon Parks* was also enhancing his early photography career into film photography and camera work, including the *Shaft* film. *Regina Jones,* in Los Angeles, used Black photographers for her <u>Soul</u> magazine. All of this created a movement of *raw but quality* visuals in representing the music and its culture, being shot through the eyes of a Black person.

There was never any resistance in content or monies available from CBS in developing this brand for our division and our artists.

Though there were no Black product managers[110] at CBS during that time, we worked with the White product managers in a smooth and soulful manner.

Magazine, radio, television and television ads helped extend the culture of the music into everyday American life. At that time, there were no budgets assigned for each project that we administered. Whatever we felt was necessary creatively and businesswise was done, with no questions asked.

We used *Ed Wright* as an independent publicity expert for the culture we were representing, though the long-term idea was to eliminate any outside press relations and publicity involvements and do everything inhouse. Eventually, *Win Wilford,*[111] was hired from Ed's company to head the Black Music Press and Publicity department at CBS.

SKY TRAUGHBER

The CBS Special Markets staff captured a quality that I was mesmerized by in my transition from disc jockey and college student to actually becoming a part of this highly respected staff. I did not realize the wide extent of this market reach until after I joined CBS and was promoted from a promotion person to product management.

The then-head of Black Music, LeBaron Taylor, gave me a stack of Black porn magazines they were buying ads in so I could take them home and get a feel of the many methods utilized to reach their consumer. Needless to say, I was a bit surprised, but thoroughly enjoyed this indoctrination study.

---

[110] A product manager at a record label is a crucial position for ensuring a well-planned coordination of visuals, marketing strategy, budgets, product inventory, publicity and artist relations, artist and manager relations, tour support, merchandising and distribution for their assigned artist roster. This importance is not exclusive to the record business, as most industries employ qualified people in this area.

[111] Win is a former bass player who performed on some of the Philly Sound music and was married to up-and-coming television and film actress *Debbie Allen* during that period.

LeBaron also encouraged the female members of the team in the headquarters offices to wear dresses and lean toward a more "professional" attire in the workplace. This impressed me, as did previously noticing women like Jo Bridges at Stax, later noticing the same in Iris Gordy, Edna Andersen, Suzanne DePasse, Simone Sheffield, Faye Hale and Billie Jean Brown at Motown.

This is somewhat contrary to the normal loosely attired record company environment. LeBaron's direction in attire was not necessarily sexist, as I noticed that the men at the CBS Special Markets department also started showing special care in wardrobe.[112] Though "clean and neat" works fine, sometimes an extra polish in attire and demeanor embellishes a culture style.

LOGAN H. WESTBROOKS

At CBS, artists would find themselves in an environment that was also becoming involved in the expression of social concerns. I produced shows for the *Congressional Black Caucus* in their early days with *Isaac Hayes* headlining and *Don Cornelius* from *Soul Train* as the Master of Ceremonies.

In fact, it was my childhood friend from Memphis, *Harold Sims*, who was a top executive at *Johnson & Johnson* who brought the idea of the Black Caucus involvement to me.

Hooking up with Motown Vice President *Junius Griffin* led to a fundraising event in Atlanta for *Coretta Scott King* featuring *Sly and the Family Stone* as headliners with *Ramsey Lewis* and *Albert King* also performing. Mrs. King presented me with an award while future United States Ambassador *Andrew Young* made another award presentation.

This was also the event where I met then-Georgia Governor and future U.S. President *Jimmy Carter*. Jimmy was impressed with what he saw and wanted to add this type of excitement to his campaign. However, he was not in the loop with any strong and profound Black

---

[112] For the most part, CBS paid higher salaries and expense freedoms than other labels, so a CBS Records person could afford this image.

entertainment culture people at this time, so I connected him with former Jimmy Smith manager and Sussex record label owner *Clarence Avant*.[113]

I did not have the kinds of brokering skills that Jimmy was looking for and Clarence was a genius in these kinds of deals. Avant is known as the Godfather of Black music. There is a documentary about his life and career that was released in 2019.

SKY TRAUGHBER
Gee, thanks Logan.

During Clarence's consulting days with President Jimmy Carter, I dated his assistant and could not hook-up with her for a week. She was escorting the First Lady around L.A. while the President was in town on business. Between you and that *Imitation of Life* movie, it's a wonder I had *any* dates during this time.

LOGAN H. WESTBROOKS
You're welcome, Sky. We all must sacrifice for the cause from time to time.

Anyway, *Peter Long* was the Executive Music Producer for the *PUSH Expo* in Chicago, an outgrowth of *Jesse Jackson's* powerful *Operation PUSH* grass root organization. Peter brought me in and CBS became a part of this event.

There were many highs in my professional career, but one of my biggest regrets happened in the early 70s in Harlem, New York. I produced a promotional concert in Mt. Morris Park (now Marcus

---

[113] Clarence Avant is considered a "godfather" of deal making. Clarence's *Sussex Records* launched the career of *Bill Withers* and Clarence would go on to found *Tabu* Records at CBS featuring acts like the *SOS Band* and *Alexander O'Neal*. Clarence would also organize the business aspects of power producers *Jimmy Jam and Terry Lewis* as well as co-promoting a Michael Jackson tour and serving on the boards of Pepsi Cola and Motown.

Garvey Park). It was an opportunity to expose new CBS product to young people in Harlem. Jazz bassist *Charles Mingus*, who was signed to CBS, put together a first-class band consisting of primarily Jazz artists. The big band sound they played had the young people ecstatic.

We also introduced the O'Jays and their new record *"Back Stabbers."* Upon hearing it, the young people were blown away. It was their first time hearing it and the first time it was played in this kind of environment. I brought in other Philly International artists as well, including Harold Melvin & the Blue Notes. Executives and the entire Philly International staff were there.

It gave the promotional staff at CBS Records national exposure for some of our hit material. The concert was held on a Saturday afternoon and it was packed. It was produced much like the Questlove documentary "Summer of Soul" which was also held outside in a park. I guess you ask what is there to regret about such a magnificent event? Well, I didn't record it, so all that musical history and documentation was lost except in the hearts, minds and souls of those who were fortunate enough to experience it.

Mingus participated in some of our other park concerts and shared his wisdom and insight into some social areas of concern in America at that time. Then, of course, acts like the O'Jays and Earth, Wind & Fire were able to spread their profound messages through the recording auspices of our division and CBS.

SKY TRAUGHBER

At one point, while a Promotion Manager in Atlanta for CBS, I was asked to represent the label in its commitment to the Jazz culture at an Atlanta news conference. I shed the normal jeans and sneaker attire of hustling records at radio on a local and regional level and donned my CBS corporate-style black and grey suit for the event. Nervous as hell at first, I then remembered *who* and *what* I was representing. Nailed it.

This lure and its operations will turn heads, bring admiration and envy from not only the Black industry stalwarts, but also the *entire* record and radio industry during that period. CBS Special Markets not only shined in its primary operations of breaking acts but in its networking and springboard operations for others.

In fact, the power being manifested at CBS Black Music Marketing may have been too much for one label to handle during that time, especially considering the tone of America, Black culture and the scramble for power transitioning into a corporate environment.

CHAPTER 10

Stax, Philly International and Invictus

LOGAN H. WESTBROOKS
Though the label had a major, primary stock-incentive deal at RCA Records worth $16 million, Stax signs a distribution deal with CBS Records in late 1972. Al Bell was impressed with Clive Davis' creative edge along with his knowledge and appreciation for the Stax sound and artists like Albert King.

The deal had two rather unusual attachments:

1. Unable to actually purchase co-owner Jim Stewart's half of the company, fearing anti-trust laws, CBS lends Al Bell $6 million to purchase Jim's interest in Stax,[114] for the distribution rights to Stax releases, thereby making Al the only 100% owner of a major Black label during this time. For the most part, this buy-out arrangement was kept confidential.

2. Clive did not consult nor inform any major CBS marketing executive of this signing. Nor was the Special Markets Division aware of this move.

No one knew, Black, Pop whatever until we were assembled for a 7:30 a.m. meeting in a Black Rock building conference room where Clive made the announcement and introduced Al Bell to everyone.

This label signing, though initiated with honorable intent and vision, will not only set forth some of the most bizarre events in music business history but will also help deliver the death blow to the most musically profound and socially-oriented deep-soul music record label, operating on a *major* level. This is not to insinuate that the

---

[114] Portions of the $6 million were also to be used for other various expansions within Stax. *Soulsville, USA: The Story of Stax Records*, Rob Bowman, 1997.

CBS deal was the *only* event contributing to the mystique and demise of Stax.

The *chain of causation* in the Stax tragedy is a long one. The highly acclaimed book, *Soulsville, USA: The Story of Stax Records* historian *Rob Bowman* and the powerful documentary, *Respect Yourself,* released after the Stax name and catalogue was acquired by *Concord Music,* offer a more in-depth chronological account of the Stax story in itself.

As in trying to understand the Motown Story, reading and viewing these releases may eliminate any need for a good shrink while in the process of analyzing what happened to the Black Music power base, owned in part or in whole, by Blacks during this time and leading to today.

The Harvard Report blueprint did not suggest any label purchase or market share to be derived from Stax in its projections for a CBS 15% market share in Black Music over the course of five years. However, in essence, the distribution deal between Stax and CBS brought a powerful Black Music consumer base as well as knowledge of *how to reach that consumer base* to the behemoth conglomerate. So, in a sense, CBS *did* acquire a market share from Stax, though the method will, to this day, remain a controversy.

Involvements in the chain of causations surrounding these events will also go beyond any job descriptions assigned to anyone associated with the CBS Special Markets Division at this time.

Following the Stax announcement in 1972, we were elated. The idea was that with some of the methods and procedures they were using, we could hopefully pick those up with CBS and do some of the same kinds of things. We thought that they were highly successful, that they were a specialized label that knew exactly what they were doing. The idea was, in bringing the might of the CBS distribution network, it would just be unlimited.[115]

---

[115] Bowman, Rob, *Soulsville, U.S.A.: The Story of Stax Records*, Schirmer,1997.

SKY TRAUGHBER

I would tell my students that if you really want to study a major part of the entertainment business, including some deal making, *go to Vegas*. Learn how to research, analyze and play the odds while also keeping some natural instinct. Coming out of a stock deal gone bad at Gulf and Western and with the new Special Markets Division in place at the world's most powerful distributor of recorded music, one can see where the Stax "gamble" at CBS would be worth a try, though the label is still feeling its way around in Black music.

Though no one in the CBS Special Markets Division would have a job description placing themselves in the middle of the legal, financial and distribution aspects of the Stax deal, the division will find itself in a position to gain from the Stax market penetration expertise.

This gain includes major labels, overall, inheriting a powerful deep-Soul artist roster including the *Staple Singers, Isaac Hayes,* the *Emotions,* the *Soul Children, Johnny Taylor,* the *Bar-Kays and* the *Temprees* with the *Emotions, Johnny Taylor,* and *Temprees* actually landing on CBS.

The Emotions and Johnny Taylor will deliver top-selling singles and albums for CBS after Stax was shut down. The CBS distribution division, though powerful in its own right, would also gain from this market penetration base, though they, like the Special Markets Division, were initially unaware of the deal.

The first screw to become loose in this seemingly tight marriage was when Stax "consultant" and *Koko* label[116] owner *Johnny Baylor* was detained by security at the Birmingham, Alabama, airport with $130,000 in cash and a check from Stax for $500,000. The FBI was called in and the IRS soon followed.

---

[116] The Koko label included Luther Ingram whose "If Loving You is Wrong" tune is one of Stax's biggest hits during that time. Johnny Baylor and Dino Woodard were originally summoned from New York to Memphis and Stax to protect the label against extortion and death threats against Stax employees, particularly Jim Stewart, by angry Black Memphis gangsters over Black ownership and money distribution at the company.

The tone of America at that time included not only a rising interest in record companies' involvement in organized crime and payola, but the FBI was beginning to pay more attention to Black social and financial organizations, categorized and filed as *Black Nationalists.* These individuals and organizations were viewed as having a power to influence the minds of others with a possible threat to "national security" and patriotism.

Allegedly, the Black Panther Party for Self Defense was now purchasing and stockpiling missile-launchers. An armed band of Panthers taking a wrong turn into the session assembly instead of the viewing gallery at the California State Assembly while Governor Ronald Reagan was giving press interviews on the state capitol lawn did not help keep the Panthers out of the FBI radar.

Chicago *Black P. Stones* gang leader *Jeff Fort* was sentenced to prison for allegedly swindling the United States government out of $1 million in the gang's job-training venture. This Chicago-based revolution in economic power will also lead to a surveillance of Stax-affiliate Jesse Jackson's half-brother's economic association with Libyan dictator and United States outcast *Muammar Qaddafi.*

Included in this file is the Jim Brown-led Black Economic Union:

> *According to the documents, the FBI had five*
> *Moles in the Black Economic Union and other*
> *groups, attending meetings and feeding*
> *information to the FBI supervisors.*
>
> *Phrases like "Agitator Index" and "Security*
> *Index" are sprinkled throughout the file.*
>
> *...though it took years, the FBI stopped seeing*
> *Brown's Black Economic Union—and to some*
> *degree Brown himself—as a threat.[117]*

---

[117] Freeman, Mike, *Jim Brown: The Fierce Life of An American Hero*, William Morrow & Company, 2006.

Though the FBI and other government agencies will ease their surveillance of this rising Black Power in the late 1970s, as the quote mentions, the intrusion will inflict its damage on the Stax/CBS relationship during that time along with other events that will contribute to the counter-clockwise turning of the seemingly tight screws of this particular venture.

Like Stax, the Kenny Gamble and Leon Huff Philadelphia International Records unit had a powerful music base, was entrenched in social causes (though not to the extent of Stax), exhibited entrepreneurship[118] and was also under a payola investigation. Unlike Stax, Philadelphia International Records will enjoy a somewhat less volatile episode of initiation into the CBS machine.

LOGAN H. WESTBROOKS

There may have been a touch of dissonance between my formal educational background and the profound street level background of Kenny and Leon, but for the most part we clicked okay. I was involved in co-coordinating the legendary *TSOP (The Sound of Philadelphia)* theme song for the *Soul Train* television show. Whereas Stax brought that soul-wrenching, raw southern sound to CBS, Philly International brought the chart-reading studio band sound of *MFSB* (*Mother, Father, Sister, Brother*).

Though Isaac Hayes initially launched the popularity of the large string and orchestra accompaniment to a tight, soulful studio band with the *Hot Buttered Soul* album of the late 60s, most of the Stax musicians themselves were not highly trained in the formal areas of orchestrations and transpositions manifested from the study of the Theory and Composition of music.

One can, however, hear and feel this formal musical ingredient in the works of people like *Booker T. Jones* (Booker T. & the M.G.'s),

---

[118] Kenny Gamble and Leon Huff joined forces with their third music collaborator, *Thom Bell,* most known for his work with the *Stylistics* and the *Delfonics* in forming *Great Philadelphia Trading.* Part of the real estate holdings of this firm becomes owning the Philadelphia International Records building in Philadelphia.

Lester Snell (The Isaac Hayes Movement) and *Ronnie Williams.*[119] David Porter and most of the Stax musicians experienced a profound early elementary, junior high and high school musical training. The *Stax Sound*, however, did not utilize consistent orchestral coloring, which usually requires a larger number and wider range of instruments and can tend to strip some soul from the music.

Philly International took its base studio band of people like *Bobby Eli, Bobby Martin, Early Young* and *Ronnie Baker* and *incorporated* the string and orchestra players with these musicians to create a singular unit, MFSB.

The *Barry White Love Unlimited Orchestra* would soon follow and this orchestra-with-rhythm-section sound would dominate a part of the Black Music sound, for the most part, until the mid-to-late 70s when Funk, Soul and Pop bands like the *Commodores, Con Funk Shun* and *Earth, Wind & Fire* arrived in prominence without orchestra.

SKY TRAUGHBER

That's what drew me to Memphis and Stax. Building on my high school symphony training, while also hitting those clubs, eventually took me to majoring in Music Theory and Composition at the University of Tennessee after a brief stint at Historically Black Tennessee State University.

Continuing to hit the clubs in and around Knoxville with people like Jimi Hendrix-styled *Jonah Ellis[120] (Jonah and the Whale)* I was ready, willing and able to jump into what Stax was doing in combining symphony, Rock and Soul.

After arriving in the Stax environment, however, my now-heightened Jazz and Acid Rock skills would sometimes conflict with the Stax feel. For instance, Stax relied heavily on a heavy "bottom up" sound that required the bass part to stay firm in a repetitious

---

[119] Ronnie also impressed the heads of Stax with his background in writing, arranging and producing advertising jingles.

[120] Jonah would go on to write and produce for acts like *The Gap Band* and *Yarbrough & Peeples.*

"pocket" rhythm, and I would "run" up and down the instrument a lot.

Nevertheless, when I heard the string and orchestra arrangements that *Lester Snell* had laid on the Temprees *Dedicated to the One I Love* hit record after I was hired to arrange their live show, I almost had a physical climax right then and there. Ladies are cool, but the music comes first. Okay…maybe a tie, sometimes.

When one takes a deep look at not only the culture but the music sound and feel of Stax and Philadelphia International entering CBS, it adds *another* link to any chain of causation of why Philly survived this marriage and Stax did not.

Not only the Stax sound but its people, overall, were an uninhibited lot. One must remember that this is still a *Paley-founded CBS Network company*. In this environment, *inhibition will trump unrestrained* when the chips are down.

This is not meant to exclude any aforementioned or still-to-come links in the Stax/CBS chain of causation factors, but is meant to illustrate that the Philly Sound was probably an easier assimilation into CBS than the Stax Sound.

In addition to being the King Label of Pop and Show Tunes, CBS was also heavily footed in a Jazz culture with its legacy of *Billie Holiday, Miles Davis, Herbie Hancock* and the like.

The Stax sound had very little or no Jazz influence, whereas Philly artists like *Billy Paul, Jean Carne* and *Lou Rawls* were drenched in Jazz-style roots. Jean Carne, in particular is an easy read in the CBS-female vocal style of high-octave stylists *Minnie Riperton, Deniece Williams* and the later addition of *Cheryl Lynn*.

Though Invictus Records interpreted Clive Davis' offer from CBS to indicate they would be a priority for the company, unlike their current experience at Capitol Records, they, too, may have hit a culture wall at CBS, especially in the earth-shaking event about to take place at the Black Rock building.

CHAPTER 11

Clive Leaves

LOGAN H. WESTBROOKS

Clive, with the Special Markets Division, was going to *do it*. Then, in mid-1973, the axiom of *"everyone* is replaceable" hit the CBS building like a rocket. Clive Davis was fired from CBS Records.

Even today, top-level dismissals are commonplace in corporate America. However, the Davis exit added a special drama to an already gripping chain of events at CBS.

First, the official reason for the Davis firing was reported as the company's discovery of "meticulous records of wrongdoing" on Davis' part and Clive was sued in a civil manner, asking him to return $94,000 of company money he had allegedly used for personal use.

Secondly, the firing mysteriously occurred during the time of a federal strike force investigation, known as *Project Sound (*also known as *The Newark Investigation)* into payola, drug trafficking and organized crime ties in the record business.[121] Remember, this is a major television and radio network suddenly terrified of losing its broadcast license.

Thirdly, the firing and investigation coincided with the CBS deals with Stax and Philadelphia International, two labels under the watchful eye of the federal strike force.

---

[121] The US government interest in entertainment "payola" actually began in 1959 with an investigation into an alleged "fix" for the television show, *The $64,000 Question.* Somehow the trail led to people like *Alan Freed,* the Rock 'n' Roll disc jockey who also had a television show and tours and *Dick Clark's American Bandstand* television show the Clark's tours, with the microscope focused on ties between *who* was allowed to perform on these shows, appear on these tours and any "special" financial arrangements out of the ordinary scope of payment for services performed. Clark emerged unscathed but Freed became the first person indicted for payola.

Fourthly, CBS was actually implicated to the strike force by Davis's CBS-aide *David Wynshaw*, who was at the time implicated in an unrelated drug charge and agreed to cooperate with the federal authorities. Wynshaw was later sentenced to a year in prison after being convicted of defrauding CBS.

Though the above events are bizarre and some believe that CBS overreacted in its handling of some of these events, the Davis firing will have a crushing effect on the Invictus relationship with CBS, and to an even greater degree, the future of Stax Records. With all due respect to the art and science of *fortune telling,* it is also hard to predict what may have happened to these labels had Clive remained at CBS. Maybe this is why we call it *drama*.

CHAPTER 12

The Fallout

LOGAN H. WESTBROOKS

In cutting the Invictus deal, Clive had promised to *"triple and quadruple"* the label's sales base through the CBS system. Clive had cut the Stax deal in private and promised Stax an equally intense expansion in album sales from their CBS alliance.

Stax product would not be distributed *by* CBS but *through* CBS, allowing Stax to retain its culture image while utilizing the CBS distribution power. Clive had also given Stax a $2.26 revenue split from the CBS album list of $5.98, an unusually high percentage for Stax, or any label during this time in a distribution deal with a major distributor.[122]

With Clive now gone, both Invictus and Stax will fall under the operations of a CBS pressing, manufacturing and branch system still immersing itself with a brand-new Special Markets Division. Neither operation was initially involved in the creative visions or financial and legal arrangements of Invictus or Stax. And neither operation was privy to nor endorsed the Stax deal.

After Clive left, I do not believe there was any intentional, concerted effort at CBS to conspire to bring these labels down. There were culture differences, and, to be frank, some racism involved, but this happens a lot in a lot of different places.

The deals and distribution events were out of my job description. Would I have liked to been involved from the outset? *Absolutely!* This was just not the case during my tenure at the label. However, I believe I was able to *stir* some interest for CBS to include Black executives in major deal-making and distribution job descriptions and positions for later years.

---

[122] The *Band of Gold* Documentary and *Soulsville* book.

The *Band of Gold: The Invictus Story* documentary producers came to my office in Los Angeles after being referred by *Clarence Tucker* of Invictus, and I gave an interview for the film. I then directed them to other key individuals who could also deliver some chronological and honest facts regarding Invictus, like *Otis Smith.*[123] The Invictus people had hired Otis from ABC Records as a key executive for the label.

SKY TRAUGHBER

In viewing the *Respect Yourself* and *Band of Gold* documentaries, reading countless other books, articles and conducting various interviews intertwined with my own recollections, there is no solid connection between the Special Markets Division at CBS and any possible conspiracy at CBS Records, itself, in what happened to Invictus and Stax.

The Special Markets Division was primarily involved in radio promotion with some marketing and advertising coordination, but not involved in the hard-core areas of deal making and distribution. Not at that time. Some of the splicing and editing in the *Band of Gold* film piece shows that someone *suggested* that Clarence Tucker of Invictus seek some input from Logan regarding an organized CBS conspiracy.

LOGAN H. WESTBROOKS

I would try and guide labels like Invictus, Stax and Philly International through the sometimes-complex maze of the CBS operations while I was at the label. I remember Invictus producer *Jeffrey Bowen*[124] coming by. But that was about all I could do outside of the radio and marketing work. I was not involved enough in the areas associated with any possible CBS conspiracy to have this type of conversation with anyone.

---

[123] Otis Smith would go on to found one of the last "soulful" labels of this era with *Beverly Glen Records* featuring *Bobby Womack*. Otis would also discover Soul and Jazz vocalist *Anita Baker*.

[124] Jeffrey would later produce some magnificent music for the *Temptations* at Motown.

SKY TRAUGHBER

Though not involved in the deal-making aspects, a *product manager* is usually a key position at a major label to help sort out some of these complexities for an artist, manager or label affiliate. The CBS Special Markets Division did not have *its own* product managers at that time and neither did Invictus, Stax or Philadelphia International.

In my product management days at CBS, as part of the Black Music Division in the late 70s, I made it a part of my business to have a contact at each of the CBS pressing plants. This allowed me to have a *direct* knowledge of pressing priorities, shipments and backlogs.[125] I could also *directly* communicate the information of demand from the marketplace to these contacts, ensuring a timely and accurate positioning of my artists' product at retail.

My artist roster at this time included acts like *Herbie Hancock, George Duke, Weather Report, Tony Williams, Ndugu Chancler, Ronnie Foster* and *Freddie Hubbard,* among others. It was business as usual, but a product manager would have wide latitude of how far they chose to go in this respect. I took the extra step from a *deep concern* for ensuring the sales availability for Black and Jazz-oriented artists at a label with no Black or Jazz sales and distribution people exclusively positioned in these areas. Not at CBS. Not at that time.

This is not to insinuate that a Black product manager, or any executive, is *necessary* for this special care in Black culture or business. It can be a choice no matter the ethnic heritage of the person involved.

Part of the imbalance of more Whites working in Black culture as opposed to Blacks working in a "raceless" culture is that some

---

[125] *Backlogs* are when there is retail and/or wholesale demand for album product but that particular album is not being actively pressed at this time. This can occur for many reasons, including a lack of communication about the demand to the pressing plant or maybe a label's fear that the demand is not real and may create a high volume of album returns, proving costly for the label. Today's "delivery on demand" model of internet purchases has somewhat diluted this model of a physical pressing dependence, though albums are still being purchased in a physical manner at retail stores.

Blacks *prefer* to become immersed in a Black culture environment instead of a "raceless" environment. It is also a known fact that powerful Black Music usually draws a significant non-Black interest. So, the log jam at Black Music from other ethnic groups is usually greater than the log jam from a diverse crowd at non-Black music cultures. Some of this may also be the difficulty of Blacks having access to some of these other culture networks.

Invictus felt that after Clive left there began a wide discrepancy between themselves and CBS over how much Invictus product would be *pressed* and *distributed* to the retail stores. This wide discrepancy will also figure into a $67 million lawsuit filed against CBS by Stax as CBS was not only withholding over $6 million due Stax in distribution *collection*s, but there would be over $5 million worth of Stax product *pressed* but still *sitting* in the CBS warehouse.

The difference in product *being pressed, being distributed* and monies *being collected* is important to understand.

Pressings are usually a result of a *demand projection*. This may result from the popularity from an artists' sales history or the *perception*, after listening to the current product and maybe consulting with the promotion people, how much product should be pressed and made available for the initial distribution period. The book publishing industry must also find a way to reach this important initial pressing figure for its retail outlets and the film industry is faced with a decision on how many prints to manufacture for distribution to theaters.

Actual distributions to wholesale and retail accounts from the record company warehouse are usually a result of the above but also includes a gauge of *actual* interest and buying patterns from the consumer. This consumer interest, through sales, may differ from the label's original perception of the product's worth in the marketplace and sometimes there is not enough promotion or a misdirected promotion effort to the marketplace that can also result in this dissonance.

You can also promote a record at radio, heavily, by various means, achieve a high level of spin rotations at a station and utilize other promotion vehicles, but you can't force consumers to purchase the music. The same holds true with how many retail outlets to service for books and how many theaters to service for a film.

<u>Collections</u> are the actual monies received from the consumer at retail and transferred back up the ladder through wholesale to the record label. These are not *account receivables,* but the actual money transfers. As of this writing, America is all screwed up, financially, due, in part, to an imbalance of its perceived receivables in relation to its actual money transfers. In contrast, the mob days in America were primarily *cash and carry.*

As in the original mob model that a large part of American corporate culture providers operates, influence flows downstream, while revenue flows upstream. As of this writing actor *Terrence Howard is* expressing a public complaint over his residuals that were expected but not received from the huge (over $300 million) revenue from the *Iron Man* film. The amount of money collected and how much expense is deducted from these collections, before itemizing and delivering any payments, can also cause some dissonance in these matters.

Payment schedules, timewise, are also a concern in the areas of distributions and collections. Monies collected but not paid promptly could be placed in an interest-bearing money account, thereby accruing additional revenue for a major company.

While the Invictus complaint with CBS hinged on not enough product being pressed, the Stax situation was somewhat the opposite. The $5 million worth of Stax product pressed and sitting in the warehouse was ordered from Stax by CBS, and financed by Stax, production wise. This depleted Stax's already struggling financial reserves,[126] and the Stax cash liquidity (available money) was furthered compounded by CBS's refusal to pay the label the $6 million due Stax from the actual collections on Stax product.

---

[126] There is some mystery surrounding the distribution of the $6 million CBS advanced to Stax, though Johnny Baylor reportedly received $2.5 million which the IRS at first confiscated as part of the ongoing investigations, then returned to Johnny after no illegal connections to the money were proved (minus the IRS normal tax deduction on legal income).

Both the Invictus and Stax problems with CBS also revolve around a culture clash between independent labels with deep-soul, an emerging R&B sound at major labels and the difference in a *push* versus a *pull* distribution philosophy. These chains of causation will figure prominently in the charges that CBS is involved in a hostile takeover conspiracy of the Soul music market, its labels and artists.

Independent labels during that time, including Stax and Invictus *pushed* their product into wholesale and retail, thereby creating a sense of urgency for these channels of distribution to help move the product. However, a label like CBS used more restraint in how much product it pressed and distributed in the marketplace, creating a sense of a solid consumer demand *pulling* the product into the distributors and the stores from the label's warehouse. A difference in the Black independent labels and a label like CBS during this time is that the Black labels knew all the nooks and crannies of how to reach their audience, ensuring that the product shipped will be sold and not returned.

This is where a coordinated understanding and belief between the supplier of the music and the distributor of the music must be on the same page, sometimes on a daily basis. The power of a distributor, in this arrangement, can overwhelm the power of the music.

Often, radio stations will discontinue the spinning of a record if it is not easily available for purchase. There are usually too many other records, *with* this availability, that can offer a credible sense of professional courtesy between the radio station and the buying appetite of its audience to use airspace for a record that cannot be found for purchase. As the Internet has changed much of this with downloads and streams, the fastest-growing physical form of recorded music, as of this writing, is vinyl, placing "push" and "pull" back in the picture of distribution models.

LOGAN H. WESTBROOKS

As I stated before, I don't believe there was any intent of conspiracy on CBS' part. However, the branch distribution system at CBS was the most racist of all the labels I had encountered during that time. This may not even be a matter of intent. One has to understand that most of the branch sales people at CBS were not "record people" from other labels but from mainstream American companies. So, as in American culture at that time, there was a dissonance in truly understanding the culture and how much power and attention it should receive.

At the same time, I remember joining some *top-level* CBS marketing people outside of a London hotel one evening, when an important figure in the England entertainment scene approached our group. The CBS person making the introductions proceeded to introduce everyone but me. I was the only Black person in the group. It upset my wife Geri—who was part of the group—more than me, and it may have been just an oversight. Then again, it may be another example of insensitivity and racism at CBS at that time, whether by intent, natural osmosis or conditioning.

Al Bell has stated in the *Soulsville* book that he believes Clive *did* read the Harvard Report and, that, in fact, Clive contributed some data to the report, some of which was lifted from his *Stax Sound in Chi-Town* research and campaign. Al presented results of this research and campaign at a NATRA (National Association of Television and Radio Announcers, Black Disc Jockeys) convention that Clive attended.

Al has also revealed that he was informed by some top-level CBS executives after Clive left that the *real* problem Stax was having with CBS, at that point, was the high percentage deal Clive had cut for the label and that if he would re-negotiate for a lower percentage, there would be more cooperation from CBS on the distribution problems.

After Clive's departure, the bulk of sorting out this dissonance while maintaining a business model for his employer—CBS Records—fell on the shoulders of Epic and Associated Labels Marketing Vice President, *Jim Tyrell,* a Black man, along with Epic Vice President Ron Alexenburg.

Al actually felt a bit slighted that he was now relegated to dealing with a *Vice President* in Jim Tyrell as opposed to a *President* in Clive Davis and a *President* he had cut his deal with.

CBS Records went through a brief period of "stand in" label heads to replace Clive before settling on Bruce Lundvall. Maybe the company felt that someone already in the day-to-day operation of marketing, like Jim Tyrrell, would be the best fit to deal with Stax during this transition period at the President level. However, on top of Clive's secrecy in cutting the deal, this period will prove to be a crucial one in terms of mis-communication and paranoia between Al and CBS at a time when both Al and CBS needed to be on the same page, musically and businesswise.

Jim was firmly entrenched in the "pull" system of distribution that would help eliminate any unnecessary return of distributed product[127] on the label's year end books. Album returns effect not only stock dividends but also employee bonus payments and employment retention.

The situation reached a point of becoming volatile when strong-arm man Johnny Baylor was assigned to represent Stax's sales and distribution interests at CBS.

> *Johnny calls me up, recounts Tyrrell and says,*
> *"You better do whatever we say. You got to put*
> *out some goods because if you don't do it, you're*
> *gonna have to take a helicopter to work."[128]*

Johnny and his partner, *Dino* (Otis Woodard), were gangsters, but *Black Nationalist* gangsters, in understanding the true potential enemy of a strong Black culture. In 1968, they may have been involved in a major physical violence disruption at the NATRA Convention in Miami, where a group of Blacks attacked anyone they felt were hurting the power of Black radio. Reportedly, Johnny and

---

[127] At this time, most labels had a generous return policy, where a retailer and wholesaler could send back any unsold product at no cost to themselves. Some of these return agreements went as high as 100%. Though the CBS return policy, reportedly, was considerably lower than 100% during this time, the company allowed an 80% return policy on Stax product, according to the *Bowman* book. If true, this would add fuel to the fire that maybe CBS was not interested in pushing sales on Stax releases.

[128] Bowman, Rob, *Soulsville, U.S.A.: The Story of Stax Records*, Schirmer, 1997.

Dino would, at the drop of a hat, go and serve as protectors for people like *Dr. Martin Luther King, Jr.*[129]

After discovering that Jim was actually associated with some of their counterparts from Harlem, they recanted the hit threat and tried to work amicably with Jim, though it would eventually not be enough to save the CBS/Stax venture.

SKY TRAUGHBER

Jo Bridges at Stax had "dropped a dime" (made a call) to Jim about me, so there was a relaxed relationship between us while I was at CBS, though he was in a sense, my *boss* in working together on my Epic acts like *George Duke*. When I saw that Jim was actually in charge of *all* the Epic releases, not just the Black product, it mesmerized me, especially with his significant bass-playing background. This was before I knew of the Stax and Invictus dramas.

The achievements of not only Jim, but people like Clarence Tucker, Al Bell, Clarence Avant, Johnny and Dino, the CBS Special Markets Division, while all of this was going on, is what not only makes warriors, but it makes heroes, in the sense that everyone has a sincere desire to achieve freedom and love in a power system possibly designed for other results.

Let's be clear, again, (if this book has nothing else, it has some damn clarity) as this co-author does not consider Johnny and Dino's violence and other activities as heroism, overall, but in a specific sense of using "whatever means necessary" to protect Black music label ownership. Death Row's Suge Knight will encounter this controversy, later. Okay, let's not call it heroism. What it should be called I have no idea, right now.

On the other hand, in February 2022, Snoop Dogg bought Def Row Records—the label that launched his rap career—which in itself displays ownership heroism.

---

[129] An interview with the late Johnny Baylor's goddaughter.

All of this also instilled in me, at a young age and into today, the need for *some* qualified and passionate *physical* Black ownership of Black culture in America. There are problems in this picture as, like everything else, physical Blackness has its flaws. But it is the painting that's planted in my head after observing and being somewhat involved in the drama.

As of this writing, there is practically *no* Black ownership in some major media and distribution areas that control how the masses view Black culture. The Internet offers some *pockets* of content and distribution, but Blacks don't own the Internet.

The Black Panther Party for Self Defense, Jim Brown's Economic Union, Jesse Jackson's Operation PUSH, Stokely Carmichael, Julian Bond and SNCC, Malcolm X and other *Pro-Black* movements of the 60s and 70s are sometimes misinterpreted as *Anti-White.*

Seriously, none of this is meant as divisive rhetoric. America must continue to allow and respect all views, or the perceived freedom associated with this country is actually going backwards, not forward.

CHAPTER 13

Africa

LOGAN H. WESTBROOKS

Not because of anything that was happening at CBS, but I was just beginning to take an interest in moving away from the core of the record business and venture into other social and business areas.

Johnny Seka, an international businessman and promoter from Senegal, West Africa, was trying to take *The Jackson 5* to Africa. Johnny and I developed a friendship in New York, including home cooked meals by my wife and just hanging out in the Manhattan nightlife. He then asked me to accompany him to Africa. He also asked New York and WBLS super jock *Frankie Crocker,* among other radio personalities, along with *Ebony, Jet, Essence* and *Soul* Magazine personnel to make this interesting trip.

Walter Yetnikoff[130] was heading the International Division of CBS Records. After I inquired about any CBS music activity in Senegal, he said that, for the most part, there was none. He then suggested that I take the trip, in part as a research project, with an eye for establishing a base for CBS in Senegal.

This conversation with Walter led to me spending six months of research with the United States International Commerce Department and various Nixon Administration aides where I received red-carpet treatment. A lot of this was primarily through my relationship with *Stan Scott,* a top Black in the Nixon Administration for Minority Affairs and my former roommate at Lincoln University.[131]

---

[130] Check out Walter's book, *Howlin' at The Moon,* for more top-level stories surrounding CBS Records.

[131] Stan graduated from Lincoln University with a B.S. Degree in Journalism and is reportedly the only reporter present at the Malcolm X killing at the Audubon Ballroom, in New York in 1965. Stan was nominated for a *Pulitzer Prize* associated with this event. Following his death from cancer, there is a *Stan Scott Cancer Research Center* in Louisiana.

Stan was part of the Scott newspaper family out of Atlanta that published the *Atlanta Daily World* along with the *Memphis* and *Birmingham Daily World*. Stan was a fully integrated Republican and good friends with eventual President George H. W. Bush. Stan's secretary made all the appointments for their office's international travel. This was near the end of Nixon's reign, and upon hearing of the tour Stan helped put the tour together, allowing us to use a similar itinerary in Africa as the Nixon administration.

I remember this being the first trip to Africa for The Jackson 5. The entourage also included the boys' father, Joe Jackson, their manager and road managers at the time along with future CBS and *Jackson* publicist from Motown.

The entourage for this trip did not stop there. Johnny Seka brought along an entourage of 10-12 members of the Black press, and freelance writer *Ronnie Claypool*[132] also accompanied us.

Just for the record, I also remember this as a time when Benjamin Hooks, a Republican, was appointed as Commissioner of the FCC (Federal Communications Commission). After his appointment, Benjamin hired *Chester Higgins* from his job as a staff writer at *Ebony* and *Jet*. Chester's son, *Chester Higgins, Jr.*, would go on to become a world-renowned photographer.

I also met African filmmaker *Francis Oladele,*[133] an independent Nigerian filmmaker and a brother-in-law to former Atlanta Mayor *Maynard Jackson,* who was helpful. Oladele became legendary as a filmmaker. His first film was *Kongi's Harvest* and was directed by Ossie Davis.

Before starting on my fact-finding trip to Africa, I spent a week in Kingston, Jamaica—Jamaica being a third-world country with a rich history of music. When I arrived, I met the principal of Federal Records and they had a studio and a manufacturing plant there that was owned by the Khouri family. They were very open and

---

[132] Ronnie would go on to become a major Broadway Producer including producing shows for *Lily Tomlin.*
[133] Francis Oladele studied photography at New York Institute of Photography and wanted to make Nigeria an *African Hollywood.*

cooperative in sharing with me the complete music scene in Jamaica. The owner's son gave me a copy of his college paper on the music business in Jamaica, which was most helpful (that report is available in my collection at Indiana University). Accompanying me on that trip to Jamaica was Francis Oladele. Francis would later be considered as a joint-venture partner for the CBS venture in Nigeria.

My first assignment for CBS International was to determine the feasibility of Black American music and the possibility of building a studio and manufacturing facility to service the market. It would also have been another outlet for Black American music on the CBS and Epic labels.

The idea was to select the most progressive African nation. Countries selected for consideration were Kenya, Ghana, Nigeria, Zaire, Ivory Coast, and Senegal. It was then decided to visit all six countries and get a first-hand look and actually meet local musicians, visit record shops and literally explore the music scene in each country. After visiting all six countries—spending a week in each— the choice was narrowed to Kenya, Nigeria, and Ghana These three countries stood out because they were English speaking, had a love for Black American Music, and all were familiar with the Jackson 5, who was signed to CBS.

Of the three countries Nigeria stood out as the first choice, being the most populous Nation with 56 million people (more than three times that now). EMI had a strong presence in all of the English-speaking countries, and was already distributing and selling Black American music, although on a very limited basis. In Nigeria, EMI and Decca had a joint venture company. EMI had a manufacturing plant in Kenya and Nigeria. This is the office I worked out of in Nigeria. Also, Motown had sent a representative who had worked in Nigeria and the Ivory Coast. His name was Gerald Theis. After careful analysis, it was determined that Nigeria should be the country to set up shop and open a recording studio and manufacturing plant.

After returning to New York and reporting on my trip to Walter Yetnikoff, he decided to put a team together to go to Lagos to confirm the feasibility. I then invited College Professor Playthell Benjamin, who was an expert on Nigeria, to come and make a presentation to the team that would be going to Nigeria. The team consisted of two CPAs from the New York CBS International office and two accountants from CBS in Israel. CBS International had a major office in Paris, France, which would be considered my regional base. The team met us there in Paris, and from there we flew on to Lagos.

The team, after spending several days in Lagos, then decided to find a joint venture partner. Naturally, Francis Oladele became a likely candidate in as much as he had volunteered to accompany me to Jamaica, and had a strong presence there in Nigeria. Also on this trip, I had arranged for two other businessmen in Nigeria to be considered for a joint venture partnership.

One was Harry Akande who later ran unsuccessfully for president of Nigeria. Akande was also a savvy businessman and was familiar with the American way of doing business. He owned the New African Technical & Electrical Company (NAFTEC), which was a representative company of General Electric (GE) America. The third individual being considered was Chief Abiola who was wealthy and owned several hotels. He was musically inclined, loved Black music, and was also a personal friend of music artists Ginger Baker and Paul McCartney.

This set the stage for the African adventure. As an international businessman, I found it necessary to actually socialize with the people I was doing business with. And I actually developed a life-long friendship with all of the Nigerian businessmen that I was dealing with. My wife Geri accompanied me on most of these trips to Nigeria, and we were invited into their homes. When they visited New York, Geri and I entertained them and their wives in our Manhattan apartment.

After carefully analyzing all the pros and cons of the potential joint venture partner, the decision was made to go with Francis Oladele's company. I was a guest at a club that he owned in Ibadan. He was instrumental in introducing me to all the top acts and local musicians in Nigeria at that time. Oladele also introduced me to Fela Kuti, the world-famous singer-musician. I wanted to get him signed to CBS, but unfortunately it didn't occur while I was there.

I spent a lot of time with Fela, and he took me to his nightclub called The Afrika Shrine. Fela's influence later spread worldwide. Years later in 2009, businessman and rapper Jay-Z produced a Broadway musical called "Fela!" that focused on Fela's life, music, and political activism.

After we had gathered all the information we needed, we returned to New York. On another trip I made to Nigeria, I was accompanied by Don Butler—a Black executive from CBS corporate—and we covered most of the same ground that I had covered before. This trip, however, was to take a look from a corporate standpoint for such a major venture as this.

On my next trip to Nigeria, I was directed to open a bank account and seek permanent housing and plan for the relocation to Nigeria for my wife and I. The fact-finding mission for a home in Nigeria are housed in my collection at Indiana University for your perusal.

Unfortunately, on that trip—which became my last trip to Nigeria in 1976—while there at that particular time on my way to the office in that Lagos GST (Go Slow Traffic) all traffic was suddenly stopped completely for a black limousine that was coming through with military personnel. In that car was the military leader General Murtala Muhammad with his driver and top aide.

While the limo was stopped at the intersection, several soldiers with long guns AK-47 assault rifles opened fire on the limo killing the military leader while they were stopped in traffic. The assassins proceeded to leave, but then turned and emptied their rifles into the car. I was stuck in this traffic while all this was going on.

Immediately, all borders were closed and no one could come into the country or leave. There was also a strong anti-American feeling in the country. Some said the CIA was involved. The most I could do was return to my hotel, the Ikoyi, and stay inside.

For the next three weeks there was a massive manhunt for the assassins, after their leader Colonel Dimka had been identified. Colonel Dimka was finally caught, tried and executed at a public institution at Bar Beach in Lagos.

While I was locked down in the hotel, I collected the evening newspapers from the day of the assassination. I then collected the morning and afternoon newspapers every day up until I left and brought them back to New York with me. Unfortunately, the person that I loaned the newspapers to has misplaced them. However, once they are found, they will be deposited in my collection at Indiana University, digitized and available for your viewing.

After the borders were reopened, I returned to New York. On my many trips to Nigeria, my friend Don Cornelius and I were exploring the possibility of showing the Soul Train show in theaters in Nigeria. I had met with a theater owner on one of my trips, and Morris Levy (a friend of Don's) gave Don a videotape player, which I carried back to Lagos with me to launch the venture.

On that last trip I determined that I would not be returning to Nigeria, so I turned that project over to a friend of mine from Chicago and her husband who worked for George Johnson of Afro Sheen in Nigeria. I never knew the outcome and of that venture. I also never got to the People's Republic of China, which would have been my next international assignment.

For several months Don Cornelius and I had been talking about the possibility of me joining he and Dick Griffey at Soul Train Records. So, on my return to New York, I resigned from CBS International and made preparations to relocate to Los Angeles. When Geri and I lived there in 1971, we had purchased a home there and had leased it out when we left.

Near the end of June 1975, Geri and my daughter Babette vacated our apartment in Manhattan and flew into Chicago. From Chicago we boarded a sleeper car train and arrived in Los Angeles on July 4, 1975. This began my stint at Soul Train Records. It was a great time with Don and Dick, the Whispers, Shalamar, Carrie Lucas, the Soul Train Gang, and many other great acts, and especially the historic show *Soul Train*.

CHAPTER 14

LeBaron, Vernon and Paris

SKY TRAUGHBER

LeBaron Taylor's move from radio to the high ranks of record labels was swift. After a storied stint in Detroit radio, followed by the same level of excellence at *WDAS* in Philadelphia, LeBaron headed a profound A&R effort in Black Music at Atlantic Records, New York. Though the Atlantic gig was brief, it produced some of the most classic recordings in early 70s R&B/Pop with acts like the *Phillippe Wynne*[134]-led *Spinners*.

Becoming the new head of Special Markets at CBS places LeBaron in a position of power that, at this time, equals the music stature he enjoyed during the brief stay at Atlantic. However, the next few years at CBS will surpass the Atlantic music model and venture heavily into the social, political and economic empowerment movements engulfing not only Black Music but also Black culture of the 70s.

Though without a formal college education, LeBaron had an articulation, class and media background that will figure heavily in embellishing what began a few years earlier at CBS with the Original Thirteen. Coming from WDAS in Philadelphia, also gives LeBaron a proud Civil Rights association with powerful Philadelphia radio revolutionaries like *Georgie Woods*.[135]

About this time, I am coming out of college with an-unheard-of degree in Music Business, along with my practical experience in

---

[134] The dynamic vocalist Wynne died prematurely in his mid-40s while performing at Ivey's, an Oakland nightclub in the mid-80s. This writer was, at the moment of Phillippe's death, at home writing music charts for an upcoming solo album and tour on Phillippe.

[135] *Georgie Woods* began as a Black Music consultant to *Dick Clark* and would develop into one of the top Civil Rights broadcasters in the nation. Repeatedly arrested for his protests and involvements with the civil disobedience activities of Dr. Martin Luther King, Jr., Woods would only return to the scene of the protest and lead yet another protest against injustices of a class and color nature.

musicianship and radio. Though the degree program, itself, was heavy in country music culture and legacy, I had, through various album credits and industry trade articles studied prolific people in Black Music like LeBaron and *Richard Mack* at CBS, *Alan Lott* at Buddha and others.

I met and interviewed with *Vernon Slaughter* and *Paris Eley* at CBS in New York and was beginning to hear about someone named Logan Westbrooks who had orchestrated much of the CBS Black Music unit but had moved on to an international post at the label.

I was confident but also in awe of actually beginning to meet and work with these people. It reached sort of a climax when I shook hands with LeBaron during my CBS interview in New York. Like everyone else, LeBaron was at first suspicious of someone like myself with a formal degree in the record business but after I was hired, hit the streets and actually got some records played, he became one of my biggest supporters. LeBaron would eventually head a CBS venture into education partnerships with then-CBS publicity agent *Sandra Trim-Dacosta*.

Before I reached CBS in my job search, I visited an airline stewardess friend in New Orleans and while she was "flying the friendly skies," I hit the New Orleans radio market looking for work. Powerful crescent-city radio jock *Donnie Brooks* picked up the phone and recommended me to *Alan Lott* at Buddha[136] New York, right there on the spot.

After joining CBS and being assigned to work the Carolinas, Charlotte and *WGIV* radio legend *Manny Clark* personally introduced me to Georgie Woods at a hotel one night after a P-Funk show. Turns out that the three of us were frat brothers, as is Vernon Slaughter.

The record industry was at this time, and should always be, to an extent, basically a street background business. However, each of these people showed an interest and a need for infusing some

---

[136] *Buddha* is one of the gems-of-Black Music labels of the 70s with acts like *Gladys Knight & The Pips, Norman Connors* and *Michael Henderson.*

educational elements into the growing sphere of Black Music and its rising influence and association with the social, political and economic empowerment of the times.

I myself would try and pass some of this on to people like *Doug Daniels*, who would go on to become a Vice President of Black Music at *Interscope*. Doug was a student at *Clark University,* in Atlanta, during my brief CBS stay there, and would come by the office to pick up some wisdom. This is not to say that one must have *either* a street or education background, but *recognizing* the wisdom of *each* does serve a purpose if one is able to connect the dots.

LOGAN H. WESTBROOKS

The now LeBaron-led BMM (Special Markets is now known as *Black Music Marketing*) Department at CBS will break or revive important acts like *Bill Withers, Tyrone Davis, The Emotions, Heatwave, Mtume, Johnnie Taylor, Gladys Knight and the Pips, Archie Bell & the Drells, Regina Belle, Wynton Marsalis and Teddy Pendergrass*. They will also embellish the *Original Thirteen*'s involvement in the Congressional Black Caucus and Coretta Scott King's Atlanta organization. As the CBS Black Music Division influences the formation and operation model of Black Music departments at other major labels, the *stakes* of this power base being in control will also rise.

The *Harvard Report* projections for a five-year profit in Black Music[137] are on schedule but there is still no one from the Black Music Division firmly entrenched in A&R or distribution, though *Dr. George Butler* was lured from his dynamic days at *Blue Note* to head the powerful *CBS Jazz and Progressive Music* A&R unit. LeBaron, for the most part, was not reporting to the CEO of CBS

---

[137] The CBS, Inc., public financial records are not broken down by musical genre within the record division. However, a review of these records shows a considerable rise in income for the record division during the mid-70s, reflecting not only the label's meteoric rise in Black Music but the label's overall industry-leading sales during this period. The entire record industry was only reaching its first $1 billion yearly mark, but it was growing at about a $200 million a year pace versus a decline of about $200 million a year the industry will show at the turn of the century.

Records, creating a layer that must be dealt with for top-level decisions regarding this important era of Black music.

Whereas the early years of BMM were "open budget," the rise of the artist roster from a few acts to close to a hundred and the BMM department, itself now employing close to thirty or more warriors, now requires a closer scrutiny of how the money is spent. Having layers of approvals helps in the oversight necessary for an efficient operation but it can also cause some mis-reads and differing opinions of intent along the way.

The Stax, Invictus and payola episodes are also still floating around in everyone's minds.

SKY TRAUGHBER

The Stax episode and CBS's involvement in the episode seemed to be a sensitive and "hush-hush" matter in the department, at least from what I could pick up on. Of course, I was a bit naïve to the whole chain of events and a bit sensitive, myself, coming from a Stax background. Okay, I was *pissed.*

All I really wanted to do after college graduation was work at Stax, and now here I was sitting on the payroll of its reputed oppressor. At the same time, I was *proud* to be a part of the personnel comprising the department. Dr. Jekyll and Mr. Hyde stuff.

I distinctly remember my first meeting in New York with the entire staff from around the country. Someone, maybe *Emma Garrett* from Miami, inquired about the truth of the CBS/Stax episode. *Russell Timmons,* from LA and a former Stax person, listened intently.

LeBaron diplomatically diffused the discussion, guaranteeing everyone that CBS did not destroy Stax, but he did not go into any detail. That's one thing about LeBaron. He could master a presentation with superb communication skills, leaving everyone satisfied and wanting to go do something positive, but still wondering exactly what was said, like Obama or my Vice President of Faculty at Berklee, *Dr. Larry Simpson.*

I also remember a New York meeting a few months later. This is a meeting where staff members across the country were directed to drop whatever records they were promoting, or whatever, and charge a flight to New York on the company American Express. It was time to *raise some hell* to the CBS brass about some things. By now I had gained a bit more confidence at being a part of the department and stepped to the mic to complain about CBS "*…not putting any money back into the Black communities that it was drawing a large part of its income from…*"

I will never forget the look on the faces of the CBS brass attending the meeting.[138]   They thought I meant payola until LeBaron diplomatically explained that I was speaking of scholarships, legitimate business investments, training and the likes. My payola days with CBS would come later.

Inheriting Richard Mack as the National Director of Album Promotion, LeBaron soon adds Vernon Slaughter as the National Director of Singles Promotion and Paris Eley as the department's first in-house Product Manager.

The Black Music Marketing field staff expands to include *Eddie Sims and Mike Bernardo* in New York, *Don Eason, Jimmy Starks, Frank Chaplin, T.C. Thompkins and Greg Peck* in the Midwest, *Curtis Mobley* and *Caesar Hancock* in Texas, *Charles Miller* in Memphis, *Freddie Richardson* in Washington D.C., *Jheryl Busby, Doug Wilkins, Michael Johnson, Maurice Warfield, Myra Weston* and *Craig Neely* on the West Coast.

Like the original Special Markets radio promotion staff, they must work *all* CBS labels (Columbia, Epic, Philly International and other Associated labels) while their Pop counterparts only work *either* the Columbia or Epic rosters. In addition, they must maintain a now-industry leading professional stature of class and Black Music/ Culture, empowerment poise both inside and outside of CBS.

---

[138] I remember CBS Marketing VP *Jack Craigo* attending this meeting. When Jack would see me later at meetings, he would encourage me to stick with my guns. Jack went on to be a top exec at RCA Records and is probably one of the best marketing people ever to work records.

Yeah…the double-duty thing was kind of disturbing, especially when you would see your Pop and Rock counterparts only working one label. But as Professor Hunt said in the beginning of this book…" running a little faster, jumping a bit higher…" and we still delivered.

The Pop and Rock promoters also utilized the secretarial staffs in the branches. Sometimes there would be some awkwardness as to their responsibility to the Black Music releases. However, my boss at the time in Atlanta, Fred Ware, strongly stated for his people to not depend on any branch secretaries to communicate with and/or gather crucial airplay reports from Black radio stations. *Take care of your own business* was the message. When appropriate it is a timeless and universal message.

LOGAN H. WESTBROOKS

In New York, it was a new day at Black Rock. *Marie Sellers* now coordinates all the radio airplay and chart data while *Beverly Paige, Wayne Edwards* and *Steve Manning* join Win Wilford and Sandra Trim-DaCosta in what is becoming an embellishment of the ground-breaking Motown Artist Development department[139] and is known at CBS, at this time, as *Press and Publicity*. Steve Manning is actually an "exclusive" press agent for *The Jacksons* at CBS, much like *Liz Rosenberg* will become at Warner Brothers for *Madonna* in the 80s. *Guy Spellman* and *Rita Roberts* will join later as product managers as will *Jerome Gasper* in Epic A&R.

The CBS West Coast building also finds itself with a Black Music staff covering Product Management, Press and Publicity and Artist Development and includes *Harold Coston, Billie Spencer, Vaughn Thomas, Gerry Griffith, Carmel Kim, Marsha Smith, George Wannamaker, Pat Thomas, Alicia Johnson, Gene Shelton, Myrna Williams, Carolyn Van Brundt* and *Orlando Imala*. At the CBS branch in Encino, Doug Wilkins, Myra Weston, Maurice Warfield

---

[139] Motown is considered the first record label to have an "Artist Development" department as separate from the other departments with an intense focus on developing an artist's appeal outside of the music. The Motown Charm School served as an attachment to this focus.

and future MCA/Motown President Jheryl Busby will operate their radio relations work.

Many of the above people will go on to help lead the Black Music Divisions and operational areas in places like Warner Brothers, MCA/Universal, Atlantic, GRP, Capitol, A&M. LaFace, EMI, Casablanca, Solar, Motown, Geffen, Dream Works, Tabu, N-Coded Music. Marsha Smith, for instance, will join longtime Vee-Jay Records and Motown veteran Ewart Abner at Stevie Wonder's Black Bull Music in the early 1980s. Later, she went on to Warner Brothers Television and ABC-TV where she held various positions in their publicity departments.

The Black Music Marketing experience at CBS in the mid-to-late 70s was becoming not just a job but *CBS Black Music University, Inc.* However, a key anonymous BMM executive, in 1981, shortly after the department was essentially integrated into CBS Records, revealed to Sky during a business meeting that he was glad the department was integrated into the label's overall operations.

He was tired of daily battles involving racism, equal pay, budgets, support staff and resources. Another now-retired anonymous "Original Thirteen" BMM member told Sky, in an interview for this book, he does not miss the high-pressured weekly conference calls and constant threats of job insecurity from others who wanted your job. Guess *"every"* story has two sides.

SKY TRAUGHBER
Yeah. Logan was the first professor I saw with a Black Music background when he taught at *California State University* in the late 70s, early 80s. I believe that my ability to teach at a high level at three of the top Music Business programs—*Middle Tennessee State, Northeastern University* and *Berklee College of Music,* in Boston— for close to twenty years along with hooking up some things between Berklee and the *Harvard Law School Legal Center* for recording and film affairs is, in part, due to the education I received from the people, business and dramas associated with *CBS University.*

One morning, leaving my Westwood apartment for the short drive to the CBS West Coast building for work, while in awe of the snow-covered mountains against the sunshine, I wondered, as still a country boy, "What am I doing here? Then it hit me. Doing a job, getting paid *and* receiving an education. Just different than the Stax and Country music eye-openers.

One of the first bits of education I received was the reality that while I was part of the most powerful corporate label Black Music entity in the industry, it was still *a part of* CBS, which was not a Black entity. This came in the form of a "schooling" I received from one of the veteran staff members assigned to room with me during one of the first New York meetings for the entire staff.

This person—book honoree Armand McKissick—explained to me in a very serious manner that LeBaron had actually fired one of his top staff members, only to have the firing overruled by CBS. Supposedly this person was behaving in a manner that not conducive to the professional image LeBaron wanted his Black Music staff to project, both inside and outside of the company. The fact that maybe someone was "falling off the wagon" did not matter to me.

The *real miracle* in America is that *every* Black man is not running around on some sort of drug or alcohol, *heavily*, and toting a gun. What bothered me was "…who's *actually* in charge of this thing…?" Power by permission is different than power by choice.[140]

In recognizing this dissonance between the *perceived* and *real* power in Black Music at major labels there would be a requirement of *honor, respect* and *loyalty* among the tight circle of Black Music executives. Otherwise, one may be viewed as an infiltrator. Practically every Black Nationalists organization during this period had to caution themselves in this manner. Vernon and Paris will find themselves no different in this caution.

---

[140] In a *PBS Documentary*, the Reverend *Al Sharpton* voiced a belief that James Brown's IRS and payola battles with the US government were founded, in part, on this power of choice exhibited by James. James Brown, single handedly, stopped a potential Boston riot after Dr. Martin Luther King, Jr.'s assassination, which, to some, exhibited a power of choice as James did not need anyone's permission or assistance in influencing people's behavior in this manner.

Vernon Slaughter and Paris Eley's elevation to Vice Presidents of CBS Black Music will bring in a new era to the division. Vernon will head Columbia with Eddie Sims while Paris spearheads the Epic and Associated Labels side of the company with Don Eason.

After his CBS college rep days while playing football in Nebraska, Vernon held down the important album-breaking territory of Washington, D.C., as part of the *Original Thirteen* staff. Washington, D.C., (also known as *Chocolate City*) radio, for the most part, then and now revolves around the *Howard University-owned WHUR-FM*. Black Music, and the record industry as a whole are, at this time in the 1970s, moving away from a singles and AM radio-based industry and into the far-reaching world of FM radio.

A wider sound spectrum, in technology, and a wider tolerance for longer playing and more mature and revolutionary lyrics and instruments helped define this era of the record business as much as anything else.

With Howard University and a *White* House residence in a predominantly *Black* city, Washington, D.C., is a hotbed for ushering in the new FM radio revolution. This is not to say Black AM radio is not a major source of revolution and intellectual thinking. Black AM radio could be counted on, during the Civil Rights battles, to give crucial up-to-the-minute accounts of the movement. Black FM radio is now adding something else to the mix.

Though I was an AM radio jock while in college and still respected the AM community, I would sit in my Atlanta apartment, while being a CBS promotion person, like a *consumer,* and just listen to *V-103,* programmed by *Scotty Andrews*, all night. *Barbara Taylor* and *WWDM,* in Sumpter, South Carolina, would blast *"the big DM"* sound all over the South with 100,000 mega-watts of now-polished soul.

LOGAN H. WESTBROOKS
With Vernon's album promotion expertise along with a brief stint as *Vice President of* CBS *Jazz and Progressive Music Marketing* and Paris' background in Black radio, creatively extended into a

profound Product Management setting, the CBS Black Music Division is now ready to explode its power on the industry without having to prove as much as the Original Thirteen and LeBaron Taylor eras.

After the Original Thirteen laid the groundwork for credibility, the LeBaron era had to show that the division could continue to operate itself in a businesslike manner *within* CBS. At times, this created some dissonance among some members of the department over *how far* the Black Music department must go in proving this without neglecting its own needs and cultural strength. This is another reality of being homeless in terms of renting space versus owning the lot.

Motown was now struggling to keep pace but still reminded everyone who they were with offerings like "Got to Give It Up" by Marvin Gaye. *Richard Pryor* was dropped from the Stax integration into CBS, due to content differences, but prepares to enter his own major film production deal and will hire Jim Brown to put it all together.

The FBI surveillance and infiltration of the Black Economic Union had inflicted its toll on Jim's masterpiece of Black Power and now Jim is looking at other options to keep the flame alive.

Everything is now *bigger*. Bigger artist rosters. Bigger executive staffs. Bigger budgets. Bigger payoffs. Bigger fears.

SKY TRAUGHBER

After a few months at CBS, I was called into my Branch Manager's office and told by he and others that I was not spending *enough* money! Though I was getting records played with hustle and sales presentations, it seems that everyone else was spending much more than me.

After they schooled me on the personal as well as the professional benefits of this model, I gave it some intelligent, prudent, open-minded thought and decided, *"...okay...we can roll like that."*

LOGAN H. WESTBROOKS
Even with all this power in its infancy, no one, including *The Harvard Report* could predict the dynamic duo looming backstage that are about to take front stage and contribute, arguably, to the loss of the "soul" of Black Music:

Disco & Cocaine.

CHAPTER 15

Disco and Everyone Ducks

SKY TRAUGHBER
Good times can blind even the clearest of eyesight. With annual revenues increasing by $200 million a year and Black Music in the forefront, the club scene is a natural habitat for not only exposing acts, but also for feeling the funk with groups of people in the same mindset.

For the most part, people don't go to clubs or dance with an eye for purchasing what they are dancing to. The music just feels good and makes that rump hump. Even if one is a bit challenged in that body area, they still shake whatever they've got.

As opposed to the adult-music club liquor of the *Prohibition and Post World War II* eras and the marijuana and acid of the *outdoor and sunshine mind-expansion* era of the 60s, it seems everyone in the late 70s just wants to dance all night and not really think about a lot of serious s**t.

Guns, protests and government oversight are replaced by corporate three-piece suits, homes and credit cards. As an accompaniment to a natural rush or in an attempt to extent the dopamine rush that accompanies some feel-good music and life, cocaine is only an obvious choice for many.

On the music side, this equates to a "four beat-bass drum" style of production that, as *Grateful Dead* leader *Jerry Garcia* described: "Even White people can feel where it is..."[141] Though the snare drum will still hit hard on the two-four-counts at times, nearly *every* record of this period is based on the "bass-drum-on-every-count" bottom-up sound.

---

[141] *History of Rock 'n' Roll* Documentary, 1995.

Many prolific recordings will emerge from this style, including hits from *The Bee Gees, Donna Summer, The Village People, The Trammps, KC & The Sunshine Band* [142] and others.

Kenny Gamble and Leon Huff intentionally cut tunes on artists like *The O'Jays, Patti LaBelle* and *McFadden & Whitehead* for CBS in this club-beat style.[143] Some of the *overall* music offerings during this period, not just at CBS, were great. Some were not.

As a fading musician, but emerging producer and A&R executive during this time, I can attest to the value of having the feel of your audience bouncing around the studio. It is no secret that some rappers smoke *big weed* in the studio. However, *cocaine* can affect *perceptions* differently than weed. People do blow to feel good, in spite of reality.

In a studio environment, one needs a clear perspective on what is sounding good and what is not. Doing blow during the playback, as opposed to the recording, may add some good perspective. The audience may be listening or dancing to the music under this influence, so you feel the music as they will probably feel it, in its finished condition. This is not to insinuate any particular artists, producers or whatever. Just making an informed point.

Yes, I am getting the hell out of this discussion. And no, I will not get into today's culture of Ecstasy, Oxycontin and everything else and the music.

However, I will add that when I discovered that CBS/Epic had taken the profound, smooth but southern soul-and romantic Stax group, the Temprees, and put them in a music bag of releasing "I Found Love on a Disco Floor," during this time, I figured *someone* was on *something.* On the other hand, the Columbia-inspired string-and orchestra sounds on deep soul merchant Tyrone Davis' "In the Mood" during this period is impeccable, maybe because it is a ballad and does not sacrifice the bottom-up soul. It lets the string and

---

[142] KC's record label, *TK Records,* out of Miami, used some HARD vinyl on their records that would give a club jock extra security in playing the grooves to death.
[143] Rock 'n' Roll/Make it Funky, Episode 8 (TV) Yvonne Smith, September 27, 1995/PBS TV, The Paley Center for Media.

orchestra take the bottom and Tyrone's voice to another place. "The Groove Line" (long disco version) by *Heatwave* on Epic/CBS goes beyond description in its Euro but American funk bottom-up sound, set against powerful but simple orchestrations. More Dr. Jekyll and Mr. Hyde stuff.

LOGAN H. WESTBROOKS

For the most part, Black Music, to this point, does not have an extremely high rate of returned albums back to the record company from the wholesale and retail distributors because of low sale-through demand. This adds to the high-profit margin of the music that many majors are now adding to their operations, but still not necessarily spending the same amount of dollars as being spent on their Pop and Rock acts.

Some of this discrepancy between spending and profit margin is due to either an "actual" or "perceived" high sales volume market base already enjoyed at major labels in the Pop and Rock genres of music. If not an actual sale-through, a "perceived" sale-through on Rock acts can set the scene for trade magazine ads, high chart performance and publicity bits emphasizing how an act has gone platinum (one million albums) or double platinum and the like.

An image of this nature helps sells concert tickets. Concert revenue is a major stream of income for Rock acts and can, in some cases, filter over to record sales. A lot of labels at this time would purchase, say, the remaining 200,000 units on an act needed to publicize this act as a "platinum selling artist." This helps the act but presents no profit for the record label unless the sales are recouped later.[144]

When the buying public relaxed their strong and increased buying pattern of *all* popular music during the Disco period, Black Music began to show a high rate of returned albums just like everyone else. Many major labels at this time were accepting a 100% rate on any unsold albums from their distributors and retail outlets.

---

[144] In the current economic crunch of the record business, as of this writing, many labels have instituted a *360 Degrees* contract arrangement, whereby, in return for any monies spent on an artist the label may participate in *all* incomes generated by that artist.

The meteoric rise of Black Music hits a snag that some contribute to the music, itself, as Disco is seen as a form of Black Music. As an example, Soul and R&B great Isaac Hayes passed away suddenly. Many of the reporters listed him as a "Disco artist" when recounting his storied career.

What caused the sudden and devastating turn of events in the record industry known as *The Crash of '79* is open to varied discussions, opinions and evidence of chains of causation. What *is* known is that the kids, especially, began to spend their money on *Pac-Man* instead of this repetitive-style music and that the now-widespread use of cocaine inside and outside of the industry will help lead to a period where how much gratuity is given for the airplay for a record trumps the record itself.

In defense of this practice during this period, business relationships and gratuities have been a part of the Pop music business and America, in general, for a while. On the other hand, during the interviews for this book, an informed Black Music radio promoter strongly stated that a group of powerful Black radio programmers were gathered in New York during this time.

Armed with a power to influence major labels in their business and social operations with Black music and its culture at this important crossroad, the programmers chose to be sidetracked from this mission by accepting liquor and women from the labels.

Those who *have* the most can now *give* the most and *receive* the most, big time.

PART III
The Powers That Be…Are the Powers That Be
Late 70s-90s

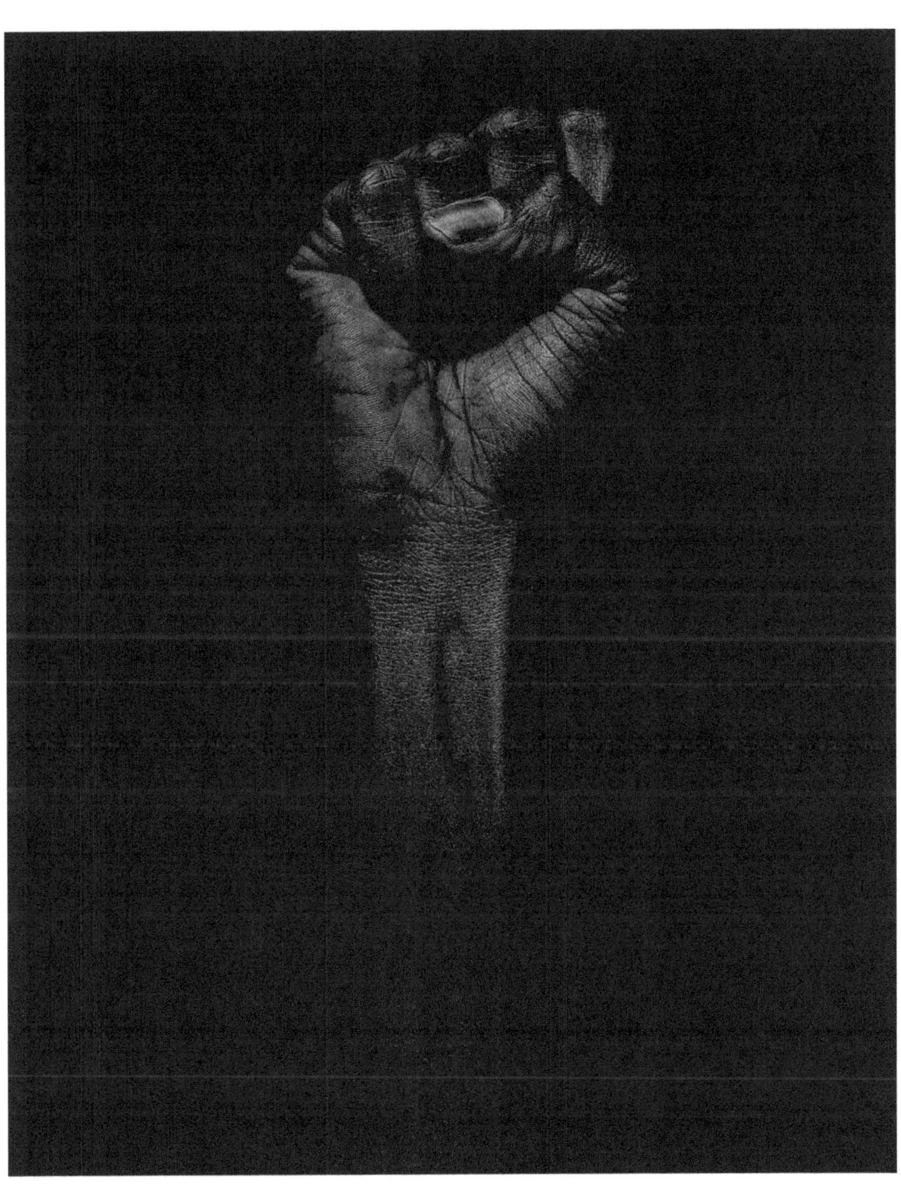

CHAPTER 16

Back "Home"

LOGAN H. WESTBROOKS
The international travel broadened me and my perspective on the world. Once I returned to the United States, I was more broadminded with a wider world view and a much greater appreciation of Black Africa.

At the same time, I had already developed an interest in real estate, education and the political direction of this country. I would check out the real estate section in the newspapers of the different cities in America that I had traveled to.

There was a Professor at *Cal State University* trying to attract non-traditional type professors to the college. *Ron Karenga,* the Black Revolutionist who helped to create the *Kwanzaa* holiday,[145] and myself were among these types of progressive thinkers recruited to teach there, as was *Diane Watson* who was on the Los Angeles City Council and later became a Congresswoman from California.

I liked *Jimmy Carter* as a person. After receiving a call from *Junius Griffin* at Motown regarding some help in Jimmy's Presidential campaign, I made the hook-up between Jimmy and Clarence Avant. However, I was becoming disenchanted with the Democratic Party, itself, and influenced by my association with Stan Scott in the Nixon

---

[145] Ron Karenga was a part of the creation of Kwanzaa in 1966 as the first specifically African-American holiday with a goal to "...give Blacks an alternative to the existing holiday and give Blacks an opportunity to celebrate themselves and history, rather than simply imitate the practice of the dominant society." Kwanzaa is also a celebration that has its roots in the Black Nationalist movement of the 1960s, and was established as a means to help African Americans reconnect with their African cultural and historical heritage by uniting in meditation and study of "African traditions" and "common humanist principles."- *Wikipedia, the free encyclopedia.*

Administration, who was a staunch Republican, I became a registered Republican,[146] though only for a short while.

SKY TRAUGHBER

I respect Kwanzaa and any movement to reconnect Black Americans with its African Heritage. At the same time, I believe Africa must be held accountable for its role in the atrocities of Black slavery in this country, such as America and the Dutch. It usually requires a *seller,* a *buyer* and a *middleman* to conduct a smooth and lucrative international slave trade industry.

From viewing Dr. Skip Gates's documentary about the African slave trade and some additional research, it appears that Africa served as the seller, America served as the buyer and the Dutch served as middlemen. There are probably differing versions of this scenario, but this is the information I found. If so, then any talk or proposal of reparations for African Americans for the effects of slavery in this country should include some reparations from Africa and the Dutch, also.

Many will say that it was long ago. Well, it appears that *AFRICAN* men have one of the lowest rates of prostate cancer in the world while *AFRICAN AMERICAN* men have one of the highest rates of this deadly disease.[147] Somewhere in the transference from Africa to America, by force, this is a still-present side effect for African American men. Just a thought, not a revolution.

Some of this thinking and discussion has probably served me well and proved controversial as a college professor, especially teaching in a popular music environment of the 1990s and into the mid-2000s.

---

[146] The powerful boxing promoter, *Don King* remained a staunch Republican, at least through the 2004 Presidential elections. His current party allegiance is unknown to this writer. At the same time, a report issued during this time showed that Don King contributed more than anyone to Historically Black Colleges and had helped create more Black millionaires than anyone. Veteran NBA player and broadcast commentator *Charles Barkley* also professed a strong allegiance to the Republican Party, until, in his words "*...they lost their minds* (after the 2004 elections)."

[147] Ellsworth, Pamela; Heaney, John; Gill, Cliff, *100 Questions & Answers About Prostate Cancer.* Jones & Bartlett, 2003.

The music business during this time, though it has sometimes projected a revolutionary and intellectual image, has also become a very conservative and closed-minded industry, for the most part.

LOGAN H. WESTBROOKS
America's movement into the 80s will prove to be a "torn" era, not only for the country and its beliefs but also for the future of Black Music and its definition of power.

After a brief stay of power by the Carter Administration, the Ronald Reagan Administration era will question the "work ethic" and "ambition" of the country's Black American population. This comes at a time when the lures of corporate jobs and power have already diluted the Black Nationalist movements of the 60s and 70s.

A new generation of Black entrepreneurs now find themselves as strong in their will and vision as Berry Gordy and Sam Cooke, but they must now balance the deck of *true ownership* with the cards truly available for such ventures in this era.

Dick Griffey and *Don Cornelius* of *Soul Train Records* are two of the new breed of Black Entrepreneurs during this time, based in Los Angeles. A graduate of the Historically Black College, *Tennessee State University,* in Nashville, Griffey parlays his business skills into becoming a top concert promoter and re-organizing Soul Train Records into *Solar Records.*

This comes after Cornelius decides to concentrate fully on television ventures, including the *Soul Train* dance-and-performance television gem which Cornelius owned until 2008. Solar (*The Sound of Los Angeles*) Records would not break as many acts as Motown, Stax and Philadelphia International, but would strongly stamp its signature on Black music with the likes of *The Whispers, Shalamar, Midnight Starr, Dynasty, Lakeside* and *The Deele.*

The Deele produces future super producers *L.A. Reid* and *Kenny "Babyface" Edmonds,* and former bubblegum-pop *Sylvers* member *Leon Sylvers* will mature into a powerful producer for many of the Solar stable of acts. Solar runs through a succession of major label distributors over the next few years, from RCA to Elektra to MCA, signaling an era of *joint venture associations* between strong Black Music labels and major distributors that have now completely cornered the muscle of retail, wholesale, radio and marketing. Some of the same muscle that labels like Stax and Motown had on their own ten years earlier.

Ownerships usually align with financial investments. As the record industry emerges from the "Crash of '79," Black Music and the music of the industry, as a whole, regain their footing, somewhat. This return to respectable sales figures will set off a chain of inflation in radio payola rates, indie promoter rates and record label perceived net worth that will continue in both healthy and unhealthy ways into the turn of the century.

The power of the major distributors will further cement their stronghold on Black Music into the mid-90s when rap entrepreneurs bring many of these distributors to their knees during negotiations. However, as in building a railroad, he who owns the tracks eventually determines which trains are allowed to run and how fast they are allowed to run.

During the time that my one-year association with Don Cornelius and Dick Griffey at Soul Train Records was nearing an end, moving into the 80s, I was venturing more heavily into full time real estate involvements and further away from the music business. I just felt that the music business, with myself, had run its course. I noticed a real estate broker had run an ad in the <u>*Los Angeles Times.*</u> The ad read only:

Joe Bradfield
Real Estate Broker

It was the *cheapest*, but to me, the most *effective* ad someone could buy. I would leave Soul Train every day and go see Joe. He essentially taught me the real estate business in Los Angeles, though I did not know at the time that he was dying from diabetes. During this period, I became an expert in buying depressed properties, rehabbing them and then turning them over. I was picking up a building a month.

Bradfield told me an interesting story that made it to the Los Angeles Times. There was a Black family that wanted to buy a house in Hancock Park, but there was a covenant to keep Blacks out of the community. At a neighborhood meeting, they said they didn't want any undesirables in Hancock Park. Bradfield hired a White couple to pose as buyers for the home, and their contract was approved.

After the sale was complete, the Black family moved into the home. That Black family was Nat King Cole. People were upset, but that's how Hancock Park eventually became integrated. White people loved to hear him sing, but they didn't want to live near him.

It was also during this time that Marnie Tattersall was working at MCA, specifically with *MCA New Ventures*—a venture to loan money to minority record companies—headed by *Norbert Simmons.*[148] MCA New Ventures was a subsidiary venture of the parent investment company, *MESBIC* (Minority Enterprise Small Business Investment Company).

The venture may have included some tax advantages for MCA but it also still offered an opportunity for aggressive and qualified entrepreneurs. I am not sure, but Jim Brown and Richard Pryor may have received some money from this venture or the parent investment company for their film projects.

Anyway, Marnie tipped me to the venture. Her job involved reviewing the many proposals that were being sent in for funding. She felt that my ability and background was on par or overreached the qualifications of most of the proposal authors. This led to the formation of *Source Records*, a joint venture with MCA Records. This also was the beginning of me owning a more widespread array of businesses including, but not limited to, the music business.

---

[148] Norbert Simmons, a former NAACP defense fund attorney, eventually owned a casino in New Orleans, *Belle of New Orleans*. He has served on the board of the Boston University Law School and has managed over $1 billion in public and private transactions. Ruth Simmons, his ex-wife is the former President of Brown University. She was the first woman and first African American to be president of an Ivy League university.

An employee at Source, who was from Washington D.C., found a powerful *Go-Go* music master single by *Chuck Brown & The Soul Searchers* titled "Bustin' Loose."[149] We picked up the single, released it and went into the studio to complete the album. "Bustin' Loose" became a huge hit with a raw Black sound when the Black sound was moving more toward Pop.

In 2002, rapper *Nelly* would use "Bustin' Loose" as a sample for his mega-hit, "Hot in Herre." Businesswise, Nelly and his people recognized that I was the legal owner of "Bustin' Loose" through the Source publishing rights. They came to Los Angeles, arranged a meeting and we worked it out so everyone could share in the success of "Hot in Herre."

In all, Source Records grossed more than $6 million during its first year of operation. I had also signed *DeBarge* at Source before their Motown days and had a single in the market. Older sister *Bunny DeBarge* was not a member of the group at this time, but had come to Los Angeles to integrate herself in the group's music sound, stability and business acumen.

After analyzing what I was doing with the group against an offer from Motown that was contingent upon getting the group released from Source, Bunny persistently but diplomatically and respectfully asked me to release the group so they could sign with Motown. As a businessman it would not make sense to me, especially a "clean" release with no backend attachments for Source.

After listening to Bunny's plea, however, and knowing that Motown and Berry might shy away from any continued indebtedness to Source on the group, I granted DeBarge a clean and non-binding release from Source so they could go to Motown. My attorney thought I had lost my mind, but sometimes you have to go with your heart. What Motown was able to do with DeBarge speaks for itself. I don't believe that Source, at that time, could have reached those heights with the group.

---

[149] "Bustin' Loose" is considered to be the first Go-Go record out of Washington, D.C. This style of bottom-up, boogie-based, call and response music would continue through the 80s with "The Butt," by *EU,* as part of Spike Lee's film *School Daze,* 1988.

SKY TRAUGHBER

Teena Marie was my first A&R priority during this time at Motown. I joined the company during the recording of her debut album with *Dick Rudolph* producing (Minnie Riperton's widower husband and ex-producer). Teena and I had begun direct discussions for her second album.

DeBarge became my second priority. They were not quite ready to record an album, so I arranged a rehearsal hall for them to rehearse and write tunes every night. During this interaction with the group, I knew immediately that one day *El DeBarge* would make a profound statement on the industry with his talent. But I also observed that Bunny DeBarge was the "glue" that held that group together, spiritually and businesswise, while she was also trying to hold a marriage together and raise her own child. The addition of her voice to the background vocals brought that "magic" that no one can explain to the DeBarge sound.

Rap has its own profound rhythms and rhymes, but the loss of the magical harmonies in Black Music of today has deprived an entire world of this magic. This is something "special" that machines, major corporations and untrained music people cannot fake. Its power transcends any earthly business or technology plan.

I was unaware of the Source signing and release, but I observed the group having a pleasant and enthusiastic vibe about where they were going. This would not have been possible without the generosity and understanding of Source Records.

LOGAN H. WESTBROOKS

Source made some great waves, but we were undercapitalized from the start. I also had to put up the collateral for the label from my personal business assets. I also had to cover the manufacturing and pressing costs that MCA carried out. So, the more successful I became with Source, the harder it was to stay in business.

We were meeting the demand of the marketplace, which was growing through pressing more records. But sometimes my manufacturing and pressing bill to MCA would come due before

MCA would cut me the royalty checks on the Source records they were selling. It was like "I owe *you* $100,000, but you owe *me* $1 million." The same type of problem Al Bell had at CBS with Stax.[150]

I ended up shutting Source down. However, I owned the Source masters so when the distribution agreement with MCA was terminated, I got the masters back. Publishing is important for licensing the *song* but masters are also important for licensing the *recording* of the song.

Major companies, at this time, were not responsible to small Black labels. I, like others, may have been ahead of my time in this respect. During my time at CBS the top level seemed to get it with a strong Black presence, and there was some racism at the branch level. However, the MCA environment, at this time, had some racism and prejudice at the top level. I am speaking of the *very* top.

I had a Rolls Royce, and I along with key Source executives would go to the weekly MCA meetings in my car. We went *strong,* businesswise. We had our facts and figures and airplay reports in order. It may have just been too much for them. I was not *the right kind of n***a* for MCA at this time, and I was not going to compromise myself for them.

However, the good part of some of the major label deals, in my view, is that almost all of the Black artists I dealt with *wanted* to be on the mother label. After Source folded, MCA picked up *Harold Melvin & The Blue Notes* as artists. I was managing Source artists, *The Valentine Brothers,* during this time. While they were on tour with *The Wiz* production, I was seeking a major label deal for them. Realistically, the tide was turning in a manner where the major labels could just do more for the artists.[151]

---

[150] People like Clarence Avant, while operating Sussex would also have distribution problems with collections versus expenses on acts like Bill Withers. Conversation between Clarence Avant and Sky Traughber, 1978.

[151] Dannen, Fredric, "Hit Men: Power Brokers and Fast Money Inside the Music Business," Vintage, 1991. Reportedly, part of the Sussex Records settlement with Bill Withers, after Bill had sued Sussex over non-payment of royalties during Sussex' collection disputes, was to release Bill from Sussex so he could sign with CBS Records.

CHAPTER 17

CBS Gets a Thrill

SKY TRAUGHBER

Moving into the 80s, CBS Records makes a move in A&R that gives a Black person the distinction of reportedly becoming the first CBS Records person to receive an *override* (profit participation on albums) bonus payment on a particular artist, as opposed to the company's practice of paying *profit sharing* bonuses[152] on overall company profits. The difference can be substantial, especially in an era where most labels are still reeling from the losses of the Disco era.

CBS Records, during this time, will also take a child star into adulthood with an album that not only lifts CBS out of the revenue doldrums, but it will resuscitate an entire industry from the bowels of revenue hell. CBS Records will also, during this period, become the primary record label focus of an expanded and expensive syndicate of independent radio promotion persons who were not only able to control the records *added* to power radio stations across the country but also able to determine which records were *not to receive airplay*.

The CBS A&R person is *Larkin Arnold*. The child star reaching maturity is *Michael Jackson*. The album is *Thriller*. The radio promotion syndicate is known as *The Network*.

Gerry Griffith, an early CBS Black Music executive, was doing West Coast Black Music A&R for CBS while I was in the West Coast building as a product manager. I remember him telling me that he was essentially doing the same job functions he had done as a product manager and did not feel he was granted the full autonomy

---

[152] "First Black Execs Persevered," *Billboard* magazine, 1997. An "override" bonus payment, in any industry assures a person a bonus payment for any particular product that they were intimately involved in and is not dependent on the company, itself, turning a profit as in a profit-sharing bonus payment arrangement.

associated with a real A&R person. So, when *Don Ellis*[153] left CBS as West Coast head of A&R to become the head of A&R at Motown, he took Gerry Griffith to essentially run the day-to-day A&R Motown operations.

Don and Gerry were impressed with my production work on *Lalo Schifrin*[154] for Clarence Avant's *Tabu* label at CBS and offered me an open A&R spot at Motown with a Staff Producer deal to boot. It was six months before my product management commitment to Vernon Slaughter was completed, but I gave two weeks-notice, had completed the album release work on my artists and worked with my replacement, Wayne Edwards,[155] upon his arrival to take over my duties. Still, kids, it is good to *honor a commitment.* To this day, my abrupt departure from Vernon still haunts me.

The person left in charge of CBS West Coast A&R after Don exited began calling Gerry and myself, separately, at Motown. These discussions involved bringing us back to CBS in A&R. I distinctly remember the call Gerry received from Vernon Slaughter informing Gerry that CBS had settled on Larkin Arnold. I don't believe it shocked Gerry that much, and I was engaged in figuring out my Motown staff producer deal with Berry Gordy.

Berry liked some of my creative and business thinking and had suggested that I produce Teena Marie. My A&R deal had been negotiated under Don Ellis and now I was essentially reporting to Berry, as Don had swiftly left Motown.

This was also a time that I was sticking my journalistic and investigative inquiries into the distribution and true ownerships ends of the Motown operation, contrary to Berry's advice not to.

---

[153] Not to be confused with the Jazz trumpeter, Don Ellis was a long time A&R person at CBS/Epic and is credited with discovering songstress Minnie Riperton at the label.

[154] Lalo Schifrin is a legend in film scoring and composition with *Mission Impossible, Mannix, Peter Gunn, The Amityville Horror, Rush Hour I &II, The Curious Case of Benjamin Button,* among his many credits. He also has a deep catalogue as a Jazz musician.

[155] Wayne Edwards will later join Larkin in A&R at CBS, eventually become the head of Black Music A&R at Capitol Records, earn a PhD and become a college professor.

Anyway, I knew of Larkin's profound credentials with a law degree from Howard University and his A&R work at Capitol Records, signing acts like *Natalie Cole, Peabo Bryson* and *Frankie Beverly & Maze.* So, there was no resentment when I heard the news, but I knew it probably represented the end of the first wave of *The Harvard Report* Black Music era at CBS. Though I was unaware of the report at that time, it just felt like the label wanted to stretch beyond its own nurturing in Black Music. Larkin was a qualified and deserving choice.

Don Ellis would eventually make the call to Clive Davis that got Gerry hired as Clive's Black Music A&R person in New York at Arista where Gerry would discover *Whitney Houston* in a New York nightclub. Gerry would then move on to head the A&R departments at Manhattan and EMI Records in New York, working under Bruce Lundvall.

After it became obvious that Berry and I could not reach a workable agreement and he made sure I had some money to re-group with, Junius Griffin and Berry's assistant, *Edna Andersen,* would take it upon themselves to place a call to Washington, D.C., Congressman *Walter E. Fauntroy* on my behalf. Though I never followed through with Walter, I moved to D.C. and shared a house with the niece and nephew of then-Georgia State Senator Julian Bond,[156] starting a relationship with Julian.

Things sometimes tend to work themselves out. Larkin has done okay, as have Gerry and myself.

Thriller set unprecedented sales records despite the top brass at CBS (not necessarily including Larkin) believing that the album's producer, *Quincy Jones*, was too "Jazz" for Michael Jackson. With the ultimate "bottom up" studio drummer, *Ndugu Chancler,* laying the one-and-three count throbbing bass drum on *Billie Jean,* Michael's songwriting and production input and Quincy taking his

---

[156] After leaving D.C., I became a consultant with Herbie Hancock's manager, *David Rubinson* and produced a taped, national radio show featuring Julian and Herbie discussing *Reaganomics,* in part, to promote Herbie's single at the time, "Everybody's Broke," featuring the dynamic vocalist and songwriter, *Gavin Christopher.*

many years of orchestration and theory to another commercial level, the success potential of *Thriller* was obvious from jump ("Billie Jean" was the first single).

With Michael Jackson as artist, writer and publisher, Quincy Jones as producer and Larkin Arnold's override bonus, *the top three earners* of this massive revenue machine are probably three Black men. Whether or not this is what *The Harvard Report* intended to accomplish at CBS, this is what happened on the business and creative side of *Thriller.* Bonus payments to *everyone* at CBS probably rose substantially that year and Michael's new manager, *Frank Dileo,* a former Epic/CBS exec (and a really nice guy in this writer's opinion) undoubtedly did well.

According to some, *Thriller* also opened doors for Black Music artists at *MTV,* which to this point had primarily programmed Rock acts. According to others it was really *Rick James* who raised the hell that opened the door for others, even though his music was not programmed at MTV.

Two of the most intelligent musicians I've ever had the pleasure of spending a few minutes with are Rick James during my A&R days at Motown and *George Clinton* of Parliament-Funkadelic. Atlanta radio station *WAOK* jock *Mark Boyd* (Dr. Feelgood) graciously allowed me to tag along to George's hotel room after a concert in Atlanta.

Though Rick and I had an awkward experience at Motown, (he had exited from producing Teena Marie after, reportedly, receiving flak from Black women about working with a White girl).[157] I learned a lot just by listening and watching him work.

There was a party atmosphere in the city the night I met George, but there were no drugs on the table and I just sat and listened to him explain to Feelgood the business and image details of a new, major Funkadelic deal he recently negotiated.

-----

[157] Just for the record, I never saw Teena Marie as a Black artist. I saw (and still see) Teena as a Carole King/Barbara Streisand combination with a strong Black edge. Really, Teena's category was undefinable.

So, yeah, I can see where Rick James would have the intelligence and leadership traits to call attention to the discrimination at MTV, though he never really benefited from the hell he raised. Rick was probably too "raw" and "ugly" for MTV as a Black artist and though MTV began after Parliament-Funkadelic's rise, they probably would have been labeled as such as well. MTV, as with the major corporations now controlling Black Music, was now emphasizing, "look" as well as, or in spite of, music, much like *The Harvard Report* categorizing section, though the report was not intended as a discriminatory tool.

This labeling would continue at major labels and the record industry for the most part until the rawness of Rap was too much to overlook in the 90s, when you would rarely see a Rock act on MTV. However, Rap would also become "polished" and somewhat "mindless" under the major labels moving into the turn of the century. He who owns the railroad tracks owns the railroad.

Thriller also gave Michael a chance to flex his muscles as a businessman. Though he credited his manager, Frank Dileo for "...turning my dream of Thriller into a reality..."[158] Michael was now being seen by insiders as more than just an eccentric entertainer. This excerpt is from the *Hit Men* book by Fredric Dannen:

> *Though the public made him out to be living*
> *on the edge of fantasy, Michael Jackson was*
> *an ambitious man with extensive knowledge of*
> *the record industry's workings. "I consider*
> *myself a musician who is incidentally a*
> *businessman"...* he [Michael] wrote.

During the time I was a CBS promotion rep in the Carolinas, Steve Manning informed me after a half-capacity *Jackson's* concert in Charlotte that I had to go to Michael's room and explain things. I figured what the hell, you've got to get fired for *something*. No way this kid (Michael was maybe 17) would understand what I was saying.

---

[158] Dannen, Fredric, Hit Men: Power Brokers and Fast Money Inside the Music Business, Vintage, 1991.

The first thing I noticed, when entering the room, was that everyone scattered EXCEPT Michael. He then approached me and calmly explained his concern. After my nervous but carefully worded analysis of the current condition of *The Jacksons'*[159] public image and how best to address it, Michael looked me straight in the eye, said he understood, gave thanks and shook my hand like a man. I have been in similar situations with a*dult* entertainers where this type of meeting did not go as smooth.

Michael had to be a man, businesswise, at an early age. The flip side to that record is that, sometimes, one reverts to being a child as an adult when one had to be an adult as a child. This reversion has cost Michael, somewhat. But he is not alone.

Thriller, by Quincy Jones and Michael's accounts in various interviews, was recorded with *intent* for every cut to be a hit single. The album accomplished this goal commercially and arguably, artistically. However, the goal accomplishment did not come cheap to CBS:

> *It is hard to imagine that any top 40 station needed*
> *to be persuaded by an indie promo man to play the*
> *singles from Thriller. Yet one Epic man admitted…*
> *that campaign cost about $100,000 and change for*
> *each single in independent promotion…*[160]

Businesswise, CBS and other major labels will become the center of attention by the FBI and the IRS, once again. This is primarily through their associations with reputed-mob affiliate and top national indie promoter *Joe Isgro.* Joe was taped, on film, with mob figures as part of an *NBC News* journalistic investigation.

---

[159] Motown continued to own the name The Jackson 5 after the group left Motown for CBS. Jermaine Jackson, who had married Berry's daughter, Hazel, remained at Motown as a solo act. CBS hired Gamble and Huff to produce The Jacksons, maybe trying to capture some of the magic that The Corporation (Berry Gordy, Hal Davis and Freddie Perren) had used in producing The Jackson 5 at Motown. Michael's voice and physical appearance were also undergoing major changes during this time.

[160] Dannen, Fredric, Hit Men: Power Brokers and Fast Money Inside the Music Business, Vintage, 1991.

The Network of national independent promoters of the 80s and 90s is reportedly the dream child of *Kal Rudman* then-publisher of the Top 40 radio tips sheet, *The Friday Morning Quarterback.* The Network will grow to include Isgro, *Frank Disipio, Ralph Tashjian* and former CBS Special Markets Original Thirteen member *Bill Craig,* among others. The power of this network could not be overlooked during this period as they, reportedly, could not only determine which records *were* played and *how many* spins they received, but also which records *were not* played or their level of spin rotation at radio stations.[161]

The costs of these spins would, reportedly, reach $250,000 per record, per radio format into the 90s.[162] Only major labels are able to afford these rates. He who owns the railroad tracks…

Just for your information, in 2012 while moderating a panel at a Berklee/Stax Academy conference in Memphis, panelist George Clinton related to me that he believes his problems at Warner Bros. began there in the late 70s after Warner's label heads found out about *The Harvard Report* and how it was being instituted at CBS.

Parliament-Funkadelic was becoming more radical/socially conscious in its music at this time and these execs feared that George would organize major label artists to boycott major labels, from their perceived impression that the study was inspiring a corporate takeover of Soul/Black music. George went on to say he had no such intention at the time. Just shows how fear can be struck in railroad owners.

I became a national indie promoter during this time for a major artist's management company and used Isgro and Bill Craig. Who didn't, if you were serious about getting hits? Joe also gave me my first production deal (outside of Motown) as a producer with his

---

[161] The U.S. payola statue allows a payment for a record to be spun on radio stations as long as the payment is reported in tax filings (by whomever receives the payment, the station or a particular person) and "disclosed" to those hearing the record. The "disclosure" language does not clearly state if these are people "hearing" the record within the station or the listening audience outside of the station. Hence, many records are heard over and over, legally, without any disclaimer of payment.

[162] Various informed sources.

LARC/MCA record label on a very talented act in Oakland, California. The group had attended *Southern University* in Baton Rouge with *American Idol* judge *Randy Jackson* and called themselves *Mellaa* (Music Encompasses Life, Love & Ascension).[163] There were bumps in the road in both ventures but for the most part Joe, Bill, LARC A&R man *Stuart Love*, and I conducted business like gentlemen.

And yeah, this era involved much cocaine and freaky women. Not that the record business never used this type of payment or entertainment. It just became *super cokey* and *super freaky* during this time. Pablo Escobar[164] was smiling. And yeah, it somewhat took the focus away from the quality of the records being promoted, though I, and I am sure others, would not touch a dog record to promote. I, personally, tried not to pay or reward any radio person with anything until after they had played the record.

At that point, if you did not reward key people, you were just out of the mix. In addition to hard work, America was built on *one hand washing the other*, in some form. Maybe if we can totally fix America, we can fix the payola activities in *everything*.

There were downsides. Many people could not break away from the sometimes draining, unhealthy and expensive pleasure or escapes of these times. I had a female friend and business associate promoter discovered naked and dead in a Los Angeles alley. Only weeks before her death I was in her office discussing airplay business as I was producing an act on the label. She did not seem herself that day. It was like she was tired of all of it. It was like she wanted to get out, but was caught up in the life. Then she was gone.

As in the mysterious Carl Proctor death in Central Park in the 70s, you can only attempt to connect the dots. This kind of s**t is not the pleasure end of this type of activity. If you want to play, you may

---

[163] Mellaa was managed by former CBS promotion man Craig Neely and Jay Ivey, of the legendary Oakland, CA, businessmen-and-brothers team of Jay, John and Fred Ivey. The brothers also owned the hot Oakland nightspot *Ivey's* during this time and were very involved in local and national social and political causes.
[164] Pablo Escobar was the infamous South American cocaine kingpin, profiled in the Johnny Depp film, *Blow*.

have to pay. Again, Vegas, the entertainment business and narcotics are a gambler's game.

LOGAN H. WESTBROOKS

In the late 80s, Bill Craig and Ralph Tashjian would plead guilty to payola/preparation of fraudulent tax returns and payola/filing a false tax return/obstruction of justice, respectively. Craig received probation and Tashjian was committed to sixty days in a halfway house.

Isgro would beat his 80s indictment but would be sentenced to fifty months in federal prison in 2000 on federal extortion and loan sharking charges. They were naughty and probably caused some grief as well as supplying some income and pleasure to some people. On the other hand, when one takes a look at the crimes of the bankers and brokers against the everyday American people of today, as of this writing…well.

Creatively, this obsession with hit singles at any cost will push record producers and label execs to new heights in recognizing instant hits. But this obsession will also somewhat diminish the artist development aspect of the record business that labels like Motown had so craftily developed, though artists like *Luther Vandross, Prince* and *Madonna* will mix singles, albums and artistry, profoundly, in the 80s. Today, a hot album cut or hot albums are becoming relics. This is not a Black Music thing, just a thing.

The transference of radio promotion power from the labels to the independent promoters, during this time, also brings up the question of just how powerful label promoters were all along, before this more in-your-face period.

You cannot separate the importance of radio from label operations no matter who the promoter is. If people hear the record and like it, they buy it. Radio programmers' power increased substantially during the 70s. The *real* power was in the Black Music departments' ability to *help connect Black Radio with the Black community.* This is usually an in-house function and can go beyond just radio and the community.

When we started the CBS Special Markets Division, *Essence* magazine was also just getting started. *Tom Rivers* was the top sales person at Essence and would come by my office frequently. We would have dinner and just hang out. Soon, I was able to turn him on to full-page ads featuring our releases. I also turned him on to the other Black label execs that pushed him some business. A lot of other Black publications and newspapers came along and received ads while we received press coverage on our acts. We also increased our time buys at Black radio.

During the *Operation PUSH Black Expo,*[165] in Chicago, I served as *Director of Artist Relations* for the event and was able to connect some of our acts to the community through the expo events.

SKY TRAUGHBER
While on tour with the Temprees, we were scheduled to perform at the Black Expo and I stayed in a hotel across the street. I had family living in the public housing units of Chicago, and I was surprised that they lived across the street from the Expo. I could walk to the Expo *and* their apartment from the hotel. The Expo was *in* the community.

LOGAN H. WESTBROOKS
All of this helps not only community relations, but it also helps to create financial economies with the community.

SKY TRAUGHBER
During my promotion days at CBS, I was aware that indies were used here and there, but I was probably a bit naïve to their actual power as they were more discreet than their presence going into the 80s. Vernon Slaughter hipped me to how some of the records I thought were being played through the efforts of the CBS Black Music Division were actually maybe *in conjunction with* indie promoters.

---

[165] The Black Expo became a yearly event while the Operation Breadbasket became a weekly operation, usually on Saturday mornings.

I believe that the CBS staff and most of the Black Music label promoters of the 70s were strong in their relationships with radio. After the Crash of '79, labels became more desperate for instant hits, thereby transferring some of the label promoter's power (and money) to the people who had more leeway at radio[166] to get things done faster. Businesswise, an indie promoter usually gets the airplay and moves on. There is not a lot of follow through connecting the label and radio to the community.

I remember CBS West Coast and Co-National Promotion Director *Doug Wilkins* with other promotion and marketing representatives attempting to unionize during the mid-80s in an effort to try and further protect their jobs and rights. It was around the time that *60 Minutes* had also run a piece about the inner workings of major labels with an emphasis on Black Music. The union never happened. As mentioned earlier, jobs and opportunities can be lost in the process of fighting the power. The effort, though, is commendable.

A good friend, *Kimberly Bridges,*[167] was affiliated, businesswise, with Black Music concert promoter *Al Haymon* during this time. Al, *W.G. Garrison* of Louisiana, *Quentin Perry* of Atlanta and other Black promoters *did* form an alliance of strength, demanding that they receive a fair shot at promoting super act Black concert tours. They, along with people like Clarence Avant, *did* succeed in gaining the promotion rights to acts like The Jacksons and Rick James.

These artists had to feel comfortable in working with these promoters, though, as they were under no legal order to do so. The concert promoters were independent and entrepreneurial and not employed or reliant on any major corporations for their livelihood. This made a difference in their stand and the attempted stand by the promotion and marketing representatives. With the concert promoters, it was just Black businessmen and Black talent working it out. On the other hand, without the power of the promotion and marketing representatives creating a radio exposure, leading to a

---

[166] Whereas a label promoter may be somewhat restricted in their promotion gifts by commerce law and/or stockholder scrutiny, labels will "indemnify" themselves from any activities that an indie promoter, that they hired, uses in obtaining airplay.

[167] Kimberly is the daughter of former Stax executive Josephine Bridges.

demand for concert tickets on artists, the concert promoters' power would be diminished. So, it sometimes required the independent *and* the job-dependent to create true and big-picture power.

The Black Promoters Collective (BPC) is, today, a 100% Black-owned business, initially aided by Logan in the early 70s while making CBS Black acts available to Black promoters. The BPC is currently (2022) promoting a packed-house New Edition "The Culture Tour" featuring New Edition, Charlie Wilson of The Gap Band and Jodeci.

A key component of this CBS aid was "tour support": whereas CBS, in the event of a concert date not fulfilling its income expectations for that date, would "subsidize" either the artist directly or the promoter to make sure the artist received their agreed upon fee for the date, though income was low for that date.

Often, for small clubs, CBS would purchase a number of tickets for the date if advance sales were not coming in as the promoter expected. Though the artist and their management would be able to plan their tour incomes more efficiently through this arrangement as a "pro," a potential "con" is that tour-support funds are often recoups (deducted) from an artist's royalty account.

When expensive videos, starting in the 1980s, were also deducted, this "draw" in attracting acts to a major label would, at times, become confusing, and cause friction and/or an audit at the label by the artist's legal representative. Another option used, through CBS Artist Development, was for artist management to submit a "shortfall" projection. For example, if the act believes they need $10,000 per night to present themselves in a quality fashion and subsist financially and the promoter could only pay $8,000 per night, CBS would cover the additional $2,000 per night for the entire tour, often paying the act up-front for this subsistence.

An act being in CBS's "Baby Act" program (for new and developing acts) often would include some sort of tour support arrangement. Getting Black acts into this program would sometimes become a challenge for CBS Artist Development staffers, product managers and artist managers. This also shows how key it was for Logan and CBS in helping Black Promoters display competence in their craft. Motown would enjoy success in serving as their acts' label, publisher, de-facto booking and tour management, but would come under scrutiny for "conflicts-of-interests" in their artist development and touring models. Some of Motown's scrutiny—much from artist confusion—was in how, reportedly, the label would "cross collateralize" various income streams (including touring) from their artists' accounts.

This means if there was a "shortfall," say in album royalties or tour expenses, these expenses could be deducted from the other income stream. Motown was, by no means, alone in this practice. It is just that public perception of Motown, being a Black-owned company, was often greater than other labels.

LOGAN H. WESTBROOKS
In 1979, the *Black Music Association* (BMA) was organized and opened its office in Philadelphia. Its stated purpose was to "Preserve, Protect and Perpetuate" the artistry of Black Music around the world.[168]

The organization was founded, primarily, by Philly International/ CBS producer and label head Kenny Gamble, media-personality Dyana Williams, and independent press powerhouse Ed Wright, formerly the primary press and publicity consultant for the CBS Special Markets Division.

Though with Kenny, Dyana and Ed's creation of BMA, President Jimmy Carter would declare June as Black Music Month in 1979. It was Dyana who worked to initiate President Bill Clinton's signing of the African American Music Bill in 2000, crystallizing what we recognize today as Black Music Month.

SKY TRAUGHBER
The Black Music Association inspired the hell out of me.

---

[168] *Black Entertainment and Music Association* Newsletter.

Ed Wright had, I believe, family in my Westwood/UCLA apartment building, and we would run into each other seemingly every week after my exit from Motown. Without his encouraging words of *"Hang in there…there is a place for you in this."* I cannot say, truthfully, which road I would have followed. And there were many roads leading to Hollywood's version of "hell" that I could have taken at that time."

The June 2019 issue of Vibe.com stated, "There was also, reportedly, a degree of splintered-agenda in the BMA leadership, contributing to its closure."

LOGAN WESTBROOKS

When I was having some problems at MCA with Source, The Black Music Association would step in. The association would serve a useful purpose in many respects during its early years.

Kenny Gamble may have contributed some seed money to get the organization off the ground, but soon the association would depend heavily on funds from the major labels. Though the association may not have been initially set up as a "watchdog" organization to monitor major labels and their dealing with Black Music, the association's efforts probably evolved into this role, somewhat, in addition to its other functions. It is hard to effectively monitor and honestly call attention to those that fund your existence. It is doable but difficult.

CHAPTER 18

Reaganomics, Diversify and Consolidate

"Reaganomics was the most serious attempt to change the course of U.S. policy of any administration since the New Deal."[169]

SKY TRAUGHBER

From 1980 until 1992 America will undergo a transformation under the administrations of Presidents Ronald Reagan and George H.W. Bush that will cement the inevitable pro-big business movements that started in the 70s.

Ronald Reagan's *Program for Economic Recovery,* in particular, questioned the underclass' dependence on government programs and work ethic, also known as "pulling oneself up by one's own boot straps."

Part of President Reagan's plan was to reduce the money supply in the market to curb inflation. Inflation actually declined from 10.4 percent in 1980 to 4.2 percent in 1988 and the unemployment rate declined from 7.0 percent in 1980 to 5.4 percent in 1988.[170] The controversy in these figures centers on *classes* of people affected, which usually finds its way to include race and attitude.

A recent FRED report shows a trend of high unemployment among Blacks during recessionary periods in America (Louis//fred.stlouisfed.org/series/LNS).

The economic strategies of the 80s, moving into the 90s, caused many people to re-think their ideas of entrepreneurship without government aid and it also caused some creative adjustments in the arts, as government spending in public school arts programs began to disappear.

---

[169] Niskanen, William A., *Reaganomics, The Concise Encyclopedia of Economics.*
[170] Ibid.

LOGAN H. WESTBROOKS

My wife, *Geri,* was teaching at a Probation Camp. Most of the students at this camp were products of various Boys Homes and had some bad experiences from those facilities. In seeing something special in Geri's teaching, they suggested that she start *her own* Boys Home. This led to the formation of our *Helping Hands Home for Boys, Inc.,* venture in 1983, a residential center for youth. We purchased a palatial estate in the heart of the Los Angeles inner city community that was once the home of boxing champion *Jack Dempsey.*

We were able to instill some progressive techniques in helping the boys overcome difficult periods of transition from childhood to adolescence. They helped Geri with various insights as well. For instance, one kid had bed-wetting problems. Some of the other kids shared their experience with this normal but embarrassing part of growing up with the kid. Maybe we can call this *associative mentorship* that did not require the intervention of an adult, but adults presented the environment for this type of interaction among the boys.

The torch of this venture was passed on to *Father Flanagan's Boy's Town,* the world-famous Nebraska youth-care organization in 1998. The Boy's Town organization has a storied national reputation for helping children.

This is just a way of a *direct* investment in the future of our youth that may include money, if that money is available but also includes the desire to help and teach.

SKY TRAUGHBER

My father[171] was a recognized juvenile court and child delinquency authority and was able to arrange for the first Black kids to be accepted into Boy's Town in the 60s. It was not easy. Sometimes a Black kid is seen as a "trouble case" when maybe their environment has just left them directionless, like any other kid. The two boys that

---

[171] The Tennessee Juvenile Court Association now has the *Charles Traughber Scholarship Fund* that assists juvenile court workers in attending various conferences.

Boys Town would not admit had lost their parents to death, were high achievers in school and had goals but lacked the environment to develop themselves in a positive manner.

I watched my father write letter after letter for the kids, and finally Boy's Town accepted them as they would any other kids who deserved their help. Between watching my father continue to write those letters under rejection and playing bass in those clubs with blistered fingers, it instilled in me a trait of continuing to work through adversity.

It also taught me to not become judgmental over society and media labels. Before becoming a professional musician in high school, I participated in sports and hung with the "thugs." They knew I was living in a different environment than they, but they also knew that we were all just kids trying to find our way in a supportive, yet oppressive society. They knew I would only go so far in certain things.

This may have helped them to think twice about risky activities but they also knew that I would not speak or look down on them because of their environment or heredity that they may or may not have had any control over. Things have not changed that much today as far as kids needing different associations that can still relate to them on an equal level of understanding and input.

LOGAN H. WESTBROOKS

My real estate ventures began to expand even further than the Boy's Home during this time with the *Crenshaw Square* (Mall) and various other buildings and properties primarily in the Los Angeles inner city. The Crenshaw Square was my first multimillion-dollar purchase and is located on Crenshaw Boulevard, a main borough in the Black Los Angeles community.

The 80s were also a time where the mood of the country was for more Blacks and minorities to become homeowners. They really let the barriers down for those willing and able to do this. However, not everyone is qualified to purchase and maintain a home. The massive real estate problems of today are due, in part, to *the powers that be* allowing unqualified people to purchase homes that they may not be able to keep or maintain. I, myself, had to pass on a gorgeous marble floored, high ceiling estate. I knew that the upkeep and utilities would be difficult to maintain. You see, if the house goes in default, it goes back on the market for another re-sell. Part of this also requires the buyer to *read* the fine print of the deal and to be honest with one's self. Still, allowing this to happen can fall on the shoulders of the powers that be.

SKY TRAUGHBER

My recent venture into screenwriting involved, at one point, having discussions with a New York investment broker who arranges deals at a minimum of a $10 million investment. It can cost that much and more to make a film, and my business plan, at that time, included the purchase of some commercial real estate among other ventures.

The most important advice I received from this broker was to *be honest with yourself* in deciding if you want to get involved in this level of indebtedness, though you have a solid plan. It takes a *risk and gambler's mentality* for true entrepreneurship but there are different levels and different ways to achieve this.

Not everyone is cut out for everything. I decided that, for now, my strongest asset in writing is the creativity and work investment along with maintaining as much ownership that is appropriate in those works, which, as intellectual properties, are like real estate in themselves.

The residential real estate thing is deep, as condos do not offer the same yard space and other amenities as a home, especially for family living. Commercial development and just basic real estate ownership is important. Though some believe that the Hip Hop era maybe over-expressed this a bit with shows like *Cribs* at every turn, at least it put this important area of personal and business power on people's minds.

The problems can begin when one does not realize that houses don't move mountains, but they offer a physical base for living, planning and expanding the moving of mountains. I believe Libyan leader

Muammar Qaddafi in his *Green Book* and *Dr. Martin Luther King, Jr.,* developed interesting philosophies on capital wealth and quality of life for democratic and capitalist societies that touch on land and physical property ownerships.

LOGAN H. WESTBROOKS

While the now-powerful MCA Records Black Music Division was spreading the *New Jack Swing* music of *Guy, Teddy Riley, Jodeci, Bobby Brown* and *Bell, Biv, DeVoe*[172] along with the more traditional Black Pop sounds of *Gladys Knight & The Pips* and *Jody Watley,* a more raw underground Black sound was about to take over the nation without using instruments and vocals as the main draw.

The MCA power was spearheaded by former CBS Black Music promoter *Jheryl Busby,* veteran promotion head *Ernie Singleton* and A&R heads *Louil Silas* and *Alonzo Miller*, a former Los Angeles radio station KACE Music Director.

The new sound of Rap and Hip Hop will bring in a new breed of Black executives/entrepreneurs whose opportunities were ushered in by the perseverance of the Black executives that came before them at major labels. However, this breed of executives and entrepreneurs will also have to overcome some obstacles at these labels in flexing their newly developed business, social and cultural muscles.

Creatively, the school arts budgets cuts in the 80s will force many of the inner city young to use their inventive and genius skills in ways that do not include the traditional musical training in vocals and using instruments.

This situation will bring about some very exciting and profound "bottom-up" efforts over the years, sell tons of records and bridge the gap between the American corporate advertising culture and Black Music. The situation will also deprive Black Music of one of its exclusive strengths from the 50s, 60s and 70s: *the ability to*

---

[172] Bobby Brown and Bell, Biv, DeVoe are re-incarnations of the talented vocal and dance group, *New Edition.*

*uniquely and soulfully perform vocally and musically in the studio
and on stage with orchestral and soulful colorings in the music.*

The introduction of a machine-oriented music machine allows
almost *anyone* to imitate what was once a treasured, learned and
experienced art, sometimes requiring years of training and Chitlin'
Circuit development. Some of these dues will also be paid in Rap
and Hip Hop and some of the works will hip a young generation to
some of the earlier legends that endured this training, like *Jay-Z's*
"Heart of the City" introducing Bobby "Blue" Bland.

The difference is short term vs *super* long term. Human beings will
always have an affinity to humanly performed and orchestrated
music. This can affect super long-term publishing rights and
incomes. Classic music tunes can sometimes have a "cover"[173] and
licensing value for fifty or more years.

Ironically, it will become some of the leaders of Rap and Hip Hop
that will fight to restore music instruction in public schools, through
political activism, after Rap and Hip Hop reached a level of power.
They did not have to do this and it sends a message about what *real*
power is.

SKY TRAUGHBER
The first time I heard "The Message" by *Grandmaster Flash & the
Furious Five* I was visiting Atlanta and riding to see former CBS
Original Thirteen member Ralph Bates, who was living in a super
exclusive section of town and co-managing Isaac Hayes.

WAOK jock Dr. Feelgood, former WGIV, Charlotte, jock Waymon
"Slack" Johnson who was the Atlanta Elektra (or EMI) promotion
rep at the time and I had to drive over the pot holes and gloom of the
Atlanta inner city enroute to Ralph's palatial dwelling. "The
Message" just captured the human experience of going from
potholes to paved roads so well:

------

[173] A "cover" is a new tune that is a re-make of a previous tune. The original writer
and publisher may remain owners of the original copyright and also receive
royalty payments from the new tune.

> *Don't push me 'cause I'm close to the edge,*
> *I'm trying not to lose my head.* [174]

Dr. Feelgood was rapping along with the rhymes. I knew something was brewing with this new music. But I was also concerned about its *real* future, musically.

Sometimes a machine and technology-oriented music style requires access. Super rapper Kanye West explains:

> *I thought back to when I was in high school: I*
> *was very into music, but the equipment was really*
> *expensive and hard to get a hold of. The basketball*
> *court at school was free. Or it was free to play a*
> *violin or a drum set, but the way music on the radio*
> *is made, there was nothing in high school that helped*
> *with that.*[175]

The U.S. Department of Education's *National Assessment of Educational Progress* has released an inconclusive report that shows music and the arts are being exposed, somewhat, in schools. But budget cuts may have hampered a *full* assessment, as of this writing:

> *In 1997, NAEP looked not only at music and visual arts,*
> *but at theater and dance. Last year, budget constraints,*
> *as well as the small number of middle-school theater*
> *and dance programs forced the government to scrap the*
> *theater and dance assessments.*[176]

The role of government in assuring education and entrepreneurship versus the role of business, itself, creating these opportunities is an ongoing debate, especially in the climate of the *Program for Economic Recovery*. As of this writing, this third turning point in the American economy (following the *New Deal* and *Reaganomics*) is funneling billions of dollars into the American and international

---

[174] "The Message" tune by Grandmaster Flash & the Furious Five, 1982.

[175] <u>USA Today</u> article: *West Drops in To Talk About Education,* Kelley L. Carter, June 10, 2009

[176] <u>USA Today</u> article: *Arts Education Not Entirely Left Behind*, Greg Toppo, 2008.

economies with a goal to filter some of the money down to smaller business entities. The SBA (Small Business Association) loans of the 70s accomplished some aspects of this goal, especially with minority-owned businesses.

"Entrepreneurs—not government programs—create businesses, jobs and growth for a city," says *Dan Gilbert*, founder of *Bizdom U*, in Detroit. Bizdom U is a non-profit, one-year program that trains and funds would-be business people to start businesses in the Motor City. Bizdom costs about $1 million a year to run and is primarily funded by Gilbert, who also owns the *Cleveland Cavaliers*. Bizdom also receives contributions from the Kauffman Foundation and the new economy initiative, a non-profit in Detroit.[177]

After this original draft, Dan Gilbert and LeBron James endured a painful parting of ways when LeBron left Cleveland for the Miami Heat. Later, LeBron and Dan reconciled, somewhat, upon LeBron's return to the Cleveland Cavaliers and brought the city a long-awaited NBA championship.

LeBron has become a much-celebrated community-oriented entrepreneur himself with his "I Promise" Elementary School in Akron, Ohio, in partnership with Akron Public School Systems. Yes, PUBLIC, not private or charter. And Yes, ELEMENTARY.

Two things are worthy of note here, with LeBron:
1. Not being afraid to serve "poor, lower-income, under-privileged" children. Just as Soul and R&B became a "kiss of death" in reaching crossover masses in popular music, the children LeBron's school is serving over recent years have become a kiss of death in many instances for politicians to attain mass-audience votes, to a degree, including liberal-leaning Obama, Hillary and Biden.
2. LeBron has stated that he and his qualified group of educators chose six-, seven-, and eight-year-olds to at least try and get to them before today's media influences get them at nine years-old.

---

[177] *USA Today* article, *Thanks to Bizdom, Detroit builds entrepreneurs, too*. Jon Swartz, April 19, 2009.

It leads one to think "…what if…?" CBS Records followed *The Harvard Report's* suggestion to invest in Black inner-city wholesale/retail distribution networks. Distribution inequality has contributed to ongoing discussions of overall wealth inequality.

Speaking of community investment, over the last 20 years or so, Harvard Law School has invested in a program at the law school named Recording Artists Project (RAP), where senior level law students with advisor Brian Price and other Harvard attorneys, offer much-needed and highly-valued assistance to domestic and international clients at pro-bono rates. We all know of tales from the beginning of Rock 'n' Roll, where potential wealth and ownership is not attained due to a misunderstanding in contracts and agreements, or a lack of qualified legal services, in the process of negotiations.

While we are on a point of equality, Black children having access to college-level Music Industry programs, such as Middle Tennessee State, Belmont, Berklee College of Music, NYU, USC, has, over the years, created preparation, knowledge, internships for non-Black graduates to secure entry-level positions, some of which are directly tied to control of Black music.

Not to suggest that non-Black graduates don't have overall qualifications, but I've endured—first hand—conflict of having contributed, somewhat, to some of my non-Black graduates gaining positions of control over Black music entities. Another Dr. Jekyll/Mr. Hyde moment.

To go further with faculty at Berklee, an organization—Association of Faculty of African Descent—was formed in the early 2000s, in part out of a concern for how Berklee's curriculum addresses Soul and R&B's contributions to early and forward-going Rock 'n' Roll. Elvis himself has admitted that some of his early stage-moves originated with Jackie Wilson. Aerosmith's front man Steven Tyler in *Walk this Way* (Stephen Davis book) explains how the band's "twos" and "fours" snare drum accent, as well as a union-band-sound, originate from his study of early Soul and R&B music.

In giving Berklee and *AFAD* credit, more Black faculty were consistently added to curriculum committees at the college, at least for a while, during my tenure there. This included me being invited to sit in on a few of these meetings. Sometimes Black faculty needs to *act* in helping to facilitate accuracies in our music's rich heritage. For instance, without this type of action, one day some history books may declare that Jay-Z and Justin Timberlake *invented* Black music. Sure, they have a part, but not its creation.

Eventually, Rap labels like *Def Jam, Bad Boy, No Limit, Cash Money, Rock-a-Fella* and others will have either joint venture or distribution deals with major labels like Sony (formerly CBS), Universal (formerly MCA), BMG and Warner Brothers.

A more independent ownership mentality and business structure will emerge with these ventures, allowing Black Music more opportunities in control and employment. However, on and off, the distribution power of the majors will call attention to *true* ownerships.

Earth, Wind & Fire will partner with their management team of *Cavallo & Ruffalo* to form *ARC Records* (American Recording Company) and distributed by CBS Records. Eventually the label folded, with Earth, Wind & Fire, reportedly, bearing the brunt of the loss. But this is part of the risk of one's attempt for true ownership.

At one point, when I was out of a job, *Monte White* (late EW&F leader, Maurice White's brother and tour manager at this time) and another ARC executive, *Maurice Watkins*, wanted to bring me into ARC. They knew I had the expertise to jump in and do the product management gig that the label needed at that time.

It never transpired, but this is what can happen in direct ownership and employment. CBS and other labels also had discussions with me during this time of unemployment, but it is a different feeling when your own people in charge of their own company also reach out.

LOGAN H. WESTBROOKS
Others will find obstacles while searching for true ownership in the 80s and 90s. In the 80s, activist Jim Brown's message transforms from Black Power to Green power, recognizing that in America's

capitalist society Blacks need financial clout. When Richard Pryor named Brown as President of his *Indigo Productions*, a $40 million film production company backed by Columbia Pictures and Coca-Cola, it seemed he would be able to help Black filmmakers and others. Then, his firing by Pryor caused many, including the NAACP, to question whether the dismissal was really Pryor's doing or a fear from the corporate backers that maybe Brown was becoming too powerful in mixing Black Power with Green Power.[178]

After going back and forth with his decision over a number of years, Berry Gordy will finally realize that Motown is no match for the distribution and green power of the major corporations and sells the label to Boston Ventures/MCA in 1988.

At one point in the 90s Def Jam will owe Sony $17 million, though they had nothing but hits with acts like *LL Cool J, Public Enemy* and the *Beastie Boys.* The costs that Sony was able to charge to Def Jam, primarily for the power of distribution, pressing and marketing, changed what would seem to be a profitable accounting for Def Jam into arrears to CBS.

Russell Simmons, the Def Jam co-founder (with Rick Rubin) was eventually able to cut deals with PolyGram and later Universal and keep Def Jam afloat before selling the label to a major distributor.

Russell publicly exposed that at times the major labels would threaten to "warehouse" or not promote Def Jam's product (much like the CBS/Stax episode) which would cause some of their artists to want out of Def Jam and maybe sign directly to the major distributor (much like Stax lost the Emotions, Johnny Taylor, the Bar-Kays and Isaac Hayes to major labels).

Russell also expressed that the deal structure that *Uptown Records* (Guy, Jodeci, Heavy D, Mary J. Blige) head *Andre Harrell* had at MCA hampered full control for Andre. Andre, who also drove a Rolls Royce and spoke out on discriminatory practices, was eventually forced out.

---

[178] Freeman, Mike, Jim Brown: *The Fierce life of An American Hero*, William Morrow and Company, 2006.

Russell was also, initially, a consultant with *Vibe* magazine, a Time Warner property until he saw their editorial control unnecessarily and falsely help create the East Coast-West Coast rapper beefs that may have contributed to the deaths of two of the most profound rap artists of all time, *Tupac* and *Biggie*.[179] Some of this "Black male-genocide" media power also contributed to monetary overtime payments to various gang-related law enforcement agencies, leading some to wonder if the continued genocide was more important to some than its decline.

As of this writing, various legislative efforts have succeeded in gaining the release of thousands of crack cocaine users and dealers who were unjustly sentenced to longer prison terms than those convicted of powder cocaine charges.[180] The prisoners being released are undoubtedly mostly Black men.

While the release is good news, the concern now becomes the country's intent and ability to assist these men in gaining the education and support necessary for legal employment. Legal and adequate-paying employment can be a basic factor in the male-esteem for a healthy contribution to themselves, a family, a culture and a nation.

Russell diversifies into advertising and media with *Rush Communications*, film with *Def Pictures* and fashion with *Phat Farm*. *Sean Combs* will end his deal with BMG and sell half of his Bad Boy record label to Warner Brothers while diversifying into television and film with *Bad Boy Films* and clothing with *Sean John*.

Diversification of Black culture can have its advantages and disadvantages. Some of this hinges on *control*. The film *Gridiron Gang* was cut at the probation camp where my wife, Geri, was teaching the key football players in the movie. Geri was interviewed by the film people about the educational aspects of the probation camp. These segments were eliminated from the film, *completely*. We understand that the film people had to do what they felt was best to sell the movie.

---

[179] Simmons, Russell, with George, Nelson, *Life and Def*, Crown Publishing, 2001.
[180] This is a controversial difference as medical and psychological studies have shown that crack cocaine is more destructive and addictive than powder.

At the same time, the educational aspect of the camp offers a balanced perspective and it could have influenced others to recognize this balance.

Another diversification and evolution matter affecting Black content and control revolves around *Congressman Conyers'* proposed bill, as of this writing, to force traditional radio stations to pay a royalty to *performers* on the recorded music that the stations play.

This law has been enacted at satellite and various other electronic radio broadcasts, recently. But as of this writing, traditional radio stations have only been required to pay a performance fee to the *publisher* and *writer* of the songs they play. Record labels have, for the most part, waived any payment for the master recording being played.

Radio advertisers became more powerful in their influence over the content of radio broadcasts in the 90s, and as more radio stations became consolidated under a few major corporations there began to be some concern over the content at Black radio.

Some of this control and consolidation was evidenced, in particular, when radio shock jock *Don Imus* claimed that his arguably demeaning references to Black women were lifted from the same music that Black radio plays by Black music artists.

Most Black radio owners say that they are hurting, financially, and cannot afford to pay the proposed artist royalty. Some have said they can't afford to pay *any* royalty to the artists and are drumming up support to oppose the bill's passage, as of this writing.

Various *Google* articles offer some interesting takes on this issue. They range from an opinion that the Black community should not support Black radio on this issue because Black radio has let down the Black community in its content and coalition with national advertisers and major labels who may not have the best interest of the Black communities at heart.

Other commentary has suggested that the Black communities, themselves, have already supported the content of Black radio by wanting to hear the controversial music and other content that Black radio broadcasts either by choice or business necessity. Many believe that this issue may be a turning point in the survival of whatever remains as true Black radio, which is still an important media outlet in Black culture.

It would be good for some sort of deal to be worked out. Though some artists of today believe they should be paid more than they are actually worth, record labels still charge costs back to the artists making it hard for the artist to see any profit from recordings and most labels still own the master after the artist has recouped their account with the label.

Unless you are a consistently touring artist or a writer or licensing yourself for advertising and the like, it is hard to make a substantial living just from a record deal. Maybe some concessions from the publishers could free up some money for the stations to be able to pay the artists. Just a thought.

The diversifications of Russell, Sean, Jay-Z & Beyonce, Master P and others in advertising, fashion, film and the radio alliances with sponsors will offer expanded cultural opportunities for the Black Music culture. In the 50s and 60s Sam Cooke and James Brown also had diversifications.

These diversifications will bring money, homes and cars to the Black culture providers involved in these diversifications. Stepin Fetchit and Nat King Cole also had money, homes and cars. The *concept* is nothing new, but the *scope* is wider and more involved. That shows progress.

However, at one point, in the 70s, there were at least two powerful *full-service* Black owned record labels, Motown and Stax, mixing music, community, radio and distribution *on their own* in a major way.[181] Today, for the most part, there are none.

---

[181] Al Bell became the 100% owner of Stax as part of the CBS deal, but he was a part owner and primary force while Stax was a full-service company with its own distribution network.

SKY TRAUGHBER

In October 2018, Congress passed and then-President Trump signed the "Music Modernization Act" primarily aiding pre-1972 releases. Pre-1972 releases include anything before midnight February 15, 1972. Post-1972 releases still have work to do.

I'm still getting calls from artists to clarify this as most music streaming rates, particularly post-1972, hover around $0.05 per stream. Today, an artist and/or artists' teams must understand that some sort of "ancillary" activity, such as touring, merchandising, and advertising, may have to surround this extremely-low income stream to earn an "American Dream" quality of life strictly from one's music. This is now true for Black, White, Orange, Purple artists and/or their team alike.

For the record, here is what the Music Modernization Act of 2018, in brief, intends to do: ("The Music Modernization Act and Its Burgeoning Impact" Knowles, Duffy, Bass, Schreihart Esquires, **www.coblentzlaw.com**, August 2018).

- Increase compensation to songwriters and streamline licensing of their music.

- Enable artists who recorded music before 1972 to be paid royalties when their music is played on digital services; and

- Enable music producers (e.g., record producers, sound engineers, and other studio professionals) to receive royalties for their creative contributions to recorded music.

The MMA is the first major legislation to affect music royalties passed since the Copyright Act of 1976.

Though "colorless" in its' nature, Black acts and writers were more prone, in many cases, for one reason or another, to not own their publishing rights, pre-and-post 1972. So, the MMA DOES enable these artists and writers more leverage to negotiate and collect royalties without being a publishing-rights owner.

Actually, when I was negotiating a record deal for an Oakland-based act with a very high-level Italian label owner in the early 1980s, he asked me: "Who owns the publishing?" to which I swiftly answered "We do." He smiled approvingly saying "It is always the Black guys who come in here without owning their songs." (He still had leverage to take a piece of the publishing, and, of course, he did).

LOGAN H. WESTBROOKS

It is finally being publicly acknowledged just how much Black artists have been cheated out of royalties for their original work and creative contributions in the music industry—another industry that often over-exploited and under-paid Black artists, writers and producers.

But, in recent years there is now a glimmer of hope. Kevin J. Greene, attorney and professor of contract music law and entertainment law at Southwestern Law School in Los Angeles has promoted reparations for Black artists who were denied fair compensation because of legal but unjust business practices.[182] He began addressing the issue as far back as 1992. His actions were very similar to that of civil rights activists from decades earlier.

The March 2022 issue of Rolling Stone magazine featured an article about his work titled "Compensation, Healing, and Closure: One Man's Quest for Reparations in the Music Business." In it, he discusses the issue of exploitation of intellectual property rights.

It is a very poignant and much needed discussion because the major record labels—through technology—have found new methods of exploitation, such as through streaming rates which are sometimes even less than a penny per stream. How can artists survive? Without the sheer will to nurture their own creative instincts and produce music in spite of circumstances, they wouldn't survive. This must change.

---

[182] Greene, Kevin J, "Copyright, Culture, and Black Music: A Legacy of Unequal Protection," *Hastings Communications & Entertainment Law Journal* 20: 339 (1999).

SKY TRAUGHBER

To take Logan's profound observations even further, let's look at a few recent examples of artists "going behind the noise," rising and winning their rights to their own material when this right has finally come due:

- On May 30, 2022, "The Grio"—an online newsletter— reported songstress Anita Baker thanking "Chance the Rapper" for being instrumental in her regaining control of her master recordings from Elektra, in 2021. Anita had tweeted her fans to not stream or purchase her "high quality, high-sales volume" albums from late 1980s on Elektra because, as by the 1976 Copyright Revision law, after 35 years, music-masters are to be returned to the artist. But Elektra was making her *fight* for it. Huh?

  Maybe or maybe not this is racial but "huh"? Even a slam dunk case has to be *fought* for? Ms. Baker also cited the "almost unbelievable" streaming rate of $0.003- $0.005 per stream her songs receive. We don't need a Ph.D. in Economics or an M.B.A. to figure out *someone* is likely getting paid in an unbalanced fashion from these low-end-of-the-food-chain rates. Hell, back in the day, with the mob, at least you could get a caddy, some jewelry, some alligator shoes, star-caliber pocket change, silk suits, maybe a house (maybe in your name). Pay attention streaming companies (or anyone else), I said *LIKELY* as my disclaimer from any potential defamation lawsuits against my shallow-but-livable teacher-retirement funds. Sue an ex-educator?

- Or maybe, as a second disclaimer there *is* a valid accounting-model where these rates are appropriate, fair and necessary to at least keep these companies in business to help expose the music to listeners. We know some companies have claimed this, but it is hard with the unregulated degree of federal law oversight in internet operations to fully know what or who to believe. This is where Americans have to continue to not only *vote* but go "behind the noise," even with legislators you voted for. Make 'em sing that Kennedy Gordy (Rockwell) Motown tune: "Somebody's Watchin' Me."

- P-Funkster George Clinton won back full copyright ownership of four top-selling Funkadelic albums in 2005.

- Kanye West settled with EMI, Universal, Rockafella and Def Jam over his publishing.[183] Again, to be clear he *settled* privately, so we don't know the details. Still, Kanye stated in numerous interviews that he wanted to expose that though he has a comparatively favorable (to himself) artist-friendly contract and actually owns some of his masters (some of this, various journalists have discovered) that if one goes "behind the noise" of fame, fortune, glitter and bling, there's more details to consider in an artist having *total* ownership of their work, even after decades.

---

[183] www.rollingstone.com>music>music-news, September 24, 2014).

CHAPTER 19

POWER 101

The journey of Soul Music and its relations with America is a highway with many twists and turns. The *Harvard Report* may have supplied a blueprint for corporate America to gain some control over Black Music and align its content with the nation's ever evolving soul and spirit.

This blueprint has also offered some *wanted* opportunities for many in Black Music. So, maybe any judgment is irrelevant. What *is* known is that when Black culture is not allowed to operate at its soulful best, on its own or within corporate America, *everyone* loses.

This book has only told a story about some warriors not satisfied with this potential loss.

It all comes down to "some things change, some things don't... unless we make them change." We believe we have helped readers to understand this and to pay attention to details. As well as critical-thinking in how we see, hear, read and write narratives, hopefully.

Even with that, today, in 2022, one thing is certain: today's music audiences *just love the old stuff*, arguably, the *good* stuff, as evidenced by, for examples, "Summer of Soul's" Oscar win, Silk Sonic's coveted Billboard Awards performance of Con Funk Shun's "Love's Train" or walking through CVS drug store hearing Philly International's "Ain't No Stoppin' Us Now" by McFadden & Whitehead blasting through overhead speakers as an inspirational anthem for today's challenges, and a continued resurgence of vinyl records sales. No matter the history, who owns it or the label it is on."

With all of this in mind, maybe the future of everything covered in this book boils down to two words: *Faith* and *Action*.

<u>THE END</u>

PHOTOS

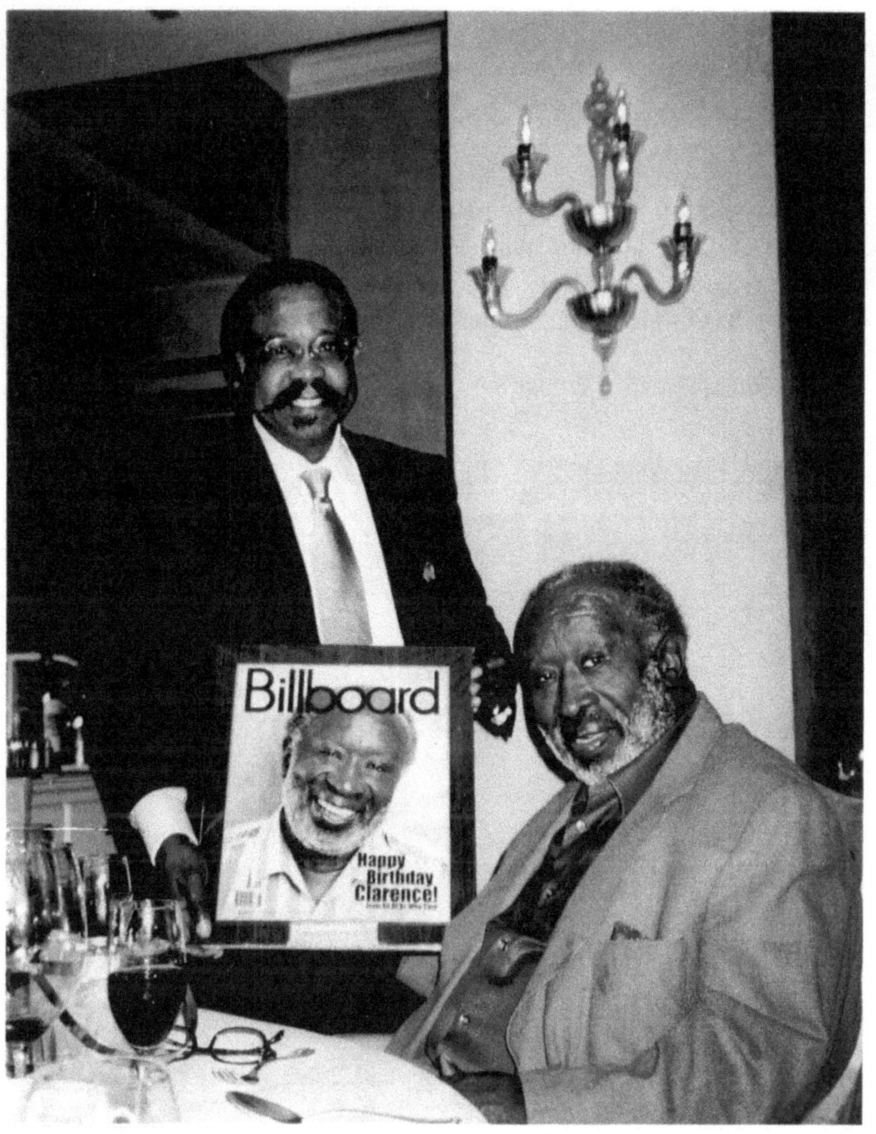

Logan H. Westbrooks (Former CBS Records Executive) and Clarence Avant (Godfather of Black Music)

Photo courtesy of Logan H. Westbrooks private collection, Indiana University, Bloomington

Sky (front center) with CBS Staffers in Chicago while consulting David Rubinson, manager for Herbie Hancock.

From Left: Artie Dunnings (Indie Rep For Cotillion Records, Greg Peck (CBS Co-National Promotions), NY Publicity Person, Glen Wright (CBS Cleveland Promotions), Mike Bernardo (CBS National Jazz Promotion Director), Doug Wilkins (CBS Co-National Promotion Director).

Photo Courtesy of Sky Traughber, 1981

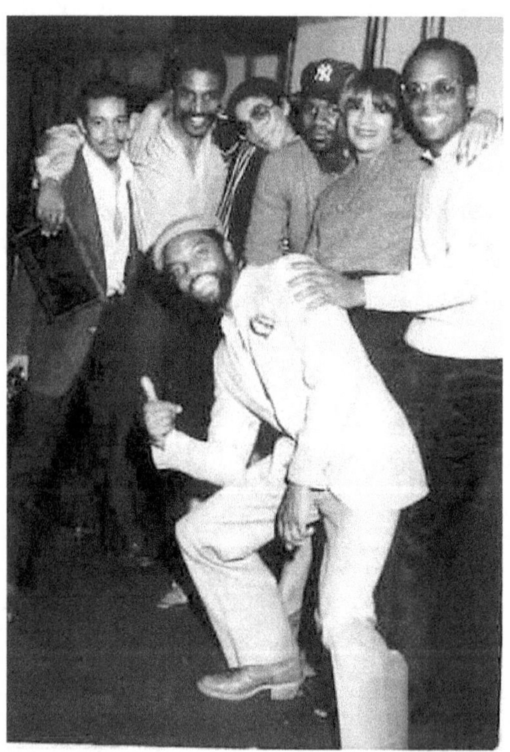

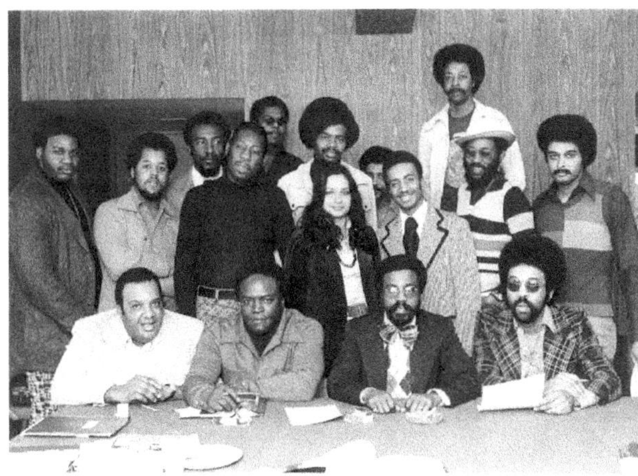

Logan Westbrooks
and CBS Staff

Circa 1973

Seated from Left: Granville White, Richard Mack, Logan H. Westbrooks, Chuck Offuitt. Standing, From Left: Glen Wright, Vernon Slaughter, Ralph Bates, Richard Outler, Bill Craig, Speedy Brown, Marnie Tattersall, Fred Ware, Armand McKissick, Leroy Smith, George Chavou, Gerry Griffith.

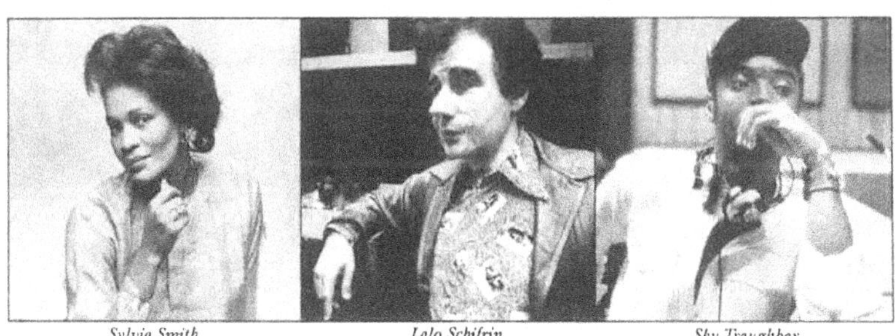

Sylvia Smith   *Lalo Schifrin*   *Sky Traughber*

Lalo Schifrin can be regarded as a "Master" of television and film music scoring with "Mannix,"
"Mission Impossible," "Medical Center," "Dirty Harry," "Amityville Horror" and "Concorde-Airport '79"
among his many projects."No One Home" combines the elements of a variety of musical directions
to appeal to a variety of listeners. NO ONE'S HOME BECAUSE EVERYONE IS IN THE
STREETS LISTENING TO THE MUSIC (AND PICKING UP THE ALBUM)!

Sky Co-Produces Acclaimed Film Composer/CBS-TABU Recording Artist Lalo Schifrin (Mission Impossible, Amityville Horror). From Left: Vocalist Sylvia Smith, Lalo Schifrin, Sky Traughber.

Sky's dual role as Lalo's Associate Producer/Product Manager was a precedent-setting ruling by CBS, Inc., benefitting future CBS staffers. Photo: 1979

Joe Mansfield co-hired Sky (with Fred Ware) in mid-1970's in Atlanta (for Carolinas) before becoming a key CBS Marketing VP in NY. Sky's background credentials helped CBS' image after "Newark Investigation" on payola. Joe Mansfield is pictured below, after speaking to MTSU RIM "Survey of Music Industry" Class (1991) while V.P. of Capital Nashville. Photo by MTSU Photographic Services

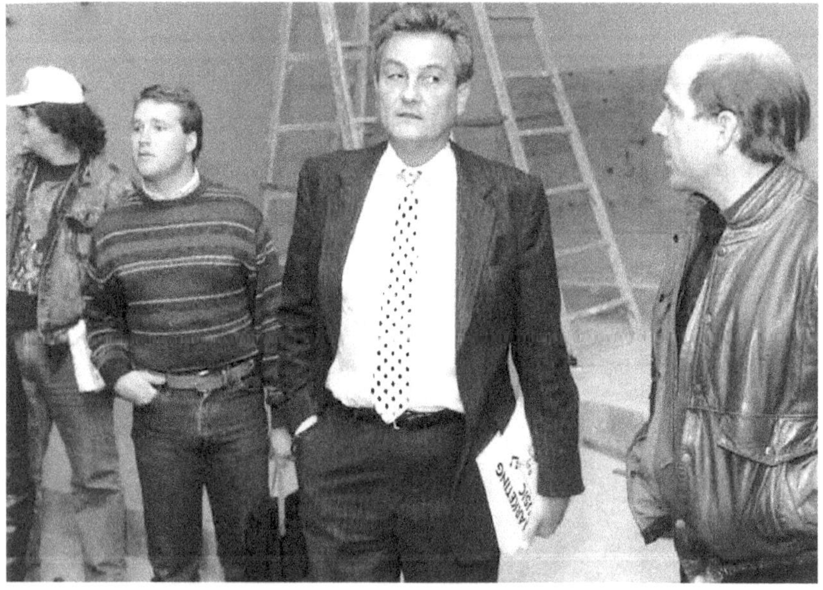

From left: Two MTSU Recording Industry Management students, Joe, Christian Haseleu, RIM Chair

Sky Receives "Black Scholarship in New England" Award from the University of Massachusetts /Boston for Master's thesis on MTV Advertising and Consumer Purchasing, including pivotal MTV policies in exposure or non-exposure of Black acts.

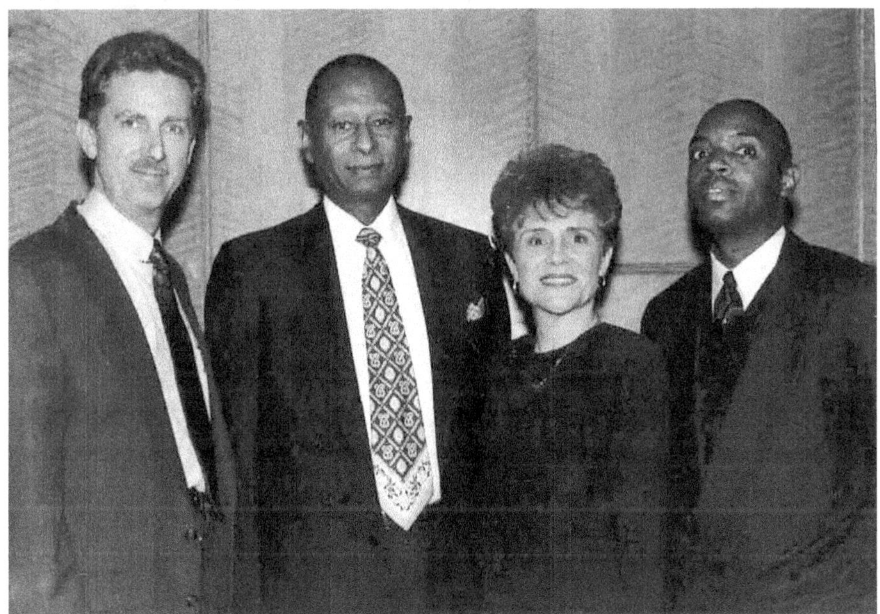

From Left: Don Gorder (Chair Music Business Management Dept. Berklee College of Music), James Blackwell (UMass/Boston Sociology Professor), Sherry Penney (UMass/Boston Chancellor), Sky Traughber

Photo Courtesy by Sky Traughber

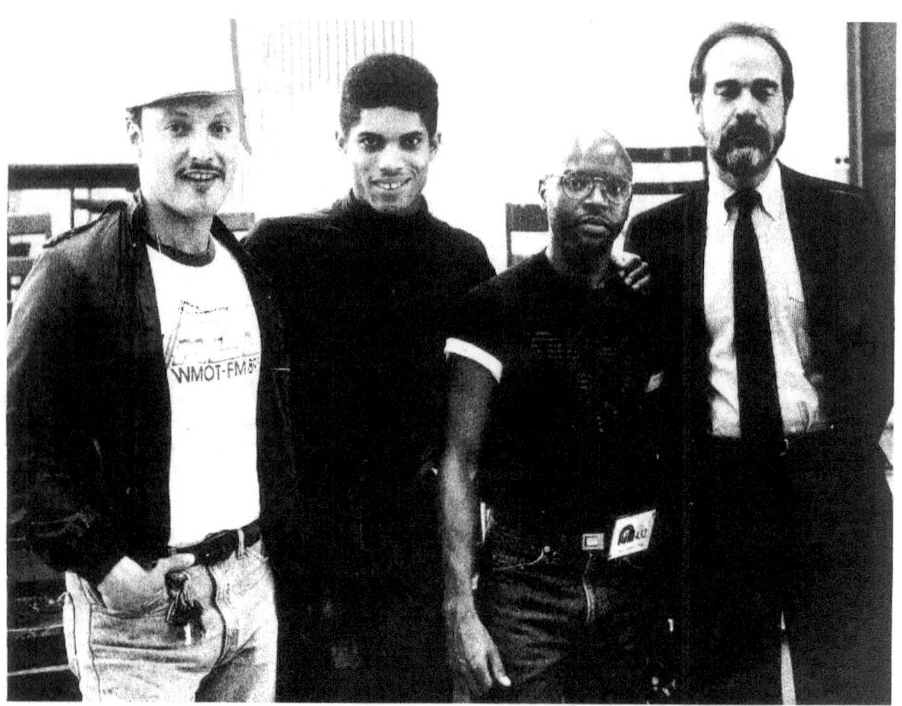

From Left: Greg Hunt (WMOT Program Director), EMI artist Stanley Jordan, Sky Traughber and Paul Wells (MTSU Center for Pop Music Director).

Sky's Middle Tennessee State University (MTSU) concert Promotion class presented Stanley Jordan in concert following Stanley's guest-lecture on ethnic challenges in jazz.

Photo by Jennifer West April 1990

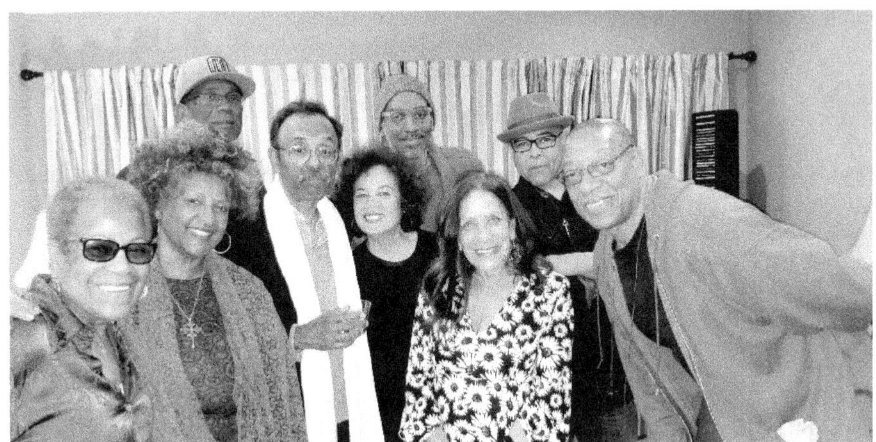

CBS Reunion remembering Ndugu Chancler, March 7, 2018

From Left: Myrna Williams (CBS Records Artist Development), Alitash Kebede (Atlantic Records), Munyungo Jackson (percussionist/producer), Bruce Talamon (photographer), Marsha Smith (CBS Records Publicity), Byron Miller (bassist), Tina Stephens (Tabu Records), Bobby Holland (photographer), Michael Williams (Founder of The Comedy Act Theater).

Photo by Jade Howard

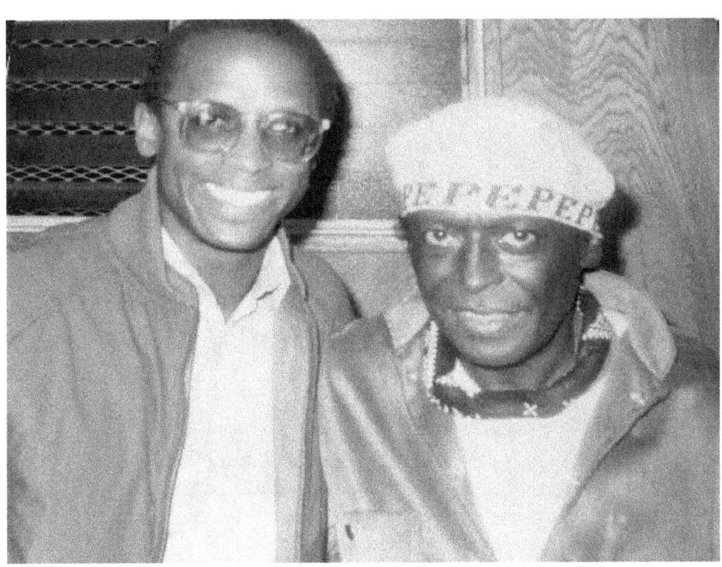

CBS National Promotions Rep Doug Wilkins and Miles Davis. Doug led a group of label radio promoters attempting to unionize in the 1980s.

Photo Courtesy by Doug Wilkins

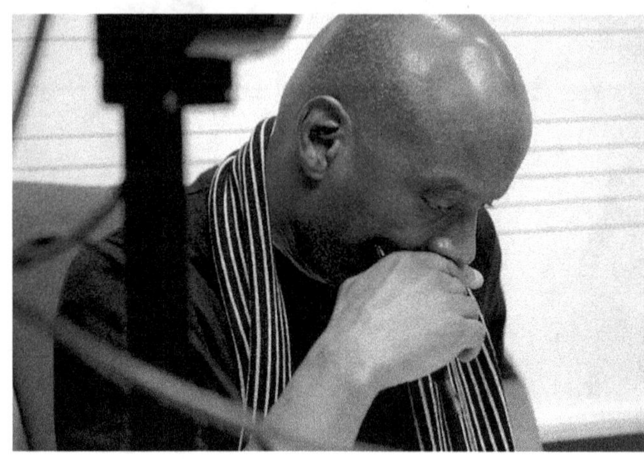

Schuyler "Sky" Traughber (Prof. Funk) ranked in the top 15% of "Influential Professors" in a Berklee College of Music student newspaper poll while developing and teaching courses in Business Management, International Record Label Operations, Concert Promotion and Creative Promotion Thru Media. He has worked as a road musician, producer and industry executive at Stax/We Produce, CBS and Motown Records.

Photo: Courtesy of Marble Mountain Records

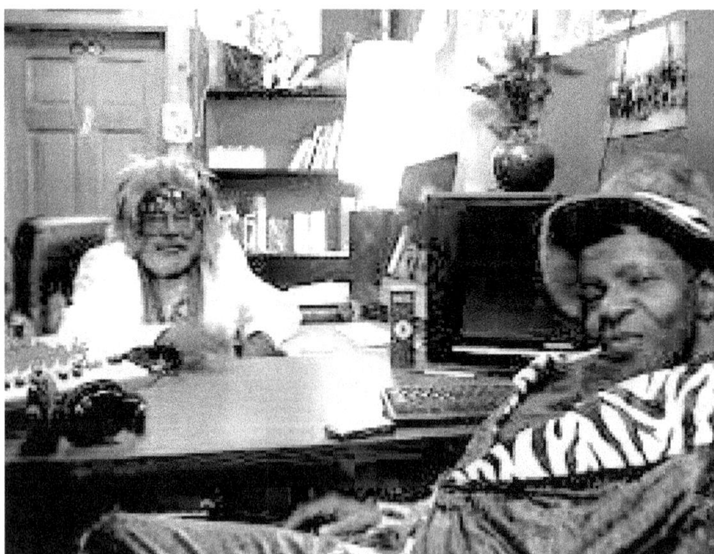

George Clinton and Sly Stone.

George had a special interest in *The Harvard Report* at Warner Brothers while Sly was one of few CBS artists that was considered a "Black act" pre-*Harvard* Report.

Photo from dublab.com

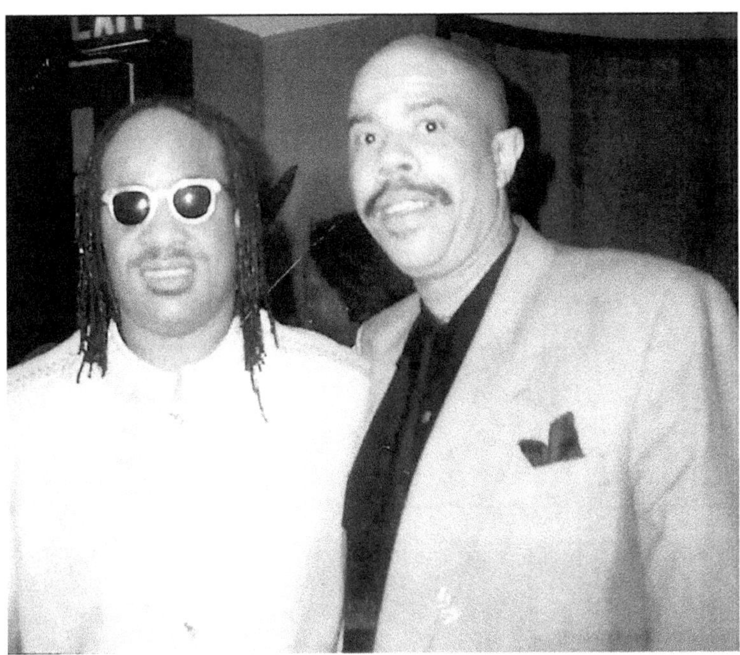

Clark "Deacon Bluz" White mentored Sky's early development in high school, and he is an African American Studies Professor and Blues Artist.

Deacon (right) is pictured with singer, songwriter and record producer Stevie Wonder (left), owner of the Urban Adult Contemporary radio station KJLH (*Kindness, Joy, Love, Happiness*) in Los Angeles, CA. Stevie was instrumental in the campaign to establish Dr. Martin Luther King Jr.'s birthday as a national holiday.

Photo Courtesy by Deacon Bluz

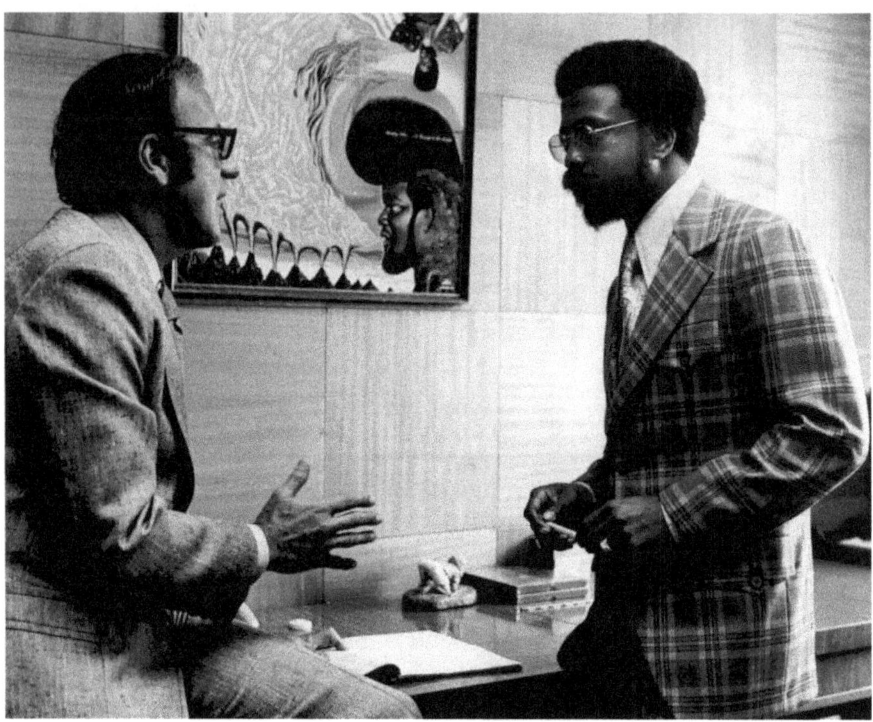

Irwin Steinberg, President of Chicago based Mercury Records in discussion with Logan H. Westbrooks. Pictured on the wall is a poster of the drummer Buddy Miles, who was an artist that was signed to Mercury Records.

Steinberg was later a part of forming Polygram Records in the 1970's and he became president of that label as well. Mercury artists included Donna Summer, Gene Simmons, Rod Stewart, Parlaiment, The Platters, The Ohio Players, Melba Moore, Little Richard and many more. Polygram would later be the record company of Tony! Toni! Toné!, Vanessa Williams and Salt-N-Pepa.

Photo: Courtesy of Logan H. Westbrooks private collection

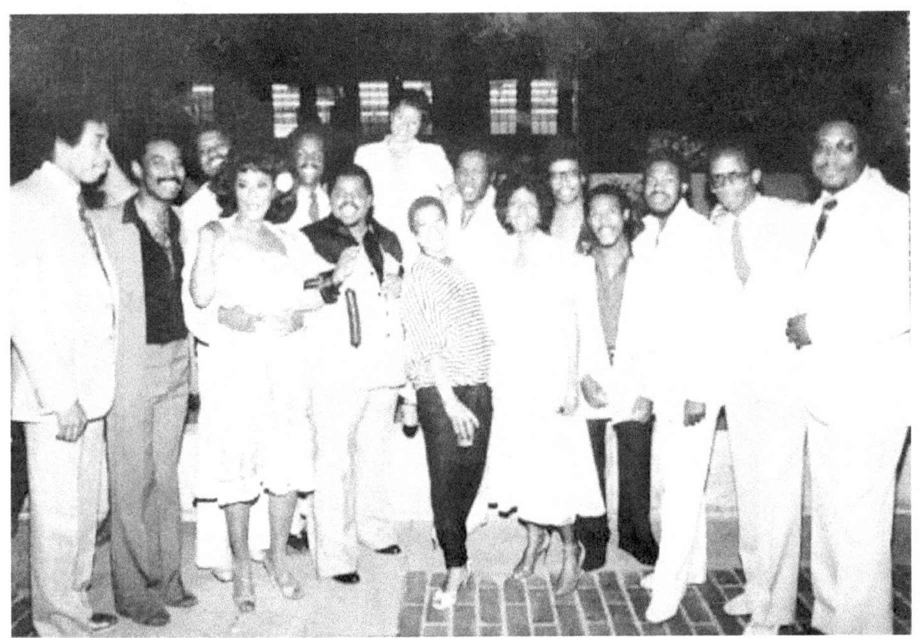

CBS Artists with label executives, Los Angeles 1980

Left to Right: Stanley Clarke, CBS/Epic A&R Jerome Gasper, Webster Lewis, Marlena Shaw, Verdine White, D.J. Rogers, Deniece Williams (back), CBS Artist Development Myrna Williams, Lou Rawls, CBS Press/Publicity Sandra Da Costa, Herbie Hancock, Rodney Franklin, Ndugu Chancler, CBS National Promotions Doug Wilkins, CBS Regional Promotions Jimmy Starks.

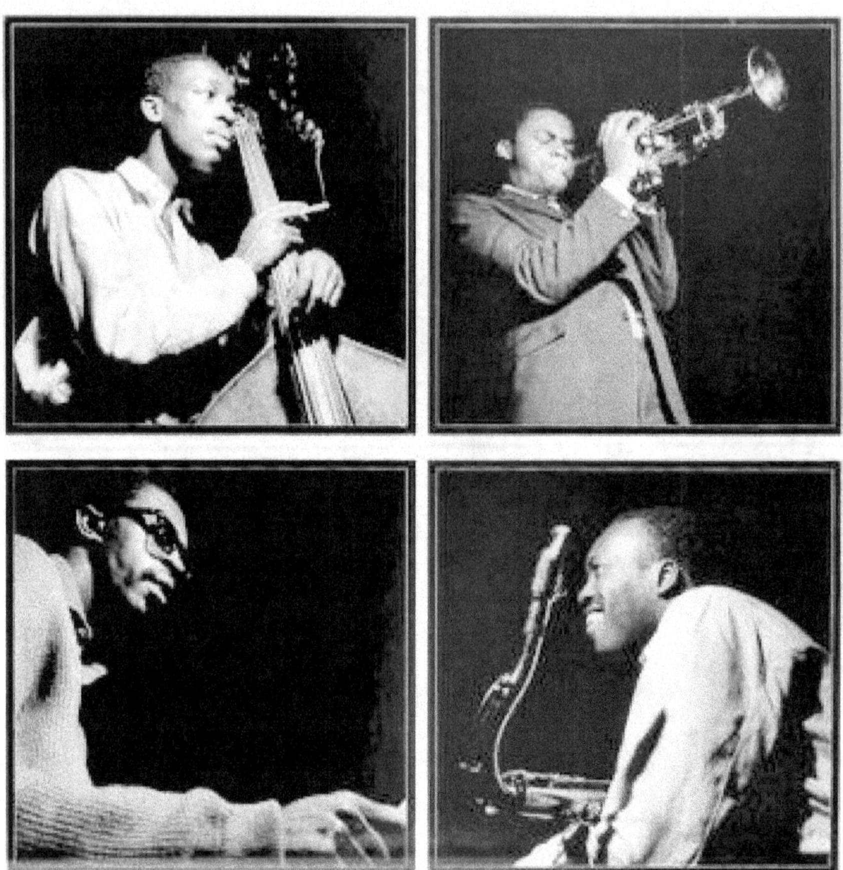

Drummer Louis Hayes (Yusef Lateef, Horace Silver, Cannonball Adderley) required Sky to learn multiple instruments when Hayes was Band Director at Orchard Knob Elementary School in Chattanooga, TN., 1961.

Hayes is pictured (bottom left) with trumpeter Freddie Hubbard (top right) who Sky later handled product management for at CBS. Others in photo are Sam Jones, bass (top left) and Hank Mobley, tenor sax (bottom right).

Photo from Kenny Drew Blue Note LP 1961 FROM: Mark W @ Durham Wasp

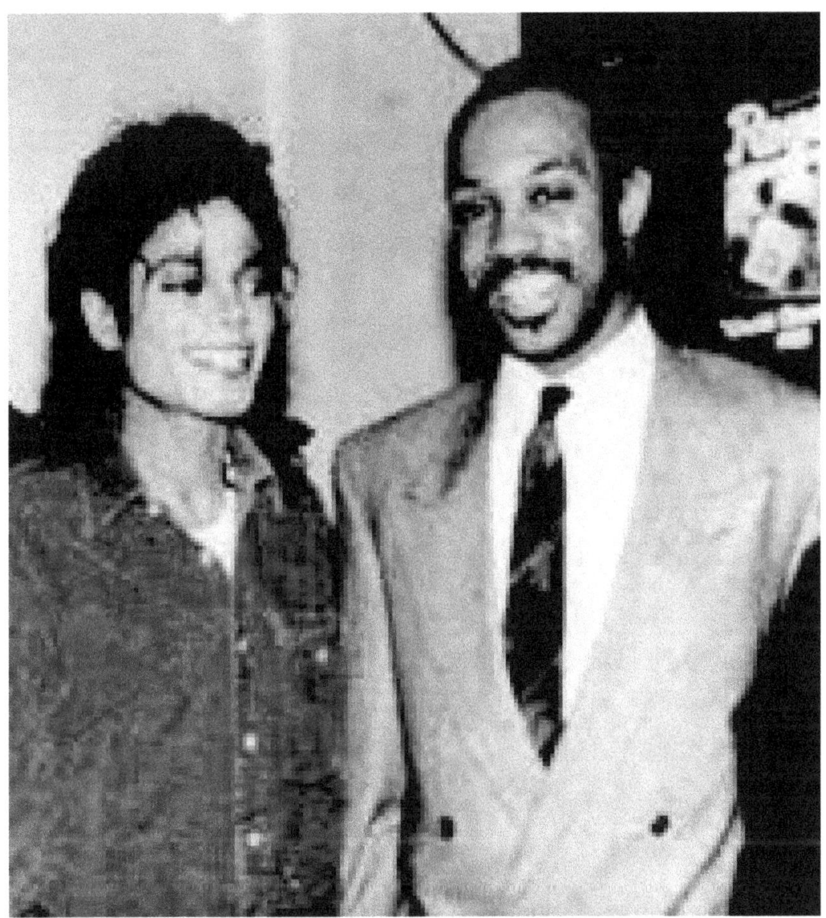

CBS/Epic artist Michael Jackson and concert promoter Al Haymon

Photo: Coli.com

In late 70s Concert Promoter Al Haymon and other Black promoters demanded that Black super-star artists use their qualified services for tour promotion. Al earned an MBA from Harvard Business School and was one of many Black promoters who handled national tours for Black superstars.

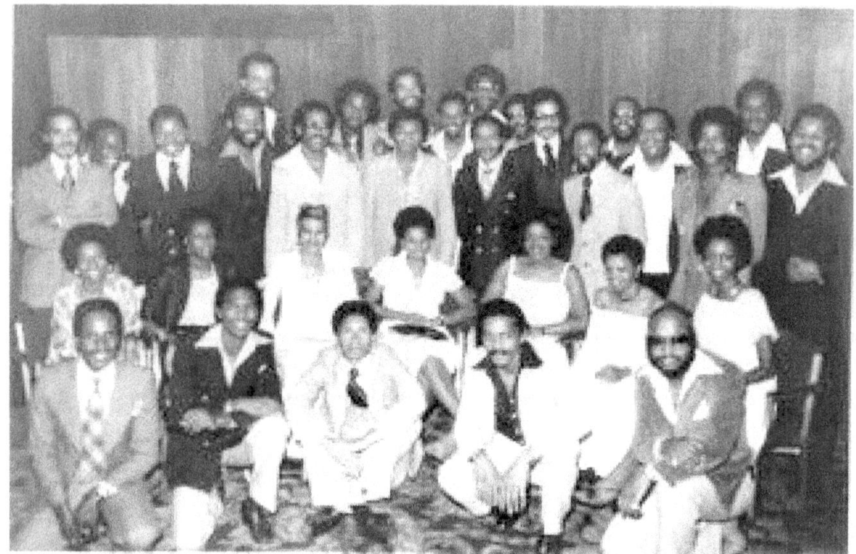

This is CBS BLACK MUSIC MARKETING, CBS Convention, London, 1977:

From Left First Row: Win Wilford, Russell Timmons, John Spears, Eddie Sims, Paris Eley

From Left Second Row: Sandra Da Costa, Emma Garrett, Mike Bernardo, Marie Sellers, Beverly Paige, Unidentified NY Staffer, Rita Roberts

From Left Third and Back Row: Charles Miller, Richard Mack, LeBaron Taylor, Don Eason, T.C. Thompkins, Frank Chaplin, Glen Wright, Maurice Warfield (back), Orlando Imala (front) Reggie Sullivan, Armand McKissick (front), Steve Manning (back), Fred Ware, Harold Coston, Sky Traughber, Vaughn Thomas, Granville White, Freddie Richardson, Curtis Mobley, Vernon Slaughter.

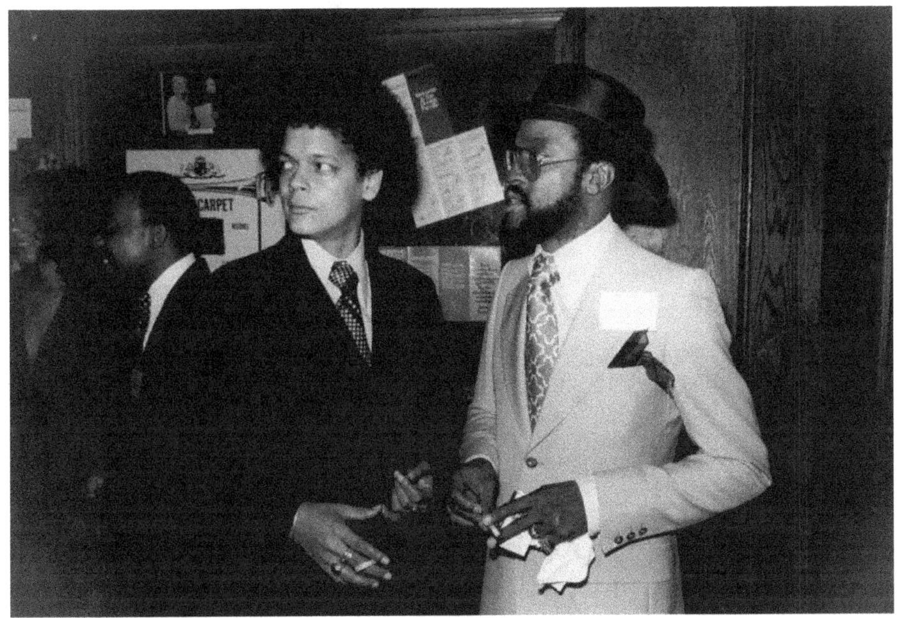

From Left: Georgia Legislator (future NAACP President) Julian Bond, CBS/ Philly International Artist Billy Paul on break from Congressional Black Caucus show produced by Logan Westbrooks with Harold Sims.

The headliner was Isaac Hayes and Don Cornelius was emcee.

Photo: Courtesy of purl.dlib.indiana.edu, Logan Westbrooks collection.

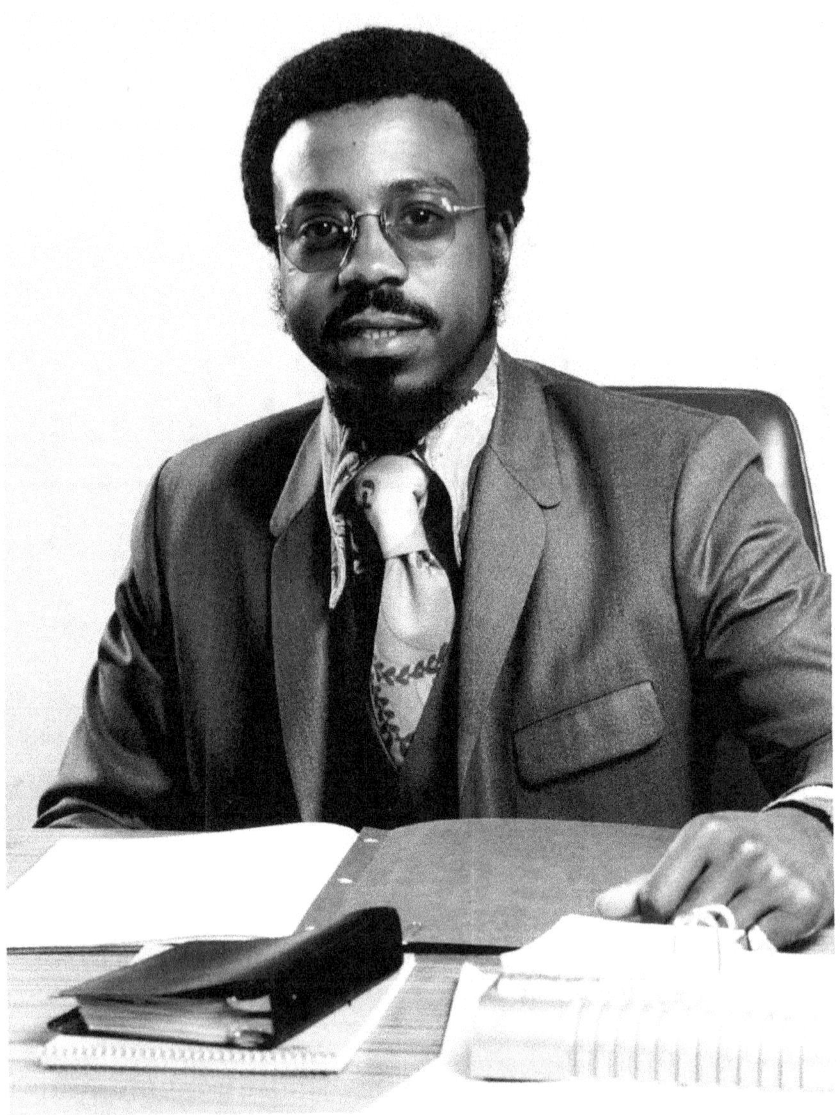

Logan Westbrooks instituted a practice of having key Black Music Marketing/CBS executives and selected artists attend Congressional Black Caucus events in the early 1970s.

After Logan departed CBS' domestic division to initiate and run CBS/AFRICA, this practice continued with Logan's CBS successors LeBaron Taylor, Vernon Slaughter and Paris Eley.

Photo: Logan Westbrooks collection

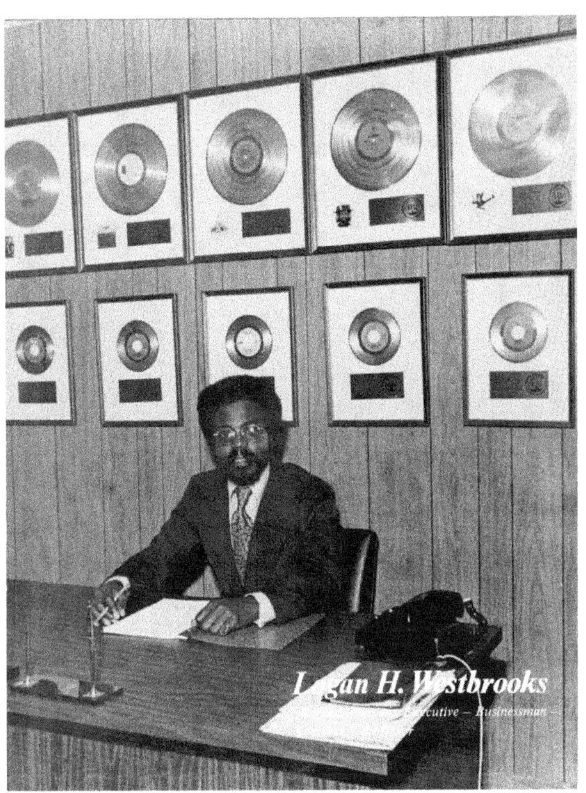

Logan made history at Capitol Records working as a Territory Salesman in the mid-1960s providing retail-positioning for artists such as The Beatles, Frank Sinatra and Lou Rawls. This position was underrepresented by Blacks in major labels at the time.

Photo: Logan Westbrooks collection, Indiana University, Bloomington

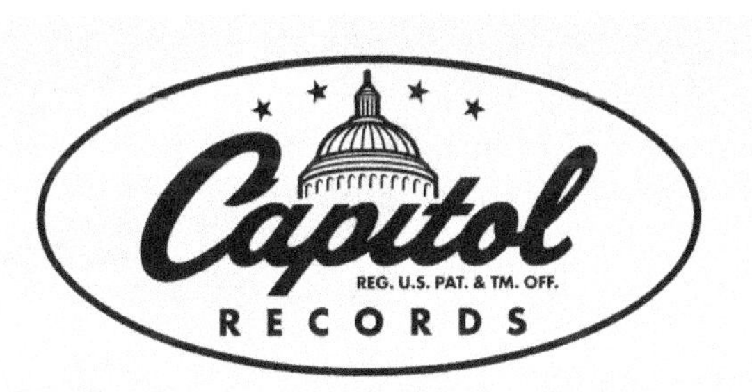

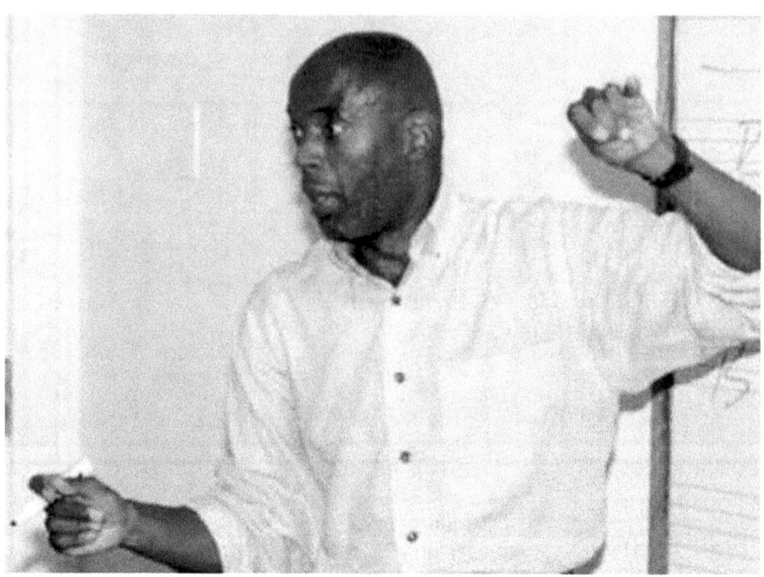

While on hiatus from the music industry in the mid 1980s, Sky unknowingly ventured into MCI (the future of music) designs, which used fiber-optic-distribution systems.

Sky worked full-time with the company in San Francisco during Silicon Valley's explosion. As today's radio playlists shrink, this type of technology (including satellites) has widened exposure for 1970s Soul/Black music.

In the 1990s Sky Traughber was a highly regarded full-time Music Business/Management faculty member in traditional classrooms as well as an instructor at Berklee's Computer Lab (pictured here).

Photo by Kim Grant

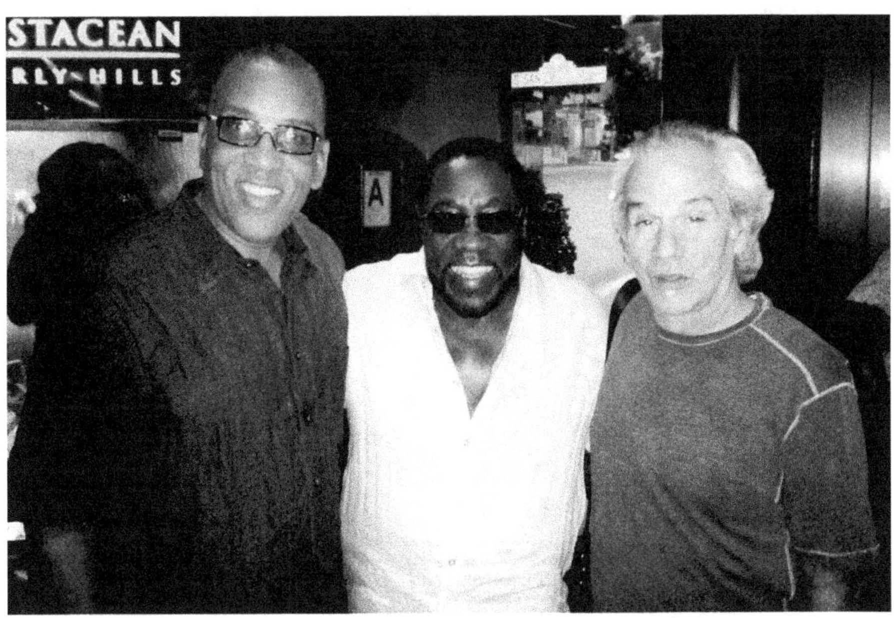

John Kellogg sponsored Sky to speak frequently on "The Harvard Report" at Berklee for John's "Business of R&B, Soul & Hip-Hop" class.

From Left: John Kellogg (former O'Jays attorney) is shown with CBS/Philly Int'l artist Eddie Levert from The O'Jays (center) Ron Hausfeld, former O'Jays tour manager (right).

Photo Courtesy form John Kellogg

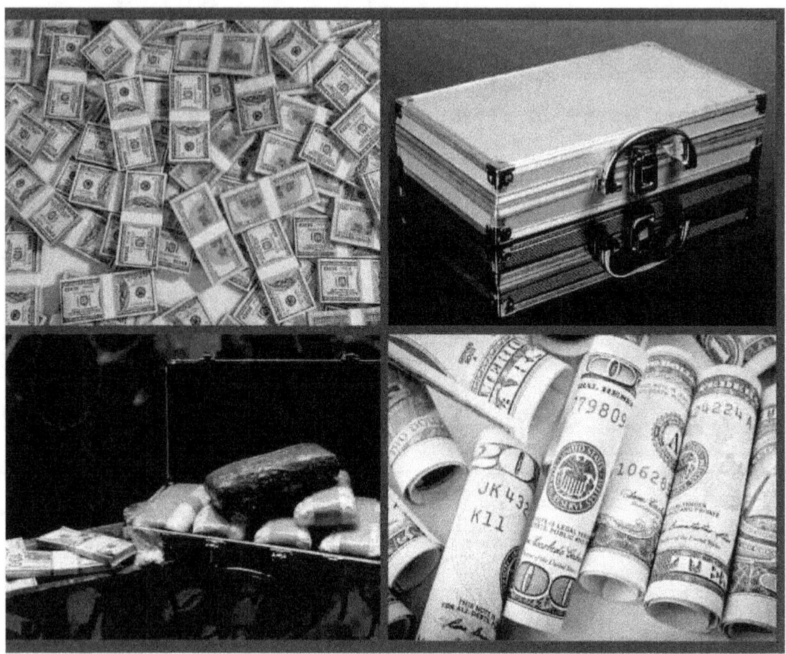

After the 1970s, cocaine and cash (as "non-traditional revenue") would have a greater impact on some Black/Pop radio playlists. Photo Collage: Canva.com

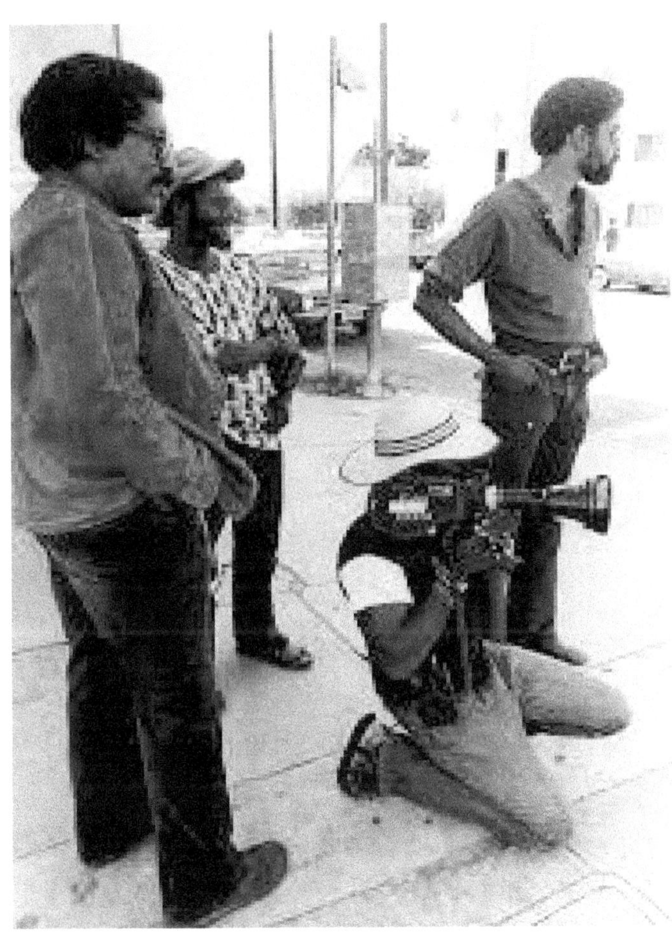

WATTSTAX
Producer Larry
Shaw with all-
Black film
crew. Watts
1972

Photo from
"Soul of Stax
Records"
concert-
coverage
article.

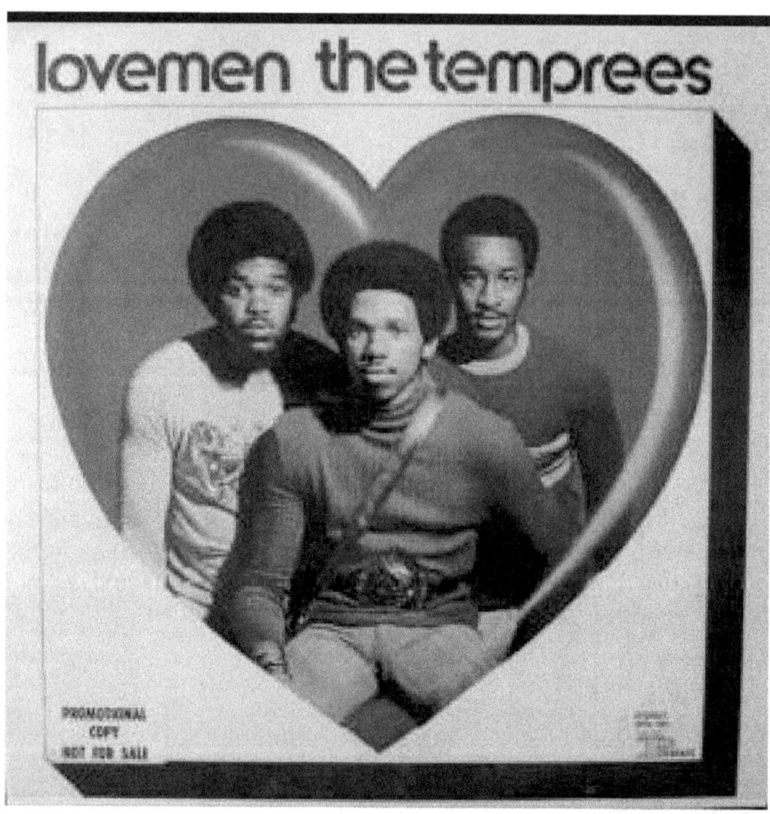

The Temprees *Love Men* LP featured a re-make of The Shirelles 1959 "Dedicated To The One I Love" recording. The Temprees 1972 version reached #17 on Billboard Soul Singles chart. The LP also resulted in a six-month tour for the group alongside top Soul/R&B acts Kool & The Gang, Earth, Wind & Fire, Curtis Mayfield and Harold Melvin & the Blue Notes. Black-Owned Queen Booking, NY, booked many of those dates.

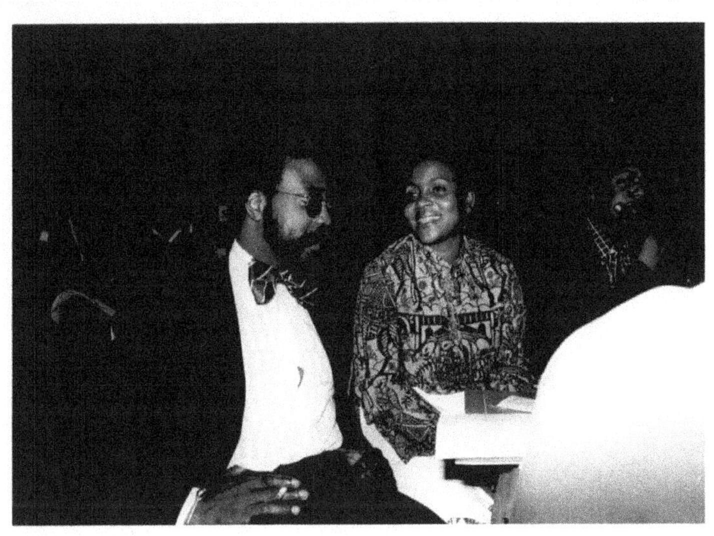

Stax Creative Director Larry Shaw and Temprees Manager/Stax-We Produce VP Josephine "Jo" Bridges presented Sky with first Stax college scholarship for study at Memphis State while playing bass on Temprees "Love Men" tour (1972-73). Ms. Bridges also wrote "Teenage Love Affair" performed by Alicia Keys.

From Left: Logan Westbrooks and Jo Bridges at a CBS event, Temprees "Love Men" LP.

Photo: Courtesy of purl.dlib.indiana.edu, Logan Westbrooks collection.

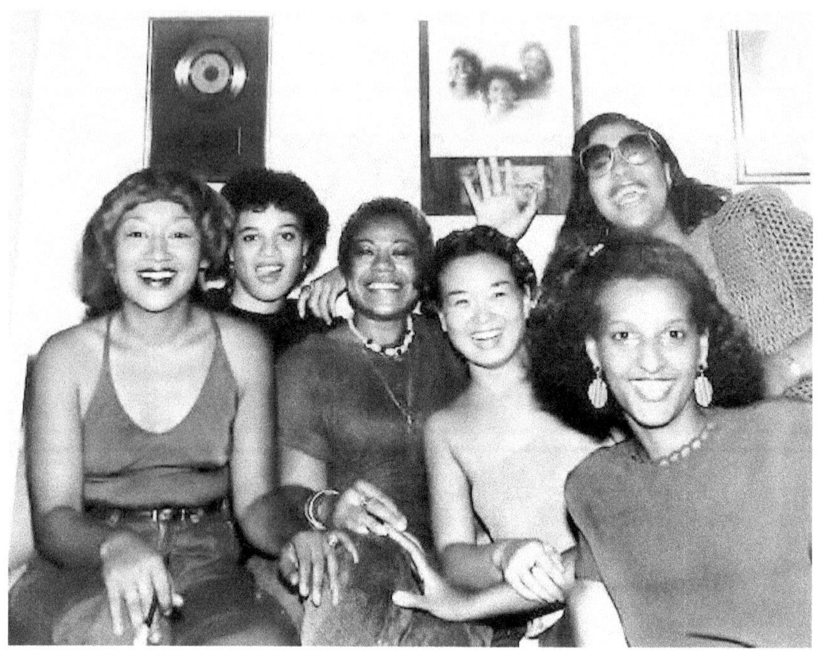

Co-workers and friends at CBS Records/Black Music Marketing office in Century City, California, 1979.

From Left: Shirley Brooks, CBS International; Marsha Smith, CBS Publicity; Myrna Williams, CBS Artist Development; Carmel Kim, CBS Artist Development; Cheryl Lynn Columbia Records recording artist (in the back); Front: Alitash Kebede Atlantic Records Promotion.

Photo Courtesy of Marsha Smith

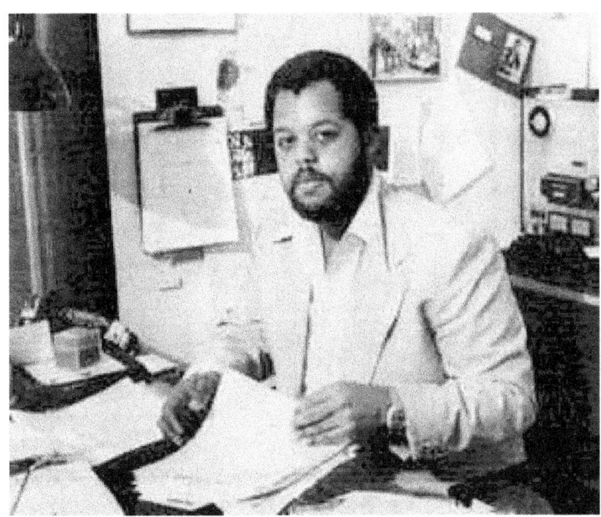

Photo from Discogs

CBS VP Vernon Slaughter required Sky, as West Coast Jazz/Progressive Product Mgr., to work from New York. This often enabled Sky to observe and work with high-level challenges for Black Music Marketing Department's New York headquarters.

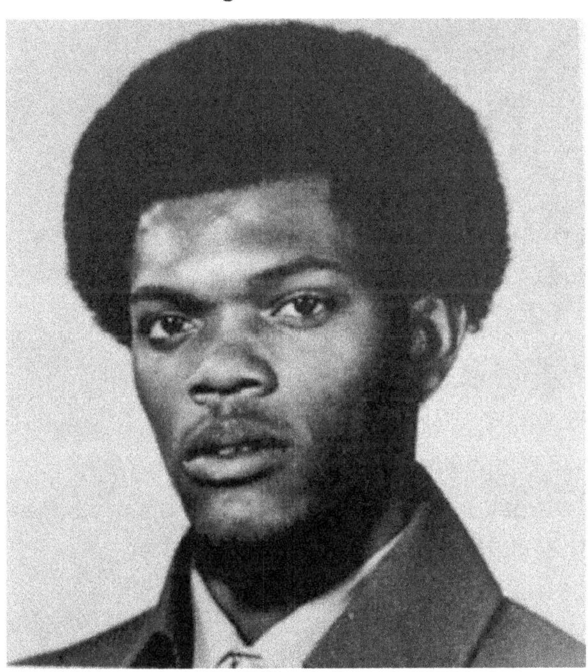

Samuel L. Jackson

Sam played trumpet with Sky and others at Riverside High in Chattanooga TN., while mentoring Sky in early development areas.

Sam's rebellion of Morehouse's governance resulted in his expulsion, as portrayed by actor Laurence Fishburne in Spike Lee's "School Daze" film. Sam continues in bringing attention to behind-the scenes power and controls, today.

Photo by Morehouse Yearbook Photography

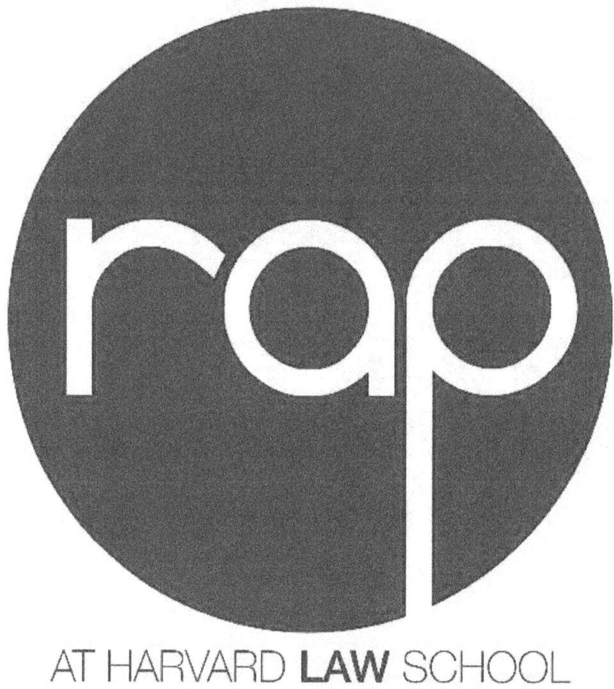

Harvard Law School offers the RECORDING ARTISTS' PROJECT for community, national and international clients, offering valuable pro bono legal services. Photo Courtesy of Brian Price/RAP

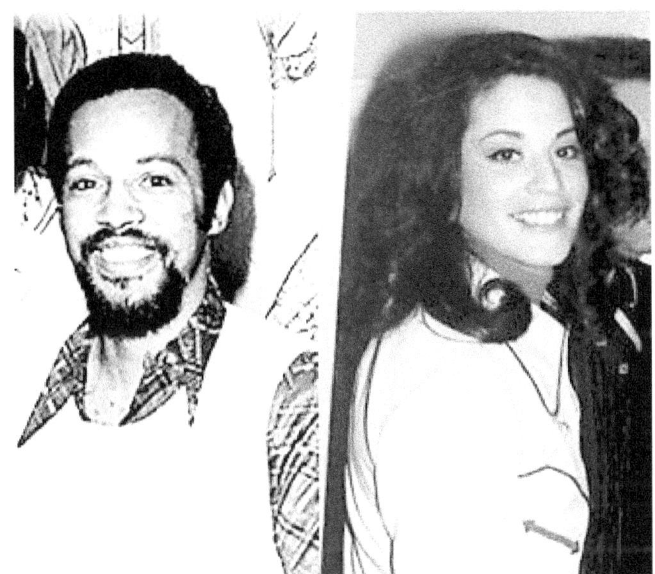

Linda Creed was a highly-valued song lyricist for the Philly Sound, writing for groups like The Stylistics among others. She worked through breast cancer in the 1970s before succumbing to the disease in the 1980s.

From Left: Philly writer/producer Thom Bell, Linda Creed

Photo from soul-patrol.com

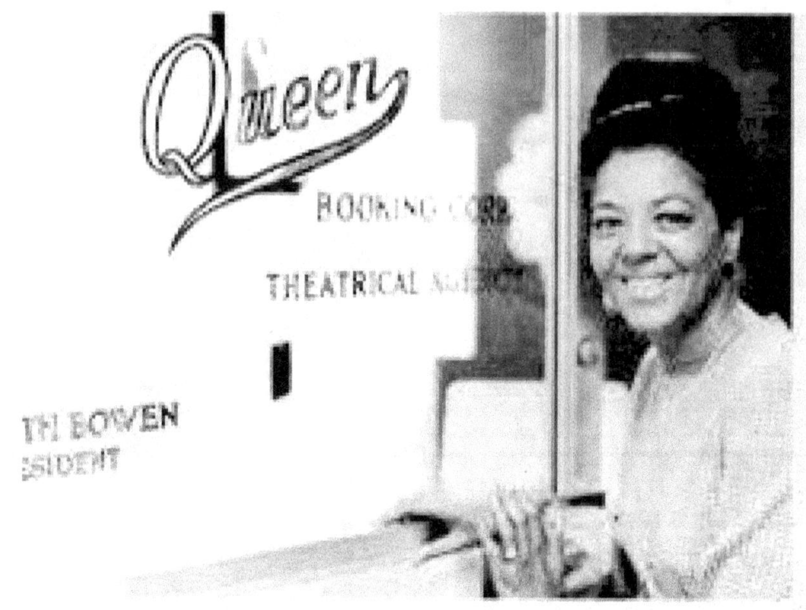

According to Wikipedia, Ruth Bowen was the first Black female talent agent in 1945, starting QUEEN BOOKING in New York 1959, handling major Soul/R&B acts into the 1970s.

Photo from Twitter.com

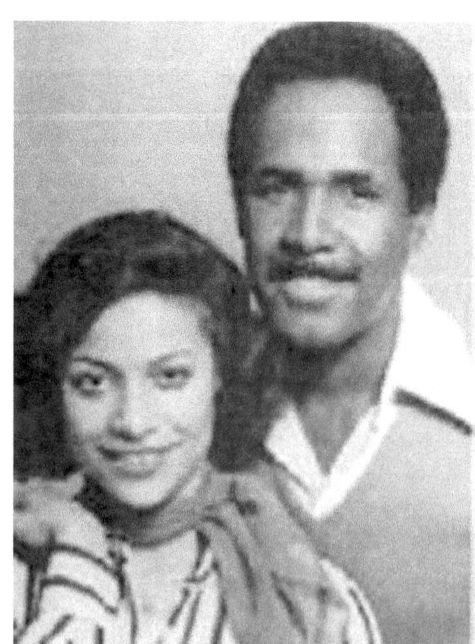

Actress, Choreographer and Emmy Award Winner ("Fame") Debbie Allen (left) with then-husband and CBS VP of Press, Publicity and Artist Development Win Wilford. The couple exemplified a 1970's New York mix of entertainment and romance.

Photo from Whodatedwho.com

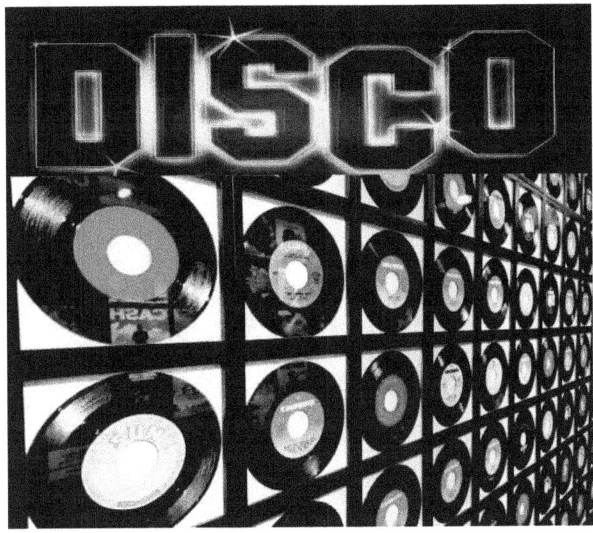

Photo collage: Canva.com

Disco provided hot moments in music and for club 12"s. However, album returns during this period caused massive label layoffs and budget cuts, known as: "The Crash of '79." Beats-per-second radio requirements altered Black Music going forward.

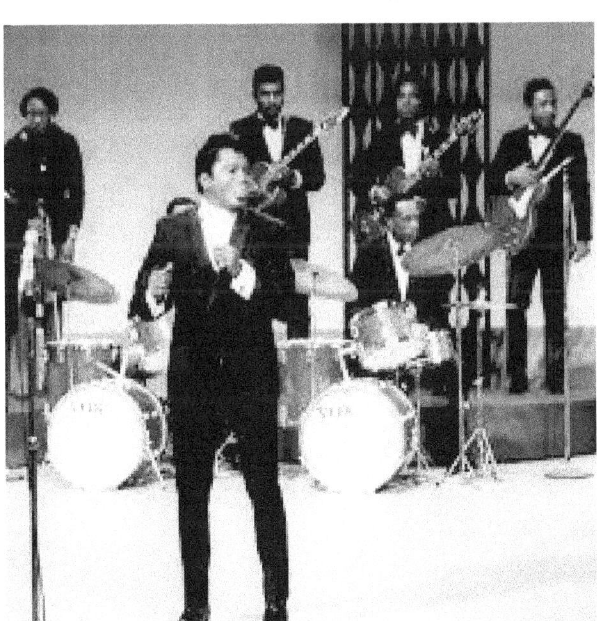

Photo from creatingthesound.com

James Brown drummer Clyde Stubblefield, (above right of Brown) is a fellow musician from Chattanooga, TN.

Clyde made an impression on Sky's understanding of Soul/Funk rhythms in the mid 1960's while Sky performed and studied with Clyde's mentor, Drummer Joe Burke.

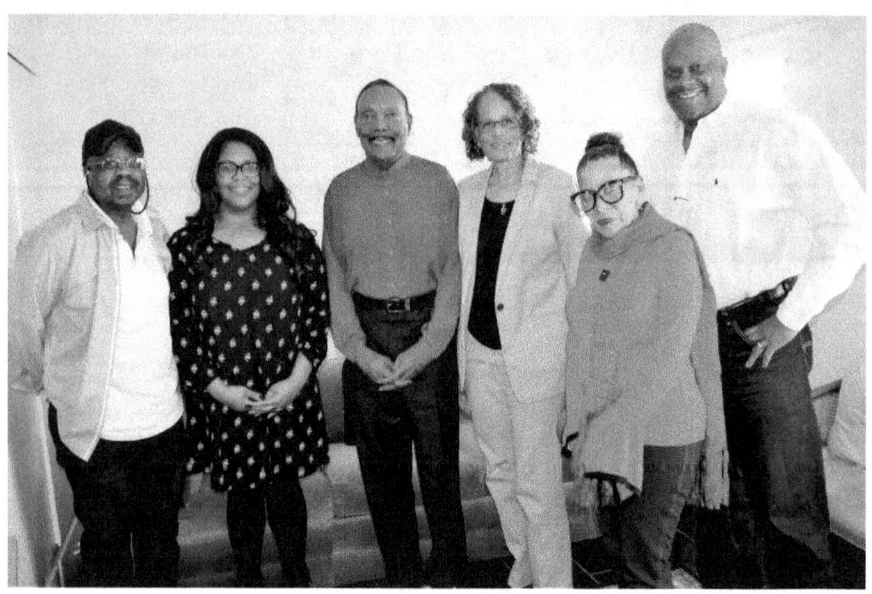

Dr. Westbrooks hosts Dr. Marquise Reed Wright, Larkin Arnold, Esq, Dr. Portia Maultsby, Tina Lousie Stephens and H. Beecher Hicks, III. The team of experts discuss key contributions to be included in the Museum of African American Music in Nashville, TN. 2019

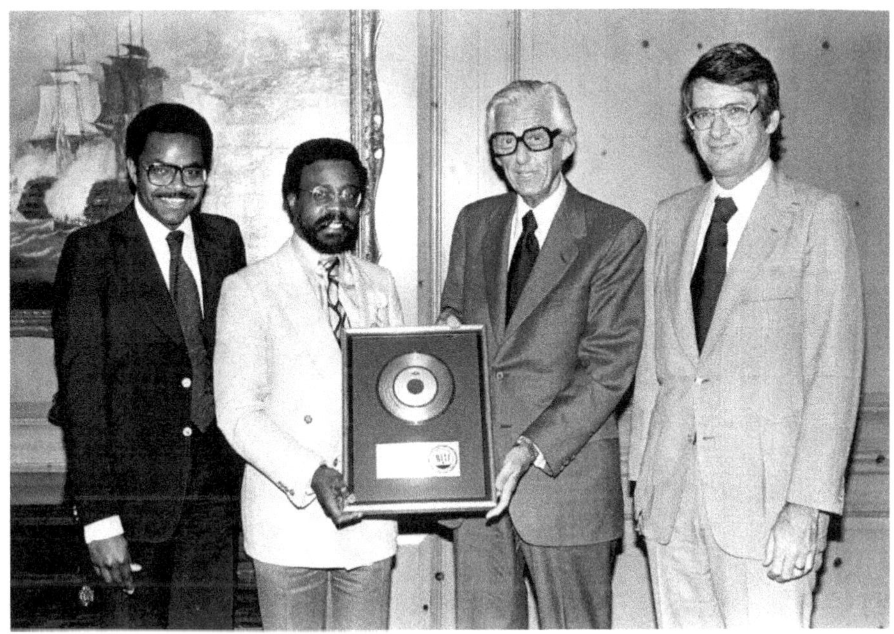

Logan H. Westbrooks presenting the first Gold Record for Source Records. From left Norbert Simmons-President of MCA New Ventures, Lou Wasserman-head of MCA Universal, and Sid Steinberg MCA Universal. 1980

Photo: Courtesy of purl.dlib.indiana.edu, Logan Westbrooks collection.

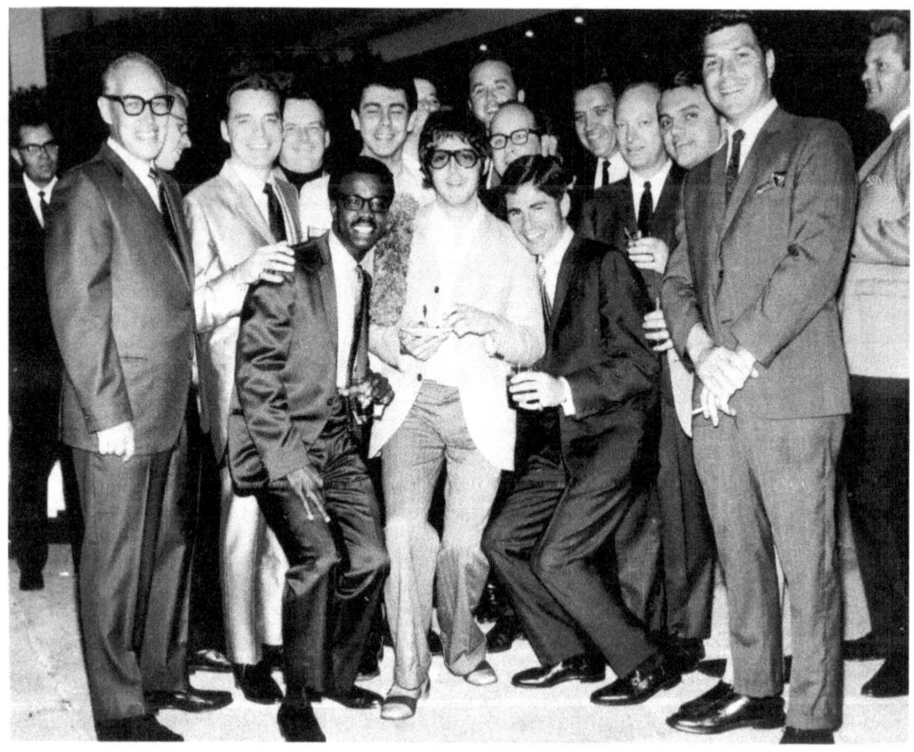

Logan H. Westbrooks next to Paul McCartney surrounded sales staff. Capitol Records National Sales Convention at Century Plaza Hotel, Los Angeles. Circa. 1970

Photo: Courtesy of purl.dlib.indiana.edu, Logan Westbrooks collection.

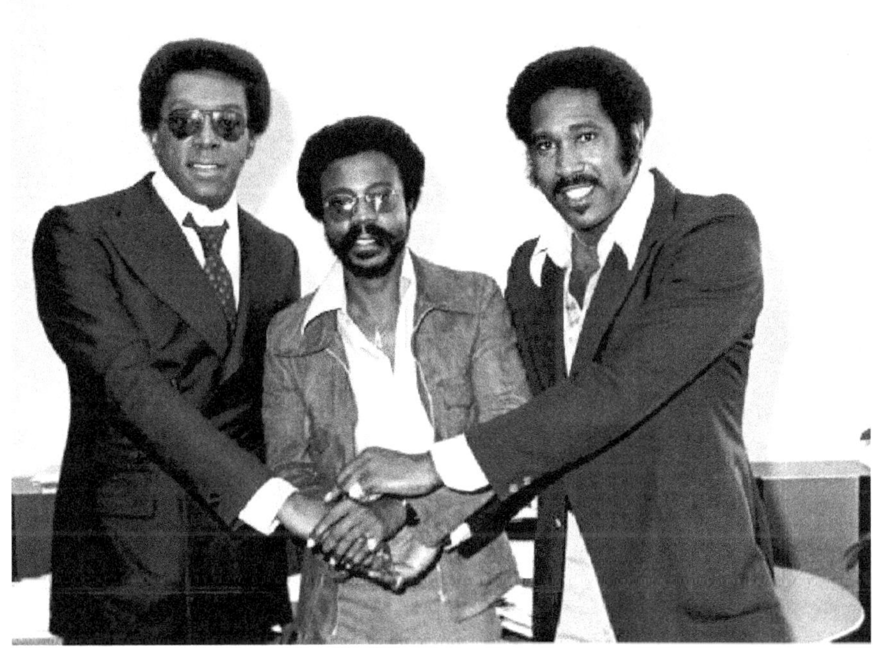

From left Don Cornelius, Logan Westbrooks, Dick Griffey in start-up mode for Soul Train Records, Los Angeles, 1976. Soul Train Records would develop acts such as Shalamar, Soul Train Gang, The Whispers and Carrie Lucas, eventually becoming Solar Records. Later, Logan will start-up Source Records hosting an artist roster of Chuck Brown & The Soul Searchers, Sharon Paige, The Valentine Brothers, Harold Melvin & The Blue Notes, Travis Biggs and Opus Seven and Smash.

Photo Courtesy of Logan Westbrooks Collection, Indiana University, Bloomington

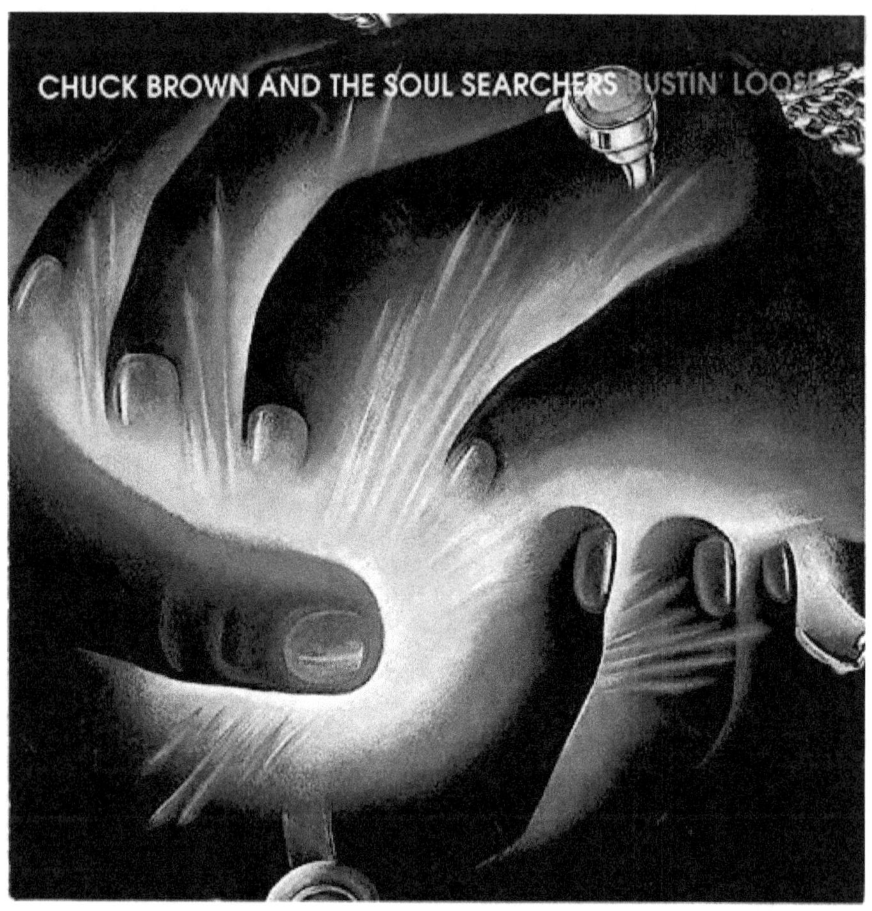

Westbrooks' Source Records presented Chuck Brown & the Soul Searchers "Bustin' Loose," creating the Washington D.C. "Go-Go" music sound in the early 1980s. Chuck/s music and vocal on "Bustin' Loose" can be traced to Fela and Yoruba music. A dispute with major-distributor MCA over pressing and royalty due dates forced Source to shut down operations after earning $6 million in its' first and only year of operation.

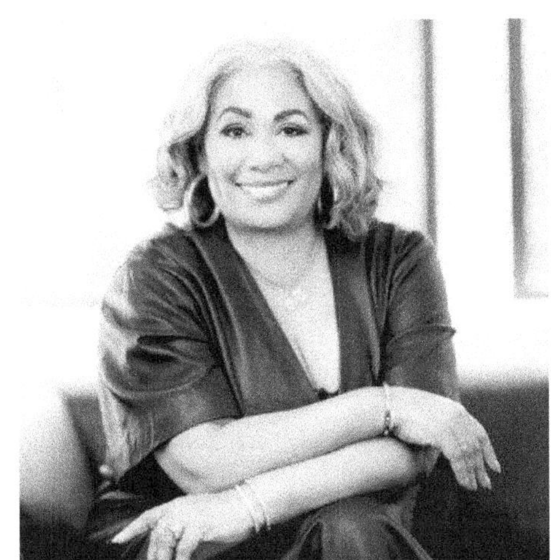

Dyana Williams co-founded the Black Music Association with Philly Int'l Kenny Gamble, Publicist Ed Wright, and others in late 1970s, as well as initiating June as Black Music Month.
Photo from: mobile.twitter.com

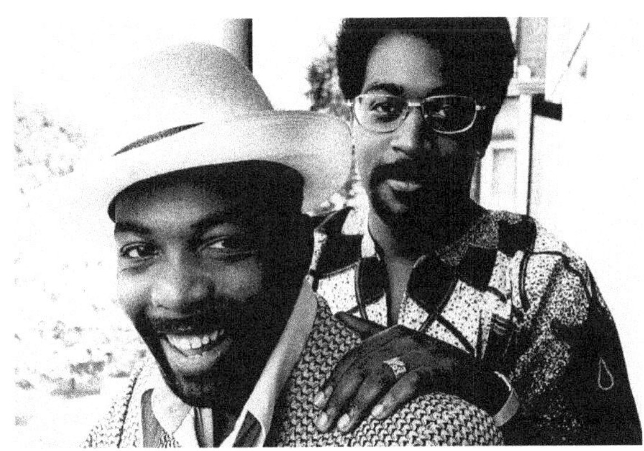

Leon Huff - Philly Sound writer and co-producer
Kenny Gamble - BMA Co-Founder, Founder/Philly Sound writer/producer.

Photo from samepassage.org

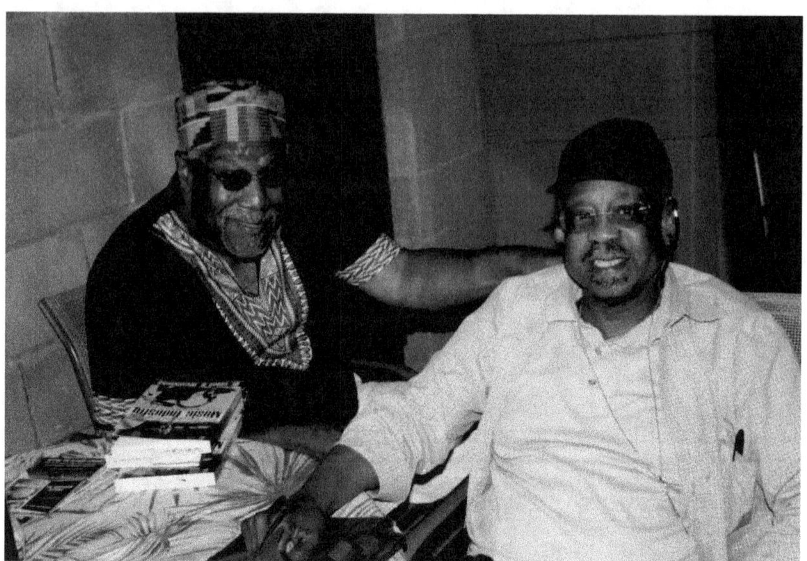

Dr. Jeff Dorsey and Dr. Logan H. Westbrooks discuss The Anatomy of the Music Industry at an event in Los Angeles, CA.

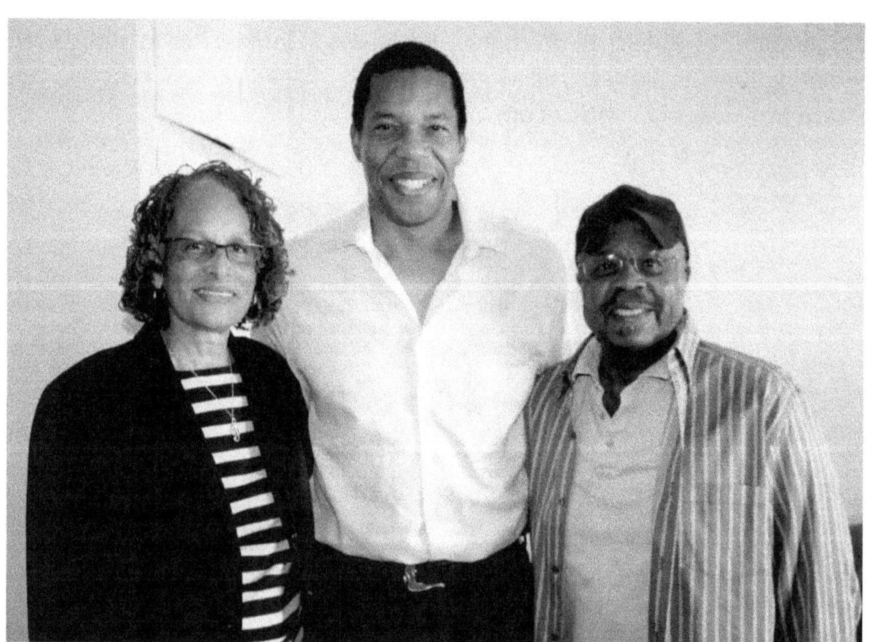

Dr. Portia Maultsby (Indiana University), Tony Cornelius (son of Soul Train's Don Cornelius), and Dr. Logan H. Westbrooks. 2017

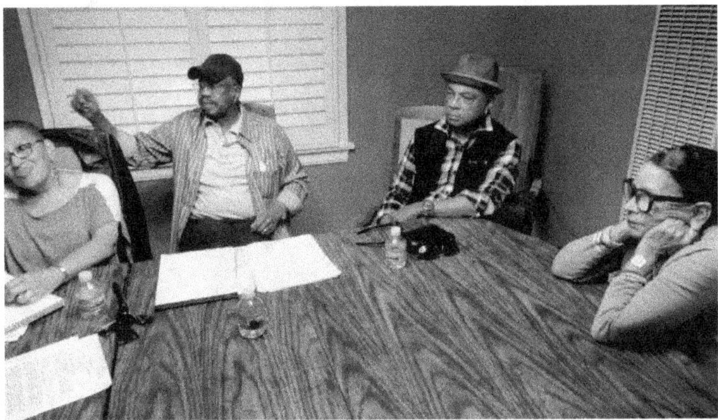

Pat Shields, Dr. Logan H. Westbrooks, Chris Jones and Tina Louise Stephens in Los Angeles at the former home of Source Records discuss the newly formed Museum of African American Music. 2017

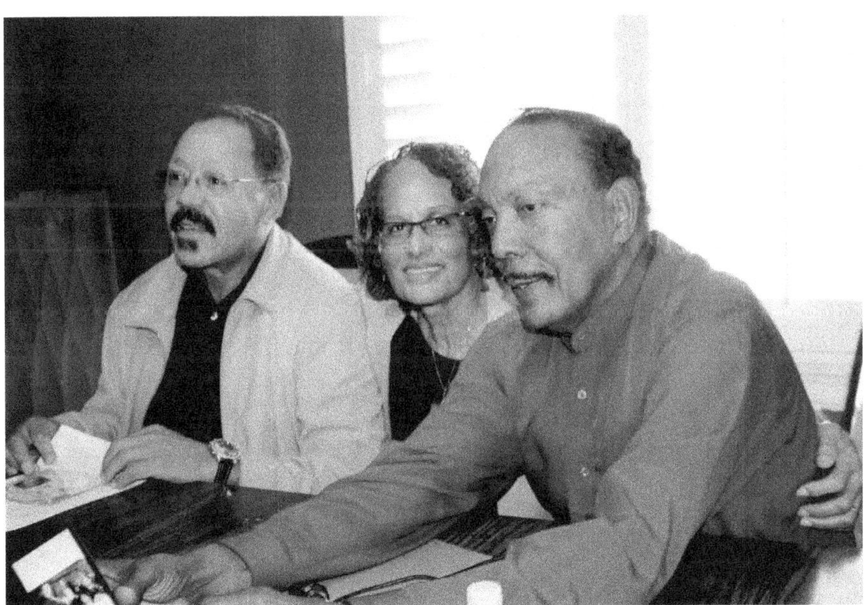

Ron Ellison, Dr. Portia Maultsby and Larkin Arnold talk about what history must be captured at the new museum of African American Music in Nashville, TN.

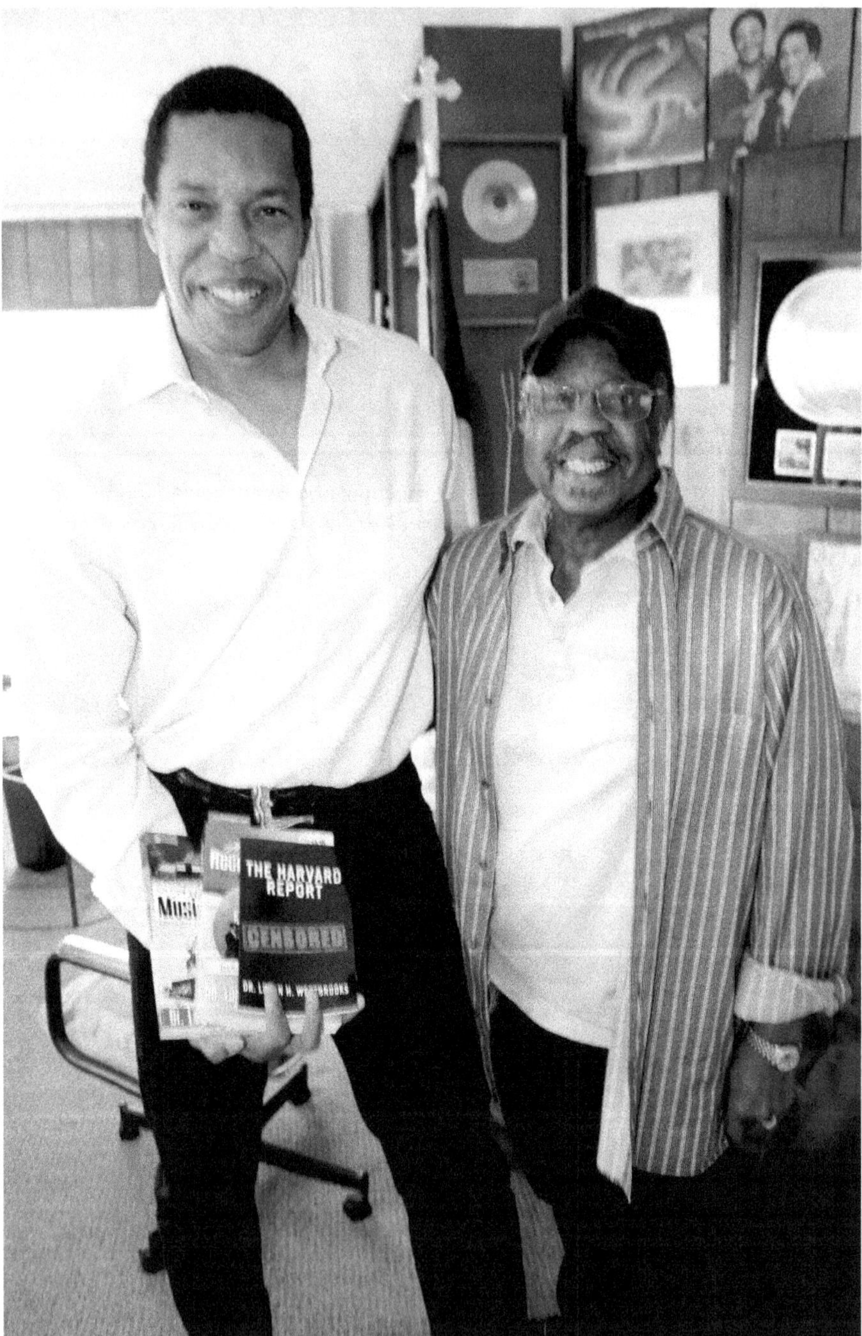

Tony Cornelius, son of the legendary Don Cornelius in the historic Source Records office of Logan Westbrooks. Los Angeles 2019.

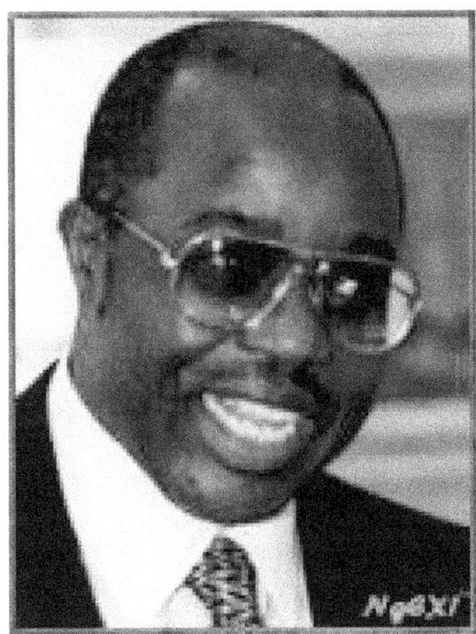

Chief Harry Akande, owned the New African Technical & Electrical Company (NAFTEC), a representative company of General Electric (GE) America.

Photo from **ngex.com**.

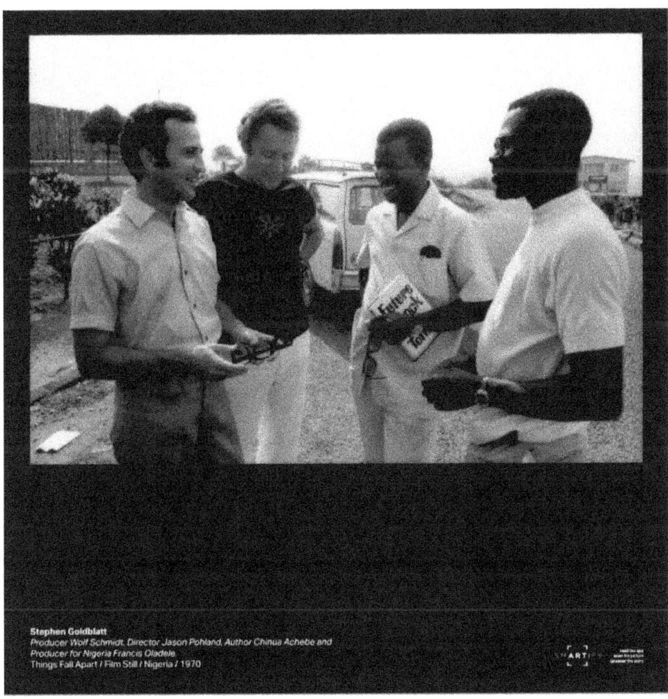

Francis Oladele on the right, legendary Nigerian filmmaker and owner of Kongi Klub in Idaban, Nigeria.

1974 poster from Francis Oladele's Kongi Klub in Ibadan, Nigeria, welcoming Americans Mr. & Mrs. Logan Westbrooks and Mr. & Mrs. Don Butler to a special event.

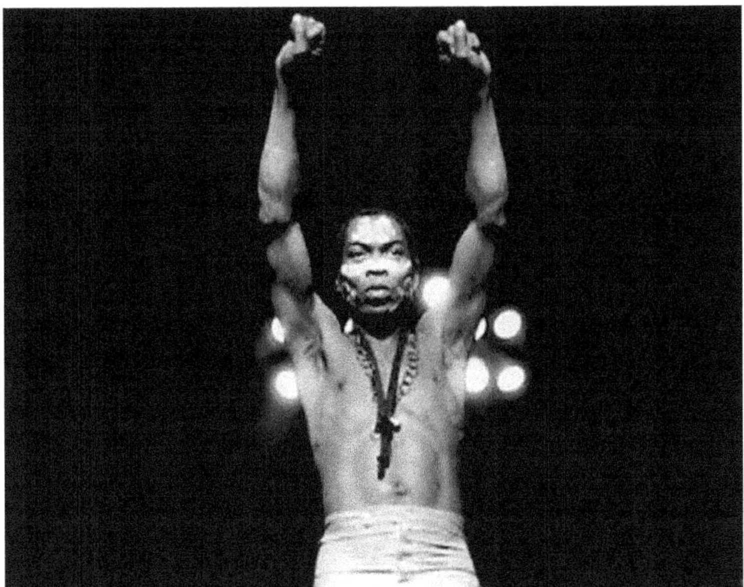

Fela Kuti was a Nigerian musician, bandleader, composer, and Pan-Africanist, who was uncompromising in his political activism. He also founded The African Shrine nightclub. Westbrooks was introduced to Fela by filmmaker Francis Oladele, and wanted to sign him to CBS Records in the early 70s. **Photo from PM News Nigeria.**

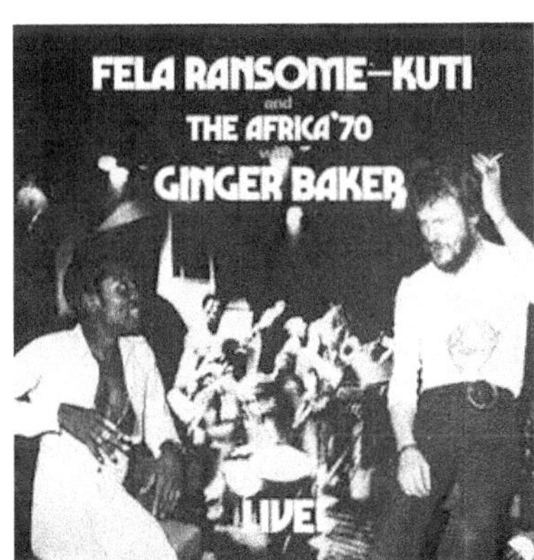

Cover for Fela's 1971 album

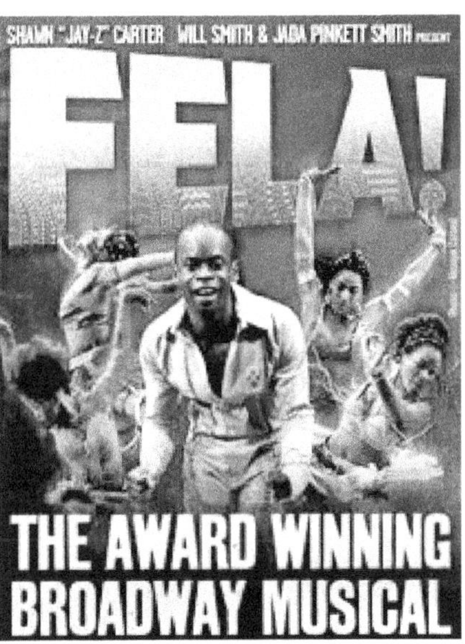

2009 poster for musical based on Fela's life

IN MEMORIAM
Promotion Managers

Rocky G
Jack Gipson
Dave Clark
George Boogaloo Frazier
Joe Medlin
William Bunky Sheppard
Jimmy B
Max Kidd
Ron Mosely
Granville Granny White
Tom Draper
Warren Lanier
Henry Allen
David Banks
Vernon Slaughter
Andre Montell
Harry Coombs
A.D. Washington
Sidney Miller
Richard Mack
Fred Ware
Skip Miller
Ralph Bates
Jheryl Busby
William Bill Hicks
Ron Granger
Ruben Rodriguez
Leroy Little, Sr.
John Hall, Jr.
Freddie Richardson
Curtis Mobley
Charles Miller
Ms. Mike Bernardo

DISCLAIMER: List may be incomplete.

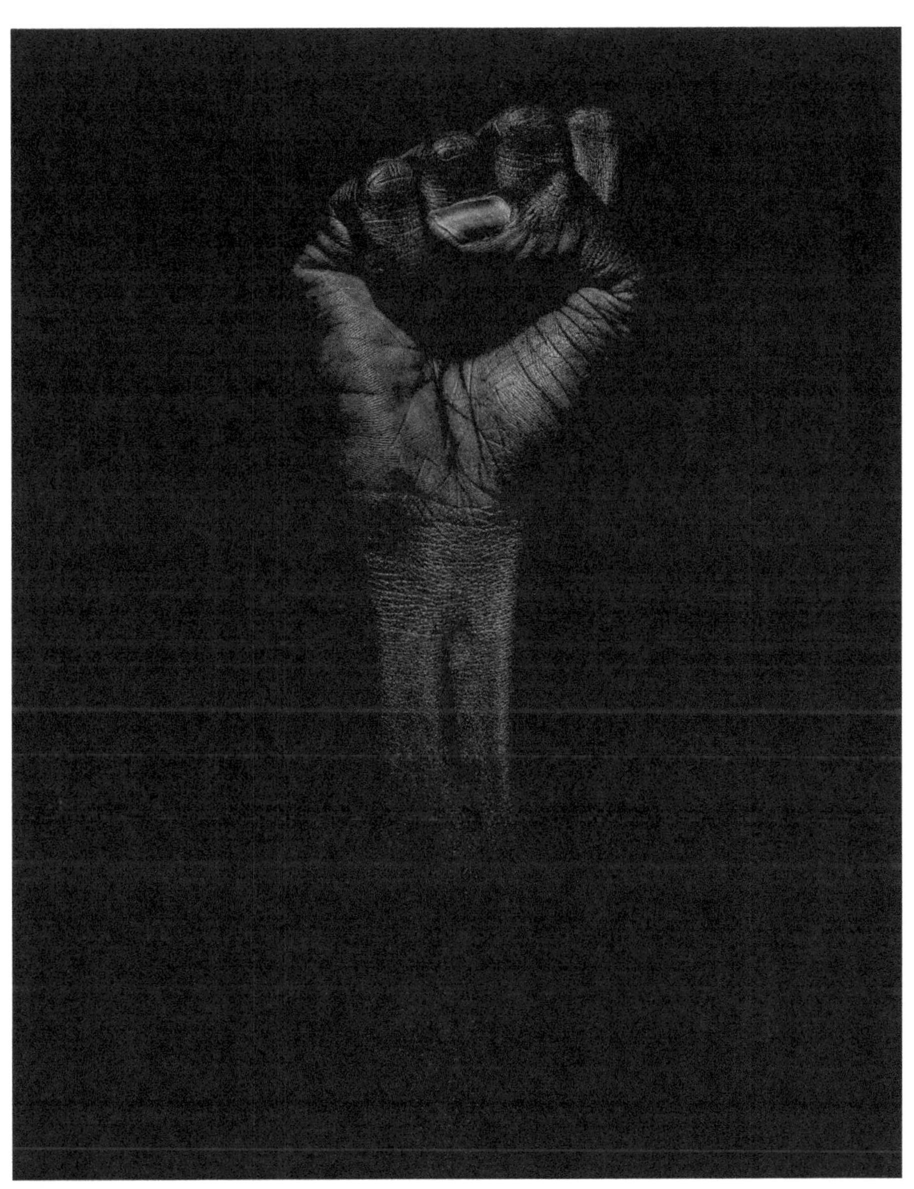

INDEX

Other books by Logan H. Westbrooks:

The Anatomy of a Record Company:
How to Survive the Record Business
Revised 2nd Edition
2017

The Harvard Report
A Study of the Soul Music Environment
Prepared for Columbia Records Group
2017

The Anatomy of the Music Industry:
How the Game Was & How the Game Has Changed
2015

The Anatomy of a Record Company:
How to Survive the Record Business
1st Edition
1981
(Out of Print)

<u>Westbrooks Curated Exhibits</u>

Original photographs, personal papers, awards, and memorabilia from Source Records and his career in the music industry are archived at Indiana University in Archives of African American Music & Culture (AAAMC) in Bloomington, Indiana.

Dr. Westbrooks is featured in a permanent video presentation about African American Music Executives in the National Museum of African American Music (NMAAM) in Nashville, Tennessee.

https://www.youtube.com/user/SourceRecordsUSA
http://www.LoganWestbrooks.com

ABOUT THE AUTHORS

DR. LOGAN H. WESTBROOKS

Dr. Logan H. Westbrooks is one of the first African Americans to work as a major label Music Executive. He's recognized as a pioneer who paved the way for the African American Music Executives of today. He is a Memphis native who attended LeMoyne-Owen College, and graduated from Lincoln University in Missouri. In 2014, he was awarded an Honorary Doctorate in Humane Letters from LeMoyne-Owen College. His career extends 50 years, and he has contributed to the success of artists such as The Jackson 5, Nancy Wilson, Elvis, Chuck Brown & the Soul Searchers, Nelly and many more.

SCHUYLER "SKY" TRAUGHBER

Sky Traughber hails from Chattanooga, Tenn. Named after Harlem Renaissance concert-pianist Philippa "Duke" Schuyler, Sky has worked as a road musician, arranger, producer and record label executive for The Temprees (We Produce/Stax Records), CBS Records and Motown Records as well as U.S. Business Rep for King Records, Tokyo. After serving as a Music Business/Management faculty member at Berklee College of Music in Boston for 15 years, Schuyler now resides in the sea-side community of Gloucester, Massachusetts, writing screenplays and giving guest college and library presentations on The Harvard Report. Sky holds B.S. and M.A. degrees in Recording Industry Management and Marketing/ Sociology from Middle Tennessee State University.